Consumer psychology for marketing

WHAT DRIVES CONSUMER BEHAVIOR?

Most people engage in consumption activities every day. Our very identities are tied up with our roles as buyers and users of goods and services. Yet how many of us understand the forces that drive our consumer choices at any given time?

In this illuminating text, Gordon Foxall and Ronald Goldsmith show how psychology can be a vital tool for making sense of consumer behavior. They argue that traditional segmentation criteria are not always appropriate in a world growing ever more fluid and complex. Instead, the motivating forces behind the consumer decision-making process must be revealed and examined. Key topics explored are information processing, the influence of personality and style on consumer choice, as well as sexual symbolism, situational and social contexts and retail environments.

Analysis is consistently tied in with the practical needs of the modern marketing manager, so offering an excellent blend of theory and practice. With real world examples and chapter summaries, this text provides an important learning resource for students of consumer behavior, marketing and psychology.

Gordon R. Foxall is Professor of Consumer Research at the University of Birmingham and Director of the Research Centre for Consumer Behaviour at the Birmingham Business School. He holds research doctorates in industrial economics and business studies, and in psychology. He is the author of a dozen books, including *Consumer Psychology in Behavioural Perspective* (Routledge, 1990), and over 150 papers and articles in leading journals. **Ronald E. Goldsmith** is Professor of Marketing at Florida State University. He holds doctorates in history and in marketing and has made numerous contributions to leading journals in the fields of consumer behavior and market research.

Consumer psychology for marketing

Gordon R. Foxall and Ronald E. Goldsmith

Routledge

London and New York

To Elizabeth, David and Andrew (REG)
To Jean and Helen (GRF)

First published 1994
by Routledge
11 New Fetter Lane, London EC4P 4EE

Simultaneously published in the USA and Canada
by Routledge
29 West 35th Street, New York, NY 10001

© 1994 Gordon R. Foxall and Ronald E. Goldsmith

Typeset in Times by J&L Composition Ltd, Filey, North Yorkshire
Printed and bound in Great Britain by
Clays Ltd., St Ives PLC

British Library Cataloguing in Publication Data
A catalogue record for this book is available from the British Library

ISBN 0–415–04673–4 (hbk)
ISBN 0–415–04674–2 (pbk)

*Library of Congress Cataloging in Publication Data
has been applied for*

Contents

Figures

Tables

Acknowledgments

We are particularly grateful to three noted marketing scholars who kindly read and commented on the manuscript: Professors Richard Bagozzi, Andrew Ehrenberg and Fred van Raaij. Gordon Foxall is grateful for permission to reproduce material first published in the *Journal of Economic Psychology*, the *International Journal of Research in Marketing*, and the *International Review of Retail, Distribution and Consumer Research*, and to his co-authors' agreement to his use of his contributions to their joint articles. Paul Hackett and Fred van Raaij were especially helpful in the earlier development of Chapter 8.

Our universities provided stimulating atmospheres for scholarship in marketing and consumer research; our wives, Liz and Jean, gave invaluable help throughout the project; and Routledge, especially in the person of Francesca Weaver, were excellent publishers. We are grateful to them all. Neither they nor anyone else who has helped us are to blame for any mistakes that appear in this book.

In a free, competitive economic world, there will be no stability in a corporation's performance if it allows its attention to be diverted from the basic business mission of serving its customers. If it consistently succeeds in serving customers more effectively than its competitors, profit will follow.

Kenichi Ohmae, The Mind of the Strategist: Business Planning for Competitive Advantage, Penguin Books, 1982: 109

Introduction

Our parents were producers. Their primary economic functioning lay in the extraction of primary resources, the fabrication of goods, and the physical distribution of products. Production will always be an essential prerequisite of consumption, of course, and for many people throughout the world it is still the source of a fundamental economic problem: acquiring enough to live on. But, at least in affluent marketing systems, it is no longer the definitive economic activity. We are consumers. Our primary economic significance derives from the purchase and consumption activities that take up so large a proportion of our waking lives. Many would say that our very identities are integrally bound up with our roles as buyers and users of economic goods and services.

A dominant, perhaps *the* dominant social and technological determinant of behavior in affluent societies has been summed up as 'consumer culture' (Featherstone 1991) and, more specifically, 'retail culture' (Gardner and Sheppard 1989). Consumption has been portrayed as a form of communication in which individuals signal their social positions, the groups to which they have managed to affiliate, and those from which they have avoided exclusion (Douglas and Isherwood 1980). Identity is frequently signalled, maybe even acquired, through the dress codes and clothing styles by which outlying social groups seek to distinguish themselves from the majority (Hebdige 1979).

> The punks, in particular, took this strategy to almost masochistic lengths. They appropriated and transformed cheap, everyday products like the bin-liner and the safety-pin into pieces of personal adornment, which made a deliberate statement about their aggressively defended cultural boundaries while, at the same time, savagely parodying the accoutrements of high fashion.
>
> (Gardner and Sheppard 1989: 45)

A profound shift has been recognized in affluent societies: from values and behavior based on the apparently fixed certainties of scientific progress, especially as manifested in industrial mass production and correspondingly by universal patterns of consumption, to individual lifestyles founded on personal tastes and preferences, eclectic patterns of purchase and consumption, and – more broadly – an approach to life that recognizes the ambiguities inherent in cultural artefacts and signs (Csikszentmihalyi and Rochberg-Halton 1981; Rudmin 1991). This move from modernity to postmodernism has far-reaching implications for consumer behavior and marketing management.

> Where the modern consumer bought goods to adorn and express a more or less consistent and recognizable lifestyle, the postmodern consumer plays with an eclectic combination of goods and services to experience a series of oftentimes inconsistent identities. Where modern market research attempted to segment the population into a set of recognizable and stable types of consumers, postmodern market research must deal with the recognition that people do not always remain true to type. Depending on shifts of mood or shifts of situation, the same individual will behave like an upscale achiever one moment, like a downscale bargain hunter the next. The same consumer will buy part of her wardrobe at Bloomingdales and part at K-Mart.
>
> (Ogilvy 1990: 15; see also Hirschman and Holbrook 1992)

Increased awareness of the more dynamic, amorphous, indeed anomic consumer behavior patterns has not, according to Ogilvy, led to specific new techniques for market analysis, segmentation and positioning. Rather, it is reflected in a new willingness to listen to the consumer and to accommodate marketing management to the emerging and fluid lifestyles of consumers rather than founding today's marketing strategies on traditional segmentation criteria that are no longer appropriate. It is, however, too early to judge whether the apparently unstoppable hedonism – assumed by many affluent consumers as a way of life – will become the socioeconomic motif of the late twentieth century (cf. Scitovsky 1992). Unsuspected and unpredicted by the new gurus of consumerism, economic recession can lead to an intractable reduction in consumer confidence and a prolonged slowdown in consumer spending, sustained in part by mass advertising that champions saving and conservation rather than spending and consumption. The application of behavioral science concepts and techniques of analysis to the interpretation of consumer behavior should nevertheless proceed with the postmodern consumer firmly in mind, if only as a working hypothesis.

How then are we to make sense of the behavior of consumers? The answers to this question are of interest not just to marketing managers but to the members of other professions concerned with providing consumer satisfaction, protection and education. In this text (which is intended for marketing managers, especially those seeking professional qualifications, and for MBA and advanced undergraduate programs) we show how psychology can help provide the necessary understanding. The book stresses the managerial implications of consumer behavior, but is also concerned with consumer research as a developing academic discipline.

Marketing texts, especially those aimed at the MBA market, tend to emphasize instant applicability of results and to give checklists and bullet-point solutions to managerial problems. We do not deride this approach and wherever possible we have presented the conclusions of research in terms that can assist the development and implementation of marketing plans. But we are aware that the conclusions drawn from research are not always as accessible as this approach suggests. The results of research are not always unambiguous; sometimes, they are plainly contradictory. Although the book is intended as an entry-level text, we have not been content merely to outline alternative research needs: where possible we draw upon the research of ourselves and others to describe in some detail either (a) how the methodologies used have implications for the interpretation of consumer behavior or marketing management, or (b) the results of recent research that has far-reaching consequences for marketing management and research, or (c) new theoretical stances that may help to understand marketing management and consumer behavior.

The book is organized in four parts:

Part I   Consumer-oriented marketing

The first two chapters present overviews of the role of consumer behavior in marketing. Chapter 1 deals specifically with the need for marketing managers to appreciate the findings of consumer research. It shows how consumer behavior concepts are related to marketing management at various stages of the product life cycle, and it sets the scene for later sections which elucidate these concepts. Chapter 2 shows how consumer behavior differs at each stage of the process in which new products diffuse through the marketplace and discusses the need for a variety of models of consumer choice.

Part II   The cognitive consumer

Three chapters follow that deal with consumer decision making and elaborate on the procedures involved as means by which consumers receive and process the information with which they are daily bombarded, and form judgments by way of attitudes and behaviors that manifest in the marketplace. The material on perception, learning and information processing is related at each stage to the needs of marketing managers. These chapters deal with topics that play an important part in the information processing models of consumer behavior which have dominated the subject over the last three decades. Our exposition is broadly linked to the sequence of cognitive decision making found in these models: perception is associated with the inputs to the information-processing system; learning is related to the processing of information; and attitude formation and change to the outputs of the process. But each of these topics is broader than this and we have not confined our discussion to the framework implied by the cognitive models. Instead, we have emphasized the general insights into consumer behavior each concept provides and its range of implications for marketing management.

Part III   The personal consumer

Consumer behavior is influenced by much more than cognitive information processing, and three more chapters deal with the consumer's personality, information-processing *style*, and underlying motivations. They consider the nature of personality, the empirical research linking traits and types of character with consumer choice in the marketplace, the influence of cognitive style on patterns of consumer innovativeness, and the ways of looking more deeply at the motivational structures that not only influence the browsing and purchase behavior of the 'big spenders' whom we shall encounter in Chapter 7, but also influence the patterns of buying and consuming that characterize all consumers. By going beyond the model of the consumer as a processor of information, a model derived from the design and operation of the computer, these chapters emphasize the part played by consumption in everyday life and in the shaping of people's lifestyles.

Part IV   Consumers in context

Finally, the book puts consumer behavior into the situational and social context that is so familiar to marketing managers and indeed to all citizens of affluent societies. The last two chapters are concerned therefore with environmental influences and social structure. Too often, the emphasis accorded the information-processing models of consumer deliberation and choice have obscured the important role played by external influences. We discuss, first, the ways in which the retail environment shapes consumer patronage and behavior: the effects of shopping malls and other architectural developments on store choice and repeat buying, and the ways in which in-store factors such as shop design and the active use of merchandising techniques affect choice. Second, we turn to the place of the consumer in the social structure, the influence of social groups on what is consumed, and the particular ways in which the family, cultures, subcultures and social class influence choice.

Part I

Consumer-oriented marketing

Chapter 1

The marketing task

CONSUMER ORIENTATION

The increasing pressures of highly competitive marketing environments make it imperative that firms understand consumers and, in particular, consumer decision making as they seek to gain competitive advantage. In a competitive economic system, the survival and growth of firms require accurate knowledge about consumers: how they buy, why they buy, and where they buy, as well as just what they buy. Hence modern marketing thought stresses the need of business managers to know who their customers are and why they choose *their* products rather than those of rival firms. Marketing is not about finding or inducing someone to buy whatever the firm happens to manufacture. Nowadays successful management depends more than ever on matching every aspect of the business – product, advertising, after-sales service and so on – to the satisfaction of consumer needs. This is the essence of consumer orientation as an integrated approach to business management.

Consumer orientation stems from the firm's adoption and implementation of the Marketing Concept, a philosophy of business organization which has four major implications:

- The success of any firm depends above all on the consumer and what he or she is willing to accept and pay for.
- The firm must be aware of what the market wants, preferably well before production commences, and, in the case of highly technological industries, long before production is even planned.
- Consumer wants must be continually monitored and measured so that, through product and market development, the firm keeps ahead of its competitors.
- Top management must achieve the integration of all components of marketing strategy (or

the four Ps: product development, pricing, place or distribution, and promotion) into a single strategic plan based upon knowledge of consumer behavior.

In a nutshell: 'to start out with the customer's utility, with what the customer buys, with what the realities of the customer are and what the customer's values are – this is what marketing is all about' (Drucker 1985: 233).

This concept of business management is not founded on altruism. It emphasizes the profitability of the firm as well as the satisfaction of buyers by showing that profits follow service. But nor is consumer-oriented management an optional extra: it is an essential corporate outlook in affluent, competitive societies in which consumers enjoy unprece- dented levels of discretionary income and the power of choice this makes possible. We may argue whether consumer orientation is ultimately a cause or a consequence of effective marketing – what is unarguable is that striving for a clear understanding of consumers' present and probable behavior, plus a willingness to respond positively to that under- standing, is a mark of the outstandingly successful business enterprise (W. Goldsmith and Clutterbuck 1985; Peters 1988; Peters and Waterman 1982).

Let us admit straightway that such firms are relatively few. Drucker expresses surprise and concern that so few business executives have taken this philosophy to heart:

> why after forty years of preaching Marketing, teaching Marketing, professing Marketing, so few suppliers are willing to follow, I cannot explain. The fact remains that so far, anyone who is willing to use marketing as the basis for strategy is likely to acquire leadership in an industry or a market fast and almost without risk.
>
> (Drucker 1985: 233)

But the difference in managerial style and its impact on sales and profits is clear as soon as one considers actual examples of business practice.

Take for instance the C5, marketed as an electric car but perceived by many people as resembling a three-wheeled cycle – pedals were provided for additional power going up hills. This short-lived product provides an example of product-oriented genius unaided by the ideas and needs of those expected to buy. Introduced into the UK car market in 1985, a C5 was advertised the following year as 'a working collector's item' (Payton 1988: 73). The C5's originator, Sir Clive Sinclair, has been described as a nonbeliever in market research, guided by the view that a market should be created after a product has been developed (Marks 1989). What research was carried out was very limited and suggested that any market would be specialized and small. An emphasis on technical product development predominated to the detriment of concept development and testing. Test marketing was entirely absent but would have assisted in the reduction of difficulties that arose after national launch, notably in distribution (Marks 1989).

By contrast, straightforward market research carried out on behalf of the sponsors of an electric car project in South Australia indicated what the carrying capacity, range and performance characteristics of an acceptable vehicle would have to be, and showed how potential consumers perceived an electric car in comparison to existing automobiles (Payton 1988; Dale 1985).

MARKET SEGMENTATION AND PRODUCT POSITIONING

The job of the marketing manager is diverse and complicated. To isolate one field of responsibility as 'the marketing task' may, therefore, seem arbitrary. Any marketing textbook shows how managers can accomplish any number of marketing tasks. Yet there is one broad area of responsibility which alone belongs to the marketing function: the creation and exploitation of marketing mixes that enhance the firm's sales position and profit performance. We have argued that this can be achieved only through consumer-oriented management. Further, we can point up two principal spheres of activity which go a long way toward defining the content of this job and which follow directly from the adoption of an outlook of profitable consumer orientation: market segmentation and product positioning. There is another reason why we focus here on market segmentation and product positioning. The first is based on the analysis of consumer groups based on the use of objective criteria: socio-demographic, economic, psychographic, geographic, or whatever. But the second is concerned with the need for marketing managers to create marketing mixes that reflect consumers' subjective perceptual and cognitive processing of information about such matters, their personal lifestyles, values and motivations. Nothing more clearly illustrates the requirement that marketing analysis, planning and control be consumer-oriented.

Market segmentation refers to the necessity of subdividing large mass markets into smaller segments each containing a relatively homogeneous group of consumers (Smith 1956). For example, consumer markets can be divided into heavy and light user segments or into segments that seek distinct benefits in their use of a product. Once a market has been thus segmented, so that the firm has a good grasp of the structure of the market to which it is selling, it is possible for the marketer to select one or more target segments on which to focus. This process of segmenting and selecting markets makes the allocation of corporate resources more *efficient* in the sense that funds and manpower are allocated to relatively smaller groups of consumers than if the whole market were the target. The practice of segmentation also makes the design of marketing strategy more *effective* because the manager has the sense of directing resources at specific and identifiable groups of people rather than at diverse collections of individuals.

Effective market segmentation is impossible without thorough consumer research that leads to an incisive understanding of the economic, social and – where relevant – psychological position of the consumer. Economic location is determined by data on income, access to credit, incidence and extent of taxation, savings and other financial commitments. Social location includes status and class position, family and other group memberships, and situational influences and cultural observances and affiliations. Psychological location includes attitudes and personality, information-processing style, innovation-proneness, and prior behavioral learning. Of the three disciplines that underlie these concepts of consumer location, sociology and social psychology rather than economics have played a decisive role in informing marketing managerial decisions. And it is on these two disciplines that this book draws predominantly to illumine consumers' decision processes and the social environment that shapes them.

Examples of market segmentation abound. To reverse recent declining revenues, the retailing giant, Sears, has begun to advertise in high fashion magazines such as *Vogue* in an effort to target fashion-conscious women with the message: 'Sears now sells stylish clothes'. Along with the new advertising, Sears is updating its selection and renovating its stores (*Wall Street Journal*, August 15, 1990). This example illustrates how a marketer segments the market, chooses a potentially profitable target (in this case younger, more affluent shoppers), and tries to position its product using a persuasive message transmitted via demographically tailored media.

Product positioning refers to the use of the strategic marketing tools, the four Ps, to give a brand a specific and often unique image or position in the minds of the consumers in each target segment. The integrated functioning of these four factors should be focused on presenting a specific target segment with a single image of a brand so that they know what the brand will do for them and how it can be distinguished from competing brands. Marketing managers must allocate limited corporate resources to the achievement of this end. That is, they must spend their limited funds in the four areas of product development, pricing, distribution and promotion with the goal of positioning a brand into a unique place in the market (Ries and Trout 1980). This is true even in highly competitive markets where much of the strategic energies of managers are focused on competitors (Ries and Trout 1986).

Market segmentation and product positioning go hand in hand. Market segmentation refers to the process of dividing the market into smaller, relatively homogeneous segments, some of which are chosen as target markets. Product positioning refers to the marketer's efforts to give his or her brand a specific position in the mind of the chosen target market segment (Ries and Trout 1981). Product positioning is the aim and inevitable result of executing a market strategy. The effect of the four Ps on consumers is the product's position in their minds. This position is how they view the brand relative to its competitors along with a set of descriptive dimensions. Since a brand's position is one of the most important factors in its ultimate success or failure, positioning is one of the most important and carefully attended to aspects of marketing.

Once a marketer has segmented the market and selected an attractive market segment to target, two decisions must be made: first, what product position will the marketer try to give the brand in the target market's mind; second, what are the best means to attain that position? Hiram Walker, for example, has made a major commitment to position its many liquor brands to consumers to strengthen lagging sales. Because Americans are drinking less hard liquor than in years past, it is important for this distiller to meet this challenge by getting drinkers to choose Hiram Walker brands when they *do* decide to drink. Their strategy is to position them as more expensive, premium liquor brands with superior quality and taste. The ad strategy is to get consumers to perceive its brand as the best in their respective categories (Strand 1988).

The core of the marketing manager's job can be viewed as the process of decision making and resource allocation in order to accomplish corporate goals of sales and profits. The tools available to the manager are these concepts of segmentation and positioning via the four Ps. In order to be successful in these tasks, however, the manager must have detailed information on consumers: what they are like, how they live, what they want from products, where and how they get their information, which prices they are willing to pay, where they shop, and what advertising will appeal to them. The decision process of the marketing manager relies on the output of marketing and consumer research for the information which guides him/her in these decision areas. And this information-based marketing decision making depends upon the behavioral sciences for its understanding of consumers.

The success of such a marketing strategy depends on managers understanding the consumer and properly executing a strategy based on this understanding. But the use of consumer behavior in the service of marketing goals goes beyond such fairly simple programs. For years, consumer researchers have sought to develop comprehensive models of consumer decision making in an effort to gain a broad perspective of this complex field. Since these models have occupied a large portion of the literature in consumer behavior and provide a useful starting point for studying consumers, the next section discusses these models.

Among those companies that have achieved marketing- or consumer-oriented management, considerable interest has been expressed in using the behavioral sciences, especially social psychology and sociology, to understand purchase and consumption. As a result, consumers' psychological backgrounds have been investigated in order to establish the extent to which factors like attitudes, motives and personality traits affect buying behavior. Social influences such as class, status and the family have also been examined for their contribution to our understanding of consumer decision making. The result has been a heightened awareness of the nature of price awareness and perception, the stimulus seeking that underlies new product search and purchase, the attitudes that determine consumers' choice of retail outlet, and the perceptual processes involved in reactions to persuasive communications. This book is concerned with concepts and variables such as these and with their usefulness in consumer research and marketing management.

THE PRODUCT LIFE CYCLE

Market segmentation and product positioning do not occur in isolation. They need to be varied over the life cycle of a product – which maps out the stages in the career of a product market from birth to decline – as consumer needs and competitive pressures are modified with the passage of time. Hence the product-market life cycle, or PLC, presents the marketing task in essence. We choose this vehicle simply because it is familiar to marketing managers and students of marketing (not because it is without criticism) and because it permits us to understand the various phases of consumer behavior in an overall, integrated context relevant to both managerial marketing and consumer orientation. The PLC describes the typical stages through which a successful product class passes (expressed in terms of unit sales) as it comes into being, thrives, matures and dies. It therefore provides a conceptual framework to discuss several topics in consumer behavior, including the development and diffusion of innovations and repeat buying. Three broad decisions dominate marketing management over the life cycle of a product:

- *Developing and introducing new products* A new combination shampoo-conditioner attracted little attention from Procter & Gamble top management when their scientists first invented it. A few years later, *Pert Plus* not only revived the poorly selling *Pert* shampoo line, it became the leading brand, with about 12 percent of the $1.4 billion US market (Swasy 1990).

- *Managing brands through growth and into maturity* In order to boost sales of its successful but venerable soft drink, Mello Yello, the Coca-Cola Company began a round of aggressive and expensive promotional efforts. In the movie *Days of Thunder*, Tom Cruise drove a souped-up Chevy Lumina with the Mello Yello logo prominently displayed on the hood. This was accompanied by a $3 million campaign including a Lumina giveaway, T-shirts, racing jackets, and a commercial starring one of the movie's characters (Konrad 1990).
- *Revitalizing old brands* Sales of the popular toy line of G.I. Joe action figures began to decline in the late 1980s. Only quick reformulation of the product ('out went combat fatigues and in came space units, jet packs, and battle copers') rejuvenated the line (Hammons 1991).

We begin with a general description of the PLC and its stages. Each of the stages in turn is then used as a managerial framework to present key topics in consumer behavior: innovativeness, repeat-buying behavior, and product demise. The PLC is one of the most important and widely known concepts in marketing because it holds the key to understanding sales and profit trends for so many products, services and brands. Figure 1.1 shows an idealized PLC. Products, like organisms, are conceived, born; sales grow rapidly for a

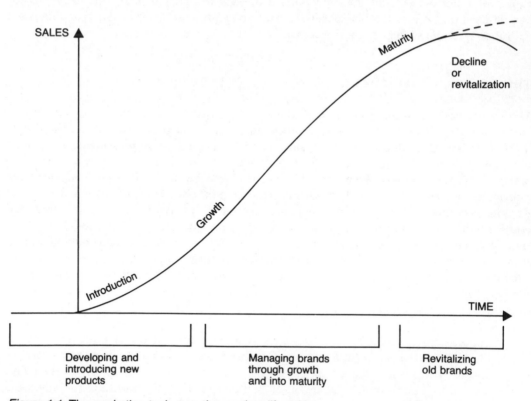

Figure 1.1 The marketing task over the product life cycle

short time, level off or plateau into flat or slow growth, and often decline as sales drop, until the product is no longer profitable. Individual product life cycles vary in form and in length of time, ranging from overnight fads to decades of consistent sales. The empirical evidence, however, suggests that the basic pattern holds for many products and brands.

The PLC reminds managers that no product sells forever and that they need to engage in constant new product development (Kuczmarski 1988). Perhaps more important, the PLC stages guide marketing strategies. These vary in emphasis from stage to stage and involve new product development, different spending levels for marketing activities, changes in the marketing mix, and decisions about what to do with declining products of brands: sell them, kill them, or revitalize (relaunch or reposition) them.

Developing and introducing new products

In reality, the life of a product or brand begins before its entry into the marketplace. Firms spend much time, energy and money on the process of delivering a new product to market. This is because few topics in business are more important than the development and successful launch of new products and services. They are the life blood of the firm; most future profits will come from products not yet in the current portfolio. In the US, for example, the average supermarket carries more than 16,000 items, a 45.5 percent increase since 1985 (Liesse 1991). Consequently, the new product development process has attracted a great deal of both managerial and scholarly attention (Foxall 1984a; Gruenwald 1988; Urban and Hauser 1980).

Essentially, new product development consists of a sequence of stages or steps beginning with product idea generation, followed by various evaluations and analyses designed to screen the various ideas for feasibility, profitability, compatibility with corporate strategy and resources, and probability of success (Kuczmarski 1988). The end of the sequence is a new product or brand launched into the marketplace. Many new product ideas are proposed by customers, sales people, managers and researchers, but few of them reach the launch stage and few of the new products appearing in the marketplace each year prove successful in the sense of either breaking even or yielding a profit (Dumaine 1991).

The new product development process can be very costly. Because the success of new products is so important to the firm, marketers should carefully and systematically research the needs and wants of their markets to enhance the chances that their brands will succeed. Much of the information about consumer needs and motivations discussed in this book bears on the new product development process as marketers strive to learn as much about their target markets as they can in order to create attractive product offerings.

The post-launch section of the introduction stage begins when the product is launched into the market, either all at once or rolled out gradually. Up to this point in time the product acts only as a cost, producing no revenue. Profits come slowly because product introduction usually entails heavy costs that must be paid back, and the product's unit costs are typically higher now than later in the PLC; rarely are new products immediately profitable. Marketers are therefore interested in accelerating the product through this stage of the life cycle so that greater sales and profits will accrue faster. Much of the success of the new product comes from accurate and effective new product development, correctly gauging what benefits consumers want from consuming the product, ensuring that it is promoted effectively, pricing it to sell, and distributing it in the most effective ways possible.

Moreover, new product success also depends on acceptance by the first buyers of the product – the innovators. This key consumer segment is vital to new product success because they are typically heavy users in the product category and therefore are likely to buy much of the product at full price, providing important revenue. Innovators are also important because they provide important feedback to marketers, pointing out product flaws and ways to improve the product early enough in the PLC to allow the marketer to make improvements and fix mistakes. Success with the innovators may result in market leadership (capturing a dominant share of 'mind') and raise effective barriers to entry that prevent other firms from easily entering the market. Finally, product acceptance by innovators legitimizes the product for later buyers and stimulates positive word-of-mouth (WOM) communication, which makes the new product more widely known and acceptable to other consumers and helps them to buy. The decision strategy followed most often by innovators has been termed 'extended decision making'. This means the innovative consumers are most likely to proceed through a careful sequence of steps in the decision process.

Managing brands into maturity

As sales increase rapidly (assuming the product has not failed with the innovators, whose rejection signals early product death), profits increase to their maximum. Not only can the firm charge a premium price, but until competitors enter the market or react to the new brand, there is little downward pressure on prices and marketing costs can be held to a minimum. Advertising support is usually very heavy to spread news of the product to the mass market. Firms increase efforts to expand distribution to more retail outlets. Of particular importance during the growth stage is the desirability of positive word-of-mouth communications about the product as the early adopters have become the target segment. Many consumers have heard about the product through advertising, personal selling or sales promotion. They wait to try the product, however, until they can get information from the innovators who have already tried it. The early adopters will act as important sources of word of mouth for later buyers as well. Thus, the topics of social communication and opinion leadership are important here. Because many of these consumers know about the product and have already tried it, their decision-making strategy is called 'limited problem solving'. This decision style uses less energy than extended problem solving because consumers have a good idea of what they want from the product and what existing brands provide. They basically choose from a reduced set of the available brands.

As the majority of consumers who are potential buyers of the product make their purchase, competitors enter the market and the channels of distribution become saturated with products, sales tend to peak and level off, and profits begin to decline slowly. The maturity phase describes many product markets. The new product or brand is no longer new to most consumers. The brand is often sold at a discount. Advertising expenditure is stable or declines, and sale promotions may increase. Many consumers are in the mode of 'routine problem solving'. They have an evoked set of brands which they consider when purchase is needed, and they select from this limited set. Brand switching is prevalent, so researchers need new theories besides diffusion of innovations to account for consumer behavior at this stage.

Hence, as a brand moves through the growth phase and into maturity, most consumption becomes repeat buying rather than trial and adoption of innovations. Market share becomes quite stable, and most of the emphasis in marketing strategy is on defending the brand from attempts by other marketers to take customers away (encouraging brand loyalty) or on attacking other brands to tempt away their customers (encouraging brand switching). Much attention is given to the perceptions consumers have of the brand (its brand image) and how this image can be enhanced, modified or extended. The concept of product positioning becomes of primary concern. This section on consumer behavior during the maturity phase, therefore, deals with the topics of brand image, product positioning, brand loyalty and switching, and repeat buying.

Revitalizing old brands

The product is now old. Both sales and profits are declining. Advertising and sales support probably are declining as well. The market is either saturated with competing brands that sell at comparable prices and/or primary demand is decreasing (e.g., black and white TVs). Consumers who buy the product for the first time are termed 'laggards' and represent little market potential. There may be shakeouts in the industry as weaker brands fail, companies withdraw from the market, brands are absorbed by other brands, etc.

Company strategies tend to focus on increasing productivity and cutting costs as the brand is milked for what profits remain. The most important decisions are whether to kill the brand, or sell it to another company, or attempt to revitalize it by repositioning it for new markets, or revitalize the product itself through redevelopment, improvements and so forth. Most consumer decision making during this stage follows the routine response pattern.

RESPONDING TO CONSUMER BEHAVIOR

Each of these tasks involves responding creatively and effectively to consumer behavior, and requires a thorough understanding of the dynamics of purchase and consumption patterns over the life cycle. Corresponding to the previous outline of the PLC stages, there are three broad components of the marketing task:

- reflecting consumer needs in new product development,
- establishing and maintaining brand loyalty, and
- ensuring consumer satisfaction during product decline.

Reflecting consumers' needs in new product development

The tasks inherent in marketing management at each of the broad stages of the product life cycle translate into the need to understand and respond creatively to three aspects of consumer behavior: reflecting consumer needs during product development, establishing and maintaining brand loyalty during maturity, and adapting to consumers' changing sources of satisfaction during the final phases of the brand's life.

Because a stream of successful new products is essential for the health of a company, marketers know that one of their most important tasks is to bring new products to market. Unfortunately, most new products fail. How can the product developer enhance his chances of scoring a hit? Researchers who have studied both successful and unsuccessful innovation diffusion have suggested that several characteristics of innovations as they are perceived by consumers play an important role in new product success (Rogers 1983).

Need fulfillment

Consumers do not buy products they do not need. What they feel they need, however, is a complex subjective assessment based on their inherent motivations and on their perceptions of the nature of the external world. For a new product to succeed, consumers must perceive that it will satisfy some need or combination of needs. The marketer therefore must try to ascertain as best he can what basic motivations can be satisfied by the product and then design the product so that it provides these benefits for the consumer. Of primary importance here is the requirement that the product be presented to consumers in such a way that they will perceive that the product will deliver the benefits they desire, or at least try it once; if it succeeds in delivering the goods, so to speak, its chances of success are good. The better it does the job marketers promise, the faster it will diffuse, other things being equal. Nevertheless, several other perceptual characteristics influence the success and speed of new product acceptance.

Relative advantage

Consumers make an assessment of whether the new product does a better job of providing benefits than existing products. Many new products fail not because they are inferior, but because they simply do not provide additional benefits to the consumer, offering no convincing reason to switch brands in the face of the risk that the unknown product will not perform as desired. The emphasis here is on the marketer's ability to improve the product and add value to it from the consumer's perspective. Other things being equal, a superior product will sell better than one that is simply a copy.

Compatibility

This perceptual characteristic refers to the consumer's belief that the new product offering will be consistent with existing values and lifestyles. New products that ask consumers to change what they consider important, or to change their usual way of living, will diffuse slowly if at all. Persuading consumers to adopt new practices, such as recycling used paper and packaging, is difficult because it calls for changes in everyday living. If consumers can be persuaded that recycling is compatible with their values, such as a healthy environment, the task becomes easier. In general, the more compatible a new product is, the fewer demands it makes on consumers to change the way they live or want to live, and the faster it will diffuse.

Complexity

As consumers evaluate a new product, one assessment they make is how complex or difficult it will be to use. This perceptual issue is especially important for durables such as appliances or other machines. Other things being equal, most consumers prefer the simple to the complex, so that marketers should strive to design their new products to be as simple as possible and promote this feature to the marketplace. The more complex a new product is, the more effort the marketer will have to devote to persuading consumers of its value. In selling their personal computers, for instance, IBM tried to overcome consumers' fears of the product's complexity by using a Little Tramp character to humanize it and show that 'everyman' could operate the device (Burstein 1983).

Conspicuousness

The more visible a new product is to consumers, the more rapidly it will diffuse. People must know about a product before they will think about buying it. Marketers often put extra effort into publicizing their new products or into other ways of making them visible, so that word-of-mouth communication will facilitate diffusion. Highly visible products diffuse more rapidly than invisible products because people can see the product in use.

Trialability

Because adopting innovations or buying new products often entails risk for the consumer, marketers try to reduce perceived risk where they can. One way is to allow trial of the new product without commitment from the consumer. Test drives of new cars or loans of complex equipment allow the consumer to experience the new product with little risk and thereby enhance the chances that it will sell. For consumer package goods, the free trial size or the sample represents a highly divisible product that can be broken into small portions so that consumers can try it with no risk. Marketers should seek new ways to use the approach to speed the diffusion of their new products.

Establishing and maintaining brand loyalty

In mature markets, differentiated competing brands will tend to assume relatively stable market shares as consumers tend to purchase the same brand (or patronize the same store) time after time. This pattern of buying the same preferred brand each time a product is purchased is called brand loyalty (Busch and Houston 1985: 221). Consumers develop repeat-buying patterns because they learn that particular brands are especially satisfying or because they come to form personal attachments to the brands. This may be because the brand uniquely provides the benefits they seek, fits well into their lifestyle, or its personality (image) matches that of the consumer. Brand loyalty can also stem from the emotional impact the brand has on the consumer or from the way the brand makes the consumer feel about himself (Liesse 1991; Schlueter 1992).

Consumers may form strong personal attachments to brands, as Coca-Cola found when the firm sought to replace Old Coke with New Coke (Fisher 1985). Sometimes, however, consumers repeatedly buy a brand out of habit or routine problem solving in order to save time and effort (Howard 1989). This repeat-buying pattern may appear to be true loyalty, but instead represents indifference on the part of many consumers. Repeat buying, whether true loyalty implying a positive emotional or affective reaction to the brand or simple thoughtless habit, reduces consumer risk and helps guarantee standards of product performance for consumers. Brand loyalty is highly valued because it facilitates segmentation based on usage and because it is cheaper to sell a product to loyal customers than to attract non-loyalists to your brand. The consumer franchise, the core loyalists, represents a key target segment for most firms, and one which they should devote maximum effort to satisfying (Peters and Waterman 1982). Consequently, the subject of brand loyalty and its complement, brand switching (which occurs when consumers buy different brands), have long attracted the attention of marketers and consumer researchers.

Unfortunately, the construct of brand loyalty has proved to be difficult to define precisely and to measure reliably. It is obvious that virtually no consumer buys the same brand every time he or she purchases, but brand selection is not completely stochastic either. Thus brand loyalty is a matter of degree – how often or what proportion of purchases are allocated to a single brand. This issue has proved so troublesome that one source details over fifty separate attempts to define and measure brand loyalty, many of which fail to yield similar results on the same objective purchase data (Jacoby and Chestnut 1978). Part of the reason this issue is so complicated is that the tendency to be brand loyal differs from one consumer to the next. Moreover, consumers in general are more loyal to brands in some product classes than in others (Alsop 1989; Bogart 1984; Howard 1989). Products that provide strong social, symbolic or emotional benefits (such as cigarettes), or that provide specific hedonic tastes (such as coffee) seem to attract more loyalty from consumers than do commodity-like products such as aluminum foil or garbage bags. Brand loyalty may also vary by purchase situation, as consumers tend to prefer certain brands for specific occasions which they would not use at other times. The fact that many consumer goods are purchased for use by different household members also makes brand loyalty difficult to define and detect.

This problem of conceptualizing and measuring brand loyalty is central to marketers' concern for their target markets and how to retain their loyal consumers. There was some concern in the 1970s that American consumers were becoming less brand loyal than before, especially as low-price generic products appeared in stores. In 1975 a survey by Needham, Harper and Steers advertising agency found that 80 percent of men and 72 percent of women agreed: 'I try to stick with well-known brand names.' In 1980, however, these figures had fallen to 64 and 56 percent, respectively (Bogart 1984: 93). Tod Johnson (1984), however, has published figures suggesting that brand loyalty for many consumer goods held steady or actually increased a little from 1975 to 1983. As the decade of the 1990s begins, concern again grows that store and brand loyalty are eroding, that images and reputations will decay in the face of price discounting by major retail chains who have come to dominate the distribution and merchandising of many consumer goods (Graham 1988; Liesse 1991). This specter of the brand as commodity frightens many manufacturers of branded merchandise. Even more frightening is the growth of the private label or 'store' brand version of a product, heavily discounted but supported by the ubiquity and reputation of the mass-market distributor, which eats into the margins of the 'name' brand product. Such challenges will surely stimulate marketers to find new ways to build loyalty to their brands.

One recent tactic for loyalty building has been termed frequency marketing: 'to identify, maintain, and increase the yield from best Customers, through long-term, interactive, value added relationships' (Colloquy 1993). FM stands for an interconnected set of programs designed to link customers with brands by engaging them into clubs entitling members to special discounts, newsletters, tie-in purchases, credit cards, promotions and other privileges. The Burger King Kids Club, for example, features characters such as Snaps, Jaws, IQ, Boomer, Wheels and Paws. Free club membership entitles members to a secret code name, a subscription to *Adventure* newsletter, and discounts with partner airlines. Kids Club meals at Burger King restaurants offer premiums like Lickety Splits (toys that are shaped like french fries and burgers), Teenage Mutant Ninja Turtles and Beetlejuice Figurines.

Repeat buying

The concepts of market segmentation and product positioning we have presented imply that the overall market will consist of relatively homogeneous segments to which marketers position brands using their marketing strategies. Although objectively there may be few differences among these brands, they will have unique images that consumers perceive and researchers can measure. This is the idea of product differentiation and brand segmentation, and it carries with it the concept we have examined of brand loyalty, that consumers form positive attachments to particular brands and limit most of their purchases in a product field to a single or a very few brands.

The topic of repeat buying is important because without some level of repeat buying, a new brand will not survive the maturity phase of the product life cycle. Most descriptions of brand loyalty and switching imply that consumers are loyal to a single brand in a product field and remain so unless competitive marketing efforts lure them to another brand. Advertising and sales promotion are emphasized as the means to persuade consumers to switch brands or stores. The picture of the market provided by aggregate purchasing data appears to show the success of these efforts as large percentages of buyers fail to purchase the same brand at each purchase. In this 'leaky-bucket' theory of consumption, advertising plays the important role of persuading non-users and other-brand users to switch (East 1990). Many contemporary observers stress the effects of sustained promotions on eroding brand loyalty, which leads consumers to become more price conscious and place less emphasis on the image of the brand itself (Liesse 1991). In this leaky-bucket theory of consumption, marketers must constantly use advertising, promotion and other marketing mix variables to replenish the loss of these old buyers with new buyers. In the light of the difficulties observed in reliably and validly defining and measuring brand loyalty (Jacoby and Chestnut 1978), another perspective may be more useful to managers seeking to understand repeat-buying behavior.

An alternative view of repeat buying is presented by Ehrenberg (1972). In a large and methodical body of research, he argues that repeat-buying behavior is more stable than this and can be described by a mathematical model. For many frequently purchased products, it appears that consumers form a stable propensity to purchase a brand or brands in a given product field much as a habit is developed. That is, consumers form relatively stable buying habits after a new product is introduced into the market or their need for an old product makes it new to them. They cease to give a great deal of thought and energy to evaluating brands in the field, and marketing efforts that cause them to 'switch' loyalty can only achieve short-run success: as the strategy ceases, consumers go back to their old buying patterns.

The work of Ehrenberg and his colleagues has shown that if we collect objective data on purchases of the same brands by the same consumers over time, we find that many markets are approximately stationary; that is, the distribution of heavy and light buyers, the rates of repeat purchase of individual brands, and the patterns of purchase by consumers can be described and predicted. Even though sales exhibit short-run fluctuations because of seasonal influences, promotional efforts or distribution fluctuations, patterns of repeat buying seem to fit well-defined models. This is because 'either the same people buy the same amount or because the increase in the tendency to buy among some people is matched by a decrease among others' (East 1990: 26). Although this approach to describing repeat buying gives little insight into why consumers buy as they do, the actual patterns of repeat purchase can be accurately described by a probabilistic model.

For periods of time larger than the average interpurchase interval for a product, a Poisson distribution provides a close approximation to brand purchase. Some consumers buy more of a product than do others, and these heavy users buy more from one time period to another. Many more consumers are once-only buyers who enter and leave the market in droves. These buyers too may buy the brand again in another time period. Hence the term 'brand loyalty' may be insufficient to describe repeated heavy purchases. Infrequent buyers may be loyal to the degree that they repurchase the brand, however infrequently. Over time, mature markets are not characterized by a continual loss of buyers. It appears that instead only a few regular buyers of a brand who buy in one period, say a quarter, also buy in the next period, indicating relatively low levels of repeat buying. But this does not mean erosion of repeat buying, for the differences in rate of repeat buying seem to account for this pattern. That is, for those heavy-user buyers in one period who do not buy in the next quarter there are many heavy-user buyers who did not buy in the previous quarter who do buy in the next. The varying purchase frequencies mean that even heavy users will not buy every consecutive quarter, but they will buy again in a subsequent quarter. Hence, marketers should spend less effort on trying to attract new users to replace old ones; they should act defensively to try to retain old, heavy and light users, who in fact have not switched brands, but who simply do not purchase every quarter.

Ehrenberg's probabilistic model of repeat buying is based on repeat-purchase data that shows that mature markets tend to be stationary, that individual purchases follow a Poisson distribution, and that long-run average purchase rates of individuals follow a Gamma distribution. The repeat-purchase rate of a brand depends on the size of its penetration (market share) and on its purchase frequency and period. The probability of making a purchase in a given period is determined by a negative binomial formula, hence the theory is termed the Negative Binomial Distribution Theory.

Empirical studies of purchase of many brands and other similar repeated behaviors (such as smoking cessation, TV watching, and participation in the London University Executive Program) have confirmed that the NBD theory provides good predictions of repeat behavior. In addition, the theory and model have revealed that sole brand loyalty and repeat purchase depend mainly on purchase frequency, but only slightly on market penetration (East 1990: 29), thus repeat purchase of a brand can be predicted accurately from knowledge of its purchase frequency and penetration. Differences in market share across brands, however, are due more to greater penetration than to purchase frequency. The model also reveals the phenomenon of *double jeopardy*, which describes the fact that less popular brands, those with small market shares (penetration), are bought by fewer people and those who do buy them do so less often (Ehrenberg, Goodhardt and Barwise 1990). As we shall see in Chapter 8, double jeopardy also applies to stores: people buy less per visit at the stores they patronize less often.

Ensuring consumer satisfaction during product decline

Products may go into a decline phase of the PLC for many reasons, including changes in market structure such as changing demographics or mobility, changes in consumer lifestyles or attitudes, technological obsolescence, legal/regulatory changes, or simply heavy competitive pressure. If the entire product category is in decline, marketers from competing companies may have to band together to stimulate primary demand. New product forms may have to be created, new markets developed, or new uses for the product discovered. If a given brand is in decline compared with competing brands, the reasons may have more to do with the brand itself. One reason a brand's share may decline relative to competing brands is that consumers may be dissatisfied with it, and this dissatisfaction may lead them to not repurchase.

Satisfaction or dissatisfaction with a brand are two of the possible outcomes of the consumer decision to consume the brand. The post-purchase evaluation after the first trial of the brand represents perhaps the key factor in a new brand's success. Regardless of the levels of advertising, promotion and distribution, failure of the brand to satisfy consumers will doom it. As the old saying goes, 'Good advertising kills a bad product'. The consumer's thoughts and feelings about the brand after consumption will be stored in long-term memory and possibly modify the evaluative criteria he or she uses to evaluate brands in the category. They may also modify the search process used to gather information, the way needs are recognized and fulfilled, or other aspects of the decision process.

Long-run satisfaction is also necessary for the brand to retain enough repeat buying to be a success. Consumers do not need to be completely satisfied to buy the brand again:

they only need to be satisfied enough, and more than with another brand (O'Shaughnessy 1987: 181). Hence, consumer satisfaction/ dissatisfaction should be continuously monitored by marketing management so that corrective action can be taken at the onset of a clear negative sales trend. In addition, marketers may want to be more proactive in enhancing levels of satisfaction so as to prevent competitors from gaining an upper hand in this important area. The process of constantly improving products and their delivery so that they increase satisfaction is a viable marketing strategy that can render valuable competitive advantage to firms that practice it.

Consumer judgments of satisfaction/dissatisfaction arise from a process of expectation formation. Consumers enter the market with expectations of product benefits and performance. Comparing the results of consumption to these expectations leads to either positive disconfirmation of the expectations (in which the brand delivered more benefits than expected) or to confirmation (where the brand meets expectations) or to negative disconfirmation (where the product fails to provide expected benefits). Obviously, the marketer wants at least to meet the expected level of performance and product satisfaction compared to competing brands. Over-satisfying consumers may be the best way for a brand to survive and forestall competitors. When consumers' expectations are not met, dissatisfaction results and unhappy consumers may complain, switch brands, and probably spread negative word-of-mouth reports about the product. Some management theorists argue that for long-run success, marketers should 'under-promise and over-deliver', thereby heightening consumer satisfaction and generating repeat buying and positive word of mouth (Peters 1988: 96). Ultimately, of course, if the product class is truly in decline, the only long-term answer is to develop new brands in new product classes – a return to the task of reflecting changing consumer needs in new product development.

SUMMARY

The guiding philosophy of marketing, the marketing concept, as well as most recent business commentators, argue that knowing and satisfying consumer needs and wants is vital to business success. Today's competitive markets force managers to take advantage of all the information they can get to help them in their main jobs or market segmentation and product positioning via four-P market strategies. To this end, a generation of consumer researchers has used the theories and techniques of the social sciences in order to understand consumer behavior.

The marketing task has been defined as the creation and profitable use of marketing mixes designed to respond sensitively to the requirements of consumers. This chapter has argued that such requirements are not static, that market segmentation and product positioning strategies are needed to accommodate the marketing offering of the firm to the demands of consumer groups at different stages of the product life cycle (PLC). The PLC describes the life of a product or brand from its inception through its introduction and spread as a viable offering in the product field. Our use of this concept has not been intended to endorse the PLC as though it were invariably an accurate descriptor of the course a product takes (cf. Dhalla and Yuseph 1976; Lambkin and Day 1988; Foxall and Fawn 1992), but as a viable means of integrating the different modes that consumer behavior takes over time and relating them systematically to the decisions faced by marketing managers (Howard 1989).

Because consumers buy brands to satisfy their needs and wants, marketers should focus much of their new product development energy on devising new brands that satisfy consumer wants better than existing brands. This strategy should enhance a new brand's chances for success. New products must win their way in the competitive marketplace by appealing to the product category innovators, the first buyers of the new brand.

Social communication and opinion leadership, consumers talking with other consumers, are major factors in brand success during the growth stage of the PLC. Once sales begin to level off, however, the brand has passed into the maturity stage. There the brand is no longer new to most consumers, and most sales represent repeat buying by heavy users. The brand's image is a principal concern at this time. The brand image or its position refers to how consumers evaluate the brand compared with competing brands in a multidimensional, perceptual space. Marketers often use marketing strategies to position their brands in the minds of consumers and perceptual mapping via multidimensional scaling techniques to measure whether their strategies have succeeded (to be discussed in Chapter 3).

Marketers traditionally have been concerned with brand loyalty, seeking to encourage repeat buying and forestall brand switching. Research on repeat-buying behavior has suggested that mature markets are characterized by a high degree of stationarity, and that patterns of repeat buying can be mathematically modeled. Market penetration and frequency of purchase seem to be the major factors in describing and predicting sales. Satisfied consumers continue to buy. Consumers may become dissatisfied with brands for many reasons. Satisfaction/dissatisfaction stems from the relative ability of brands to meet or exceed consumer expectations of how well a brand performs as a delivery system for the benefits consumers are seeking. Long-run success depends on marketers continually monitoring consumer expectations, ensuring that the brand meets these expectations, and seeking to expand the benefit delivery power of the brand. In Chapter 2 we turn to the analysis of consumer choice in behavioral science terms, showing how the decision processes inherent in the patterns of consumer behavior briefly considered above are related to one another and to the formation of attitudes and intentions.

Consumer choice in theory and practice

CONSUMER DECISION MAKING

Many fundamental facts about consumer behavior are easily ascertained just by simple observation. About eighty percent of shopping trips begin and end at home; more than half are made on foot; nearly a quarter are made by public transportation; most of the remainder involve car travel. Data such as these are often useful for planners, transportation managers and retailers. But the description of consumer movements is normally insufficient on its own for many of the other agencies concerned with the consumer. Government organizations set up to educate or protect the customer need information about the social, psychological and business forces that influence purchasing. Home economists often find that knowledge about consumer choices is basic to their work. And, as we have seen, marketing managers themselves need to be vitally and centrally concerned with the wants, needs and aspirations of their firms' customers.

Many of these groups have turned to the behavioral sciences, particularly social psychology, to understand the complexities of consumer choice. Such constructs as personality, attitude and lifestyle, social-class culture, and the social situation promise to throw light on the mass of simple facts that beset professionals in this area. But identifying and using these behavioral constructs is seldom of far-reaching help in itself. While each seems to elucidate a small aspect of consumer behavior, what is needed is an integrated framework for consumer research that shows how the concepts are interrelated and how they can be logically combined to assist not only understanding but prediction and, where necessary, intervention. In this chapter and the next, we outline some of the models that have been produced to guide consumer researchers and marketing managers in making sense of the differing patterns of consumer behavior under a variety of economic, social and behavioral conditions.

The buying process

The complexity inherent in understanding consumer behavior has led to the construction of models of the buying process that indicate the stages through which the consumer passes from the time he or she first becomes aware of a need for a product or service to the time when a product is purchased, a brand selected, and the consumer evaluates the success of his or her purchase and decides whether to buy that particular product and/or brand again. At the same time, such models usually indicate the social and psychological forces that shape the potential buyer's action at each stage in the process. The two principal aims of such model building are the prediction of future behavior, based on measurement of relevant variables, and the explanation of this behavior in terms of theoretically relevant constructs.

The more comprehensive models of the buying process are useful in specifying possible relationships between variables and in suggesting hypotheses which may be empirically tested. Most of those which have been put forward are elaborate computer flow diagrams which show the stages in the consumer's decision process and the behavioral inputs which can be used to explain his/her actions (Engel *et al.* 1968, 1990; Howard and Sheth 1969; Nicosia 1966; see also Bettman 1979).

However, despite the sophistication which has been achieved in the building of consumer models, and their usefulness in academic research, it is probably fair to say that many of them mean little in the absence of a general understanding of how customers act. We can usefully begin, therefore, with a basic outline of consumer behavior as a sequence of problem-solving stages.

Consumption is a process which begins well before a product is purchased and which extends well beyond it. Four stages can be recognized:

- the development and perception of a want or need;
- pre-purchase planning and decision making;
- the purchase act itself;
- post-purchase behavior which may lead to repeat buying, repeat sales, and disposition of the product after consumption.

Like any model of human behavior, this description simplifies and abstracts from reality. But it allows the student of consumer behavior the opportunity to isolate some of the social, psychological and business influences on consumer choice without unduly complicating the process. Its value will be seen as we follow a hypothetical consumer through the various stages involved in purchasing behavior (see Figure 2.1).

The first stage is the 'growing consciousness of a need', in which the potential customer becomes aware of a want which can be satisfied through the marketing system. There is always opportunity for firms to innovate by developing products that satisfy needs for which there is currently no adequate market offering; however, complete innovation is rare.

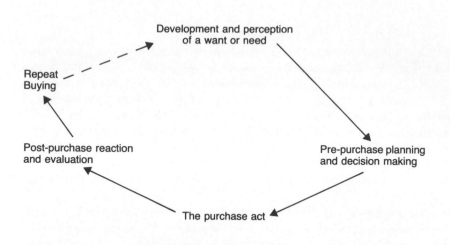

Figure 2.1 The buying process in outline

Moreover, many of the resources of the marketing manager are devoted to adapting product offerings to the particular circumstances of target segment needs and wants, not to trying to create needs and wants where none existed before. More common is the stimulation of already existing wants through advertising and sales promotion: the activation, as it were, of a latent demand. Even so-called impulse buying requires some kind of stimulus and some pattern of relevant past behavior to make the stimulus meaningful. Of paramount concern is the fact that several competing firms are trying to do the same thing. Hence the marketing manager must view all of his or her crucial product and brand decisions in the light of the intense rivalry or 'marketing warfare' (Ries and Trout 1986) that characterizes the marketplace.

Having grown aware of a want, the consumer looks for something that may satisfy it. This involves an appraisal of the products and brands on offer and available in the marketplace. Consumers are, of course, not as economically rational as economists often assume for theoretical purposes, and their knowledge of the market is usually limited. Much, if not most, of consumer market learning occurs prior to need realization as beliefs and attitudes are developed through informal exposure to sources of information (Jacoby, Hoyer and Sheluga 1980). Consumers may, moreover, be easily misinformed about what is available, its price, its reputation, and so on. The informative and persuasive functions of advertising are thus of immense importance at this stage too, but so are interpersonal influences. It may be that the desire for the product originated through the consumer's observations of or contact with another person; it is almost certain that, in the case of a fairly expensive, infrequently bought item, he or she will seek information from friends, neighbors or relatives about the relative merits of different brands (Peters 1988: 238–42).

Indeed, several studies indicate that informal, word-of-mouth communication may be much more effective than formal advertising in molding consumers' decisions (see, for instance, Price and Feick 1984).

Decisions about brand choice continue right up to the moment of purchase; even if the consumer is fairly certain of a brand before he goes to the shop, there is the possibility of his or her being influenced by point-of-sale advertising or by the salesman. Furthermore, the purchase act does not consist of a single decision, namely that of brand choice. It is a complex selection involving subdecisions regarding time and place of purchase, the possibility of mail order buying rather than a store purchase, and the method of payment, e.g., cash sale or hire purchase.

The marketing manager's interest in consumer buying does not end when a purchase has been made. Firms that survive do so because they create a degree of loyalty in their customers, because they develop groups of customers who buy the same brand again and again or who frequently patronize the same store. These customers will also spread positive information about the brand or store to other consumers through word of mouth. Moreover, sales increases are more likely to come from existing customers than from new customers (*Economist* 1992). In order for this to occur, customers clearly must be satisfied with their purchases. The company must do all within its power to make sure that its buyers are pleased with what they buy, even to the extent of reassuring them after their purchase that they have chosen the right brand. Therefore, consideration of post-purchase behaviors must take account of product nurturance activities or possession rituals such as caring for the product, improving it, talking to others about it, and finally, disposition of the product when it is used up or no longer needed (McCracken 1981).

Naturally, the consumer who becomes aware of a need may not follow all these procedures and make a purchase: lack of funds or conflicting interests may cause him or her to give attention to some other activity. But, if the consumer does go through the stages of the buying process described here, it is certain that his or her precise behavior will be modified and shaped by attitudes, self-concept, general motivation and personality, and often by social class, stage in the family life cycle and the groups to which he or she belongs (or would like to belong). Unraveling the nature of these influences on the consumer's choice is the basic task of the application of behavioral science to marketing.

HIGH INVOLVEMENT: THE COGNITIVE CONSUMER

Consumer behavior has frequently been described by analogy with the information-processing activities of computers (McGuire 1976; cf. Olshavsky and Granbois 1979). The three major 'comprehensive' models of consumer decision making (Nicosia 1966; Engel *et al.* 1968; Howard and Sheth 1969) trace the psychological state of individual purchasers from the point at which they become aware of the possibility of satisfying a material need by purchasing and consuming a product to their final evaluation of the consequences of having done so.

The assumption underlying this approach is that consumer behavior is preceded by a sequence of mental information processing. Consumers seek and use information as part of their rational problem solving and decision-making processes. Buyer behavior is 'largely determined by how the customer thinks and processes information' (Howard 1983). Consumers are credited with the capacity to receive and handle considerable quantities of information and undertake extensive pre-purchase searches and evaluations. Information is received and classified by the individual and, via mental processing, transformed into the attitudes and intentions that determine brand choice and related aspects of purchase and consumption.

In summary, the information-processing consumer is portrayed as:

- receiving information from the environment – typically in the form of an advertisement for a new brand of a fast-moving product,
- interpreting this information according to their experience, opinions, personal goods, personal characteristics and social position,
- searching for additional information to clarify the want or need so aroused,
- evaluating the alternative competing brands available to satisfy this want/need,
- developing the beliefs, attitudes and intentions that determine whether a purchase takes place and, if so, which brand is selected,
- acting upon these intrapsychic forces to purchase and use the product/brand,
- reevaluating the attitudes and intentions in the light of the satisfaction engendered by consuming the product, and
- storing the new attitudes and intentions in mind for future reference,

The consumer is portrayed, therefore, as an active part of the overall marketing system. First, he or she is cognitively engaged in responding to the marketing mix to the extent of forming and, where necessary, modifying beliefs on the basis of novel information. Second, the consumer responds affectively (evaluatively or emotionally) to each alternative means of satisfying his or her wants, taking a more or less favorable position on each brand and thereby establishing positive or negative attitudes toward it. Finally, the consumer shows a conative reaction, being motivated to buy or reject the advertised brand. His or her selection of a particular brand (or, if no purchase occurs, of none of the brands considered) is seen as the result of an intentional stance which necessarily precedes choice in the marketplace.

This reasoning is not new. The sequence of events and accompanying mental processes assumed by such models is an elaboration of the cognition–affect–conation hierarchy proposed over a quarter century ago by mechanistic models of consumer response to advertising. This, in turn, reflected the stimulus–organism–response (S–[O]–R) psychology on which cognitive science is ultimately based.

The basic sequence is shown in Figure 2.2. The social, business, political and economic environments give rise to the stimuli found in advertisements, interpersonal observations, and so on. These potential inputs must pass through the filter of the individual's selective attention and perception before they can initiate information processing. The cognitive processing of information includes the search for any relevant stored data to interpret the new inputs, the evaluation of alternative brands according to the goals of the consumer (needs and wants), and the biases inherent in past experience and its outcomes, beliefs and attitudes, and conflicting behavioral intentions. The psychological outputs of this processing are new brand beliefs, attitudes, and intentions to purchase. These intentions must pass

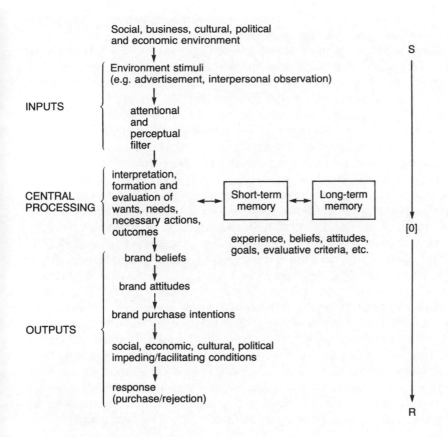

Figure 2.2 A model of the consumer choice process

through the filter of environmental and situational facilitation (is the purchase socially, economically, culturally and politically feasible and appropriate?) before the brand can be purchased. The outcomes of its purchase, especially those revealed in consumption, determine the consumer's evaluation of the brand and the likelihood of repeat purchase.

LOW INVOLVEMENT: THE UNINVOLVED CONSUMER

An obvious criticism of this approach is that it assumes too rational a consumer. Consumers are depicted as highly involved with the marketing message, able to detect important differences between branded versions of the same product, and, through a complex procedure of comparative evaluation, becoming committed to a single version of the product among many similar brands. Somehow, much of the routine purchasing undertaken by consumers every day – such as that for a chocolate bar, a breakfast cereal or a washing-up liquid – does not appear to entail so high a level of involvement and commitment. This simple observation has not gone unnoticed by consumer researchers.

Krugman (1965) suggested that high-involvement learning may be absent from most consumer behavior. Television advertising does not usually create strong pre-purchase attitudes toward brands but it generates at the most, small – possibly undetectable – changes in perception. At this stage, advertising does no more than inaugurate a process of slow and unenduring learning, which is insufficient to allow consumers to discriminate between the advertised brand and its competitors. The learning that results from watching televized commercials is, like the learning of things that are nonsensical or unimportant, *uninvolving*. It is only when the consumer is in a situation where purchase is possible that this perceptual learning comes to the fore and makes brand differentiation possible. If attitudes are formed at all during this process, it is after purchase and consumption have taken place. Even then, because of the low level of personal concern usually evoked by specific brands within a product class, brand attitudes are likely to be extremely weak.

A television viewer's degree of involvement in what he or she is watching is defined by Krugman as the number of connections they make mentally and unconsciously between what is being watched and their personal experience. Robertson (1976) uses the term 'commitment' to denote the consumer's mental reaction to a brand (rather than an item of mass communication); an individual's commitment to a brand is a function of his or her perception of the number and salience of the attributes which allow him or her to discriminate between it and other similar brands. Robertson argues that most consumer behavior in practice is based on low commitment to brands, and low involvement with advertising. In a more recent formulation, the involvement construct refers to the extent to which the consumer finds a product category interesting or exciting. Much product enthusiasm (or lack of it) has implications for both consumer behavior and marketing management (Bloch 1986; Goldsmith and Emmert 1991).

There is now a convincing volume of empirical evidence to suggest that under conditions of low media involvement/low brand commitment, consumers often:

- make far less use of information than the comprehensive models suggest,
- show little sign of pre-purchase decision making based upon the rational processing of information,
- use brand trial in order to obtain information about and to evaluate brands,
- exhibit multibrand purchasing within a small repertoire of brands that share attributes (or characteristics) common to all members of their product class, and
- are influenced in product and brand choice mainly by situational factors and in-store information sources.

Limited pre-purchase information processing

Consumer research conducted over the last decade or so suggests strongly that consumers have a very limited capacity for receiving and using information; that they do not as a rule undertake rational, comparative evaluations of brands on the basis of their attributes or make final judgments among brands on the basis of such outputs of complex information processing as attitudes and intentions.

From an empirical investigation of consumers' understanding and use of additional information about the nutritional value of food products (provided on the product labels) Jacoby *et al.* (1977) concluded that 'the vast majority of consumers neither use nor comprehend nutrition information in arriving at food purchase decisions'. An earlier study (Jacoby *et al.* 1974) reached the conclusion that, whilst the increased availability of information led to consumers reporting greater satisfaction and less confusion, it also resulted in their making less economically rational decisions. This is not to argue against the provision of information: presumably consumers need to be educated in its uses and benefits (cf. Scammon 1977). But it does suggest that the idea that consumers are natural information devourers should be qualified.

Consumers' comparatively small use of pre-purchase information is not confined to the situations in which they purchase nondurables such as food. Olshavsky and Granbois (1979) and Robertson (1976) cite numerous studies indicating that consumers drastically limit their search for information about durable products like furniture and cars, and services such as those of general practitioners. Wilkie and Dickson (1991) summarize the consistent findings of a substantial research effort by noting that most consumers for domestic appliances visit a single store, fail to consult advertising, use restricted price information, consider only one make, and employ perceptions of the manufacturer's reputation and packaging rather than make evaluations of the product/service attributes to arrive at judgments of quality. A proportion of consumers do undertake a considerable amount of pre-purchase information search, but 'on average . . . reported information search is surprisingly low' (Wilkie and Dickson 1991: 2).

The whole decision sequence assumed in comprehensive modeling appears absent from many instances of consumer buying. Situational variables, group pressures, and the physical arrangement of in-store displays influence consumer choice at the point of sale. Many purchases of a make or brand seem not to be preceded by a decision process at all, even on the first occasion (Olshavsky and Granbois 1979). There is also evidence that the expected outcomes of rational decision making – such as strong brand attitudes – are not present even when products have been purchased on many occasions (Lastovicka and Bonfield 1982; Foxall 1983, 1984b).

Brand evaluation through trial

Some early models of consumer response to advertising failed to distinguish trial from repeat purchase: they depict the effects of advertising in terms of a sequence of pre-purchase mental states which apparently culminates in the habitual purchase of the promoted brand. Lavidge and Steiner (1961) portray this 'hierarchy of effects' sequence as awareness–knowledge–liking–preference–conviction–purchase, while Colley (1961) speaks of the 'marketing spectrum' of unawareness–awareness–comprehension–conviction–action.

These early models suggested that consumers' evaluations of competing brands could be carried out even before a purchase had been made on the basis of information supplied by the marketer. The comprehensive models are more sophisticated than this, recognizing the importance of repeat buying and the consequences of initial purchase and consumption for subsequent purchase behavior. But they continue to accent the pre-purchase psychological processing of information, especially that supplied by producers, as customers' primary method of evaluating brands. Where commitment to brands is low, however, it is customers' experience with the brand that counts. Use of a brand during a period of trial, perhaps involving several purchases, eventually determines whether it becomes part of the repertoire from which regular purchases are made.

Ehrenberg and Goodhardt (1979) present a simplified model of consumer behavior that contains three phases of purchasing and consuming – awareness, trial and repeat buying. Simple as this 'ATR model' appears, it has provided a valuable device in both theoretical debate and commercial research (Ehrenberg 1974; Tauber 1981). Repeat buying, which is of enormous significance to the success of consumer products and services, is shown as a function of trial purchase and consumption. Trial itself is a function of awareness. The awareness, trial and repeat-buying approach emphasizes that awareness of a new brand, and any other mental states it engenders, is alone insufficient to guarantee adoption (repeat purchase) of the advertised brand. Rather, awareness results at best in curiosity and trial, and it is only when the brand is in use that evaluations and comparisons are possible. The ATR depiction does not rule out mental processes between awareness and trial: they might include growing interest in the brand and the formation of an evaluation of it based on the limited information available from advertising, word of mouth or observation. But such pre-purchase cognitive activity cannot be great, since the consumer has no experience of the brand on which to base an evaluation. Attitude formation and an intention to repurchase can come only after the consumer has both purchased and used the item.

Multibrand purchasing

Most nondurable product classes comprise several brands which are so similar to one another in terms of their basic attributes that consumers do not discriminate among them. Thus it is hardly surprising that consumers do not, on the whole, show total loyalty to any one brand but select from a small set of tried and tested brands that are close substitutes. There is a great deal of evidence that consumers behave in this manner. The markets for established nondurable products are characterized typically by more or less stable sales, at least in the short to medium term; the buying behavior of individuals usually involves several brand choices but the aggregate level of market sales and brand shares is stable and predictable. Customers may change brands often – the vast majority frequently do make substitutes – but not in the sense of irrevocably switching brands, never again buying that which is 'rejected' (Ehrenberg 1972). Buyers of a given product class typically choose several brands over a sequence of purchases.

Table 2.1 summarizes this multibrand purchasing for ready–to–eat breakfast cereals over a typical quarter year. Various proportions of those respondents who purchased Nabisco Shredded Wheat during this period also purchased other brands during the same thirteen weeks. Similar duplication of purchasing is also apparent for the other brands. There is no indication here that the majority of consumers are brand loyal in the sense of always purchasing a particular brand. Nor is any immutable brand segmentation suggested. Consumers buy brands from their repertoire, 'some perhaps less often than others, but each fairly consistently over time' (Ehrenberg and Goodhardt 1979). In the absence of some radical change in the behavior of a manufacturer – such as the introduction of a more acceptable brand into a complacent market – patterns of repeat buying tend to be predictable in the aggregate, even though individual customers appear to be buying haphazardly from week to week or month to month.

Table 2.1 Duplications for Kellogg's brands

Weeks 1–13		Corn Flakes	Rice Krispies	% who also bought Kellogg's Special K	Raisin Bran	Froot Loops	Bran Flakes
Buyers of:							
Nabisco Shredded Wheat	%	33	29	18	13	5	5
Kellogg's Corn Flakes	%	(100)	27	13	12	7	5
Kellogg's Rice Krispies	%	29	(100)	18	14	10	5
Kellogg's Special K	%	22	26	(100)	16	6	6
Kellogg's Raisin Bran	%	30	31	24	(100)	6	5
Kellogg's Froot Loops	%	27	33	14	9	(100)	4
Kellogg's Bran Flakes	%	28	27	23	11	5	(100)
Average Kellogg's Brand*	%	27	29	18	12	7	5

Source: Ehrenberg, A. S. C. and G. J. Goodhardt (1979), *Essays on Understanding Buyer Behavior*, J. Walter Thompson Co. and Market Research Corporation of America. Reproduced by permission.
Note: * Excluding the 100%s

The incursions of Rowntree's Yorkie into the molded chocolate bar market and Tetrosyl's Tetrion into the do-it-yourself filler market are obvious examples of abrupt changes in consumer behavior but they are the exception rather than the rule. Some consumers, of course, are totally loyal in the sense that they buy only one brand and never try its competitors; but they make up only a small proportion of most markets (clear exceptions are the markets for alcoholic drinks and cigarettes).

It is, therefore, unwise to generalize too much about the nature of consumer loyalty. Recent studies based on supermarket scanner data show great complexity in how consumers buy frequently purchased, low-price items. At least four distinct buying strategies characterize consumers within a product category (*Economist* 1992):

• *Long loyals* are committed to one brand regardless of price or competition.
• *Rotators* care little about price but like to switch brands for variety.

- *Deal sensitives* switch among a small set of brands, almost always buying the one on special offer.
- *Price sensitives* purchase the cheapest brand.

Proportions of consumers in each category differ from one product field to another, so a consumer who is deal sensitive for, say, coffee, may be long loyal for paper towels.

Situational influence

Wilkie and Dickson (1991: 21–2) propose an empirically based framework for understanding consumers' information search for major domestic appliance purchases. This framework recognizes that:

- *situational factors shape wants and needs*: a specific precipitating circumstance, such as the breaking down of a refrigerator, or a house move, motivates most sales of these products and 'the resulting physical, social, economic, and psychological situation severely constrains the choice';
- *store and brand choice reflect experience*, prior knowledge and predispositions: search for information is often limited because consumers have personal knowledge of stores, faith in manufacturers and retailers, high levels of satisfaction with previously purchased appliances, and trust in the competitive economy;
- *in-store information sources are often paramount*: consumers rely heavily on sales persons for information and influence, for legitimizing the purchase, making it socially acceptable and respectable, and additional services such as arranging credit, delivery and so on;
- *the consumer decides, in-store, whether to pursue further information*: if the in-store and other pre-purchase sources of information are adequate, no further seeking of information is likely; however, if the consumer is not satisfied with the amount of information or the trustworthiness of its source, he or she may decide to postpone a purchase and continue the search.

MODES OF CONSUMER BEHAVIOR

To concentrate exclusively on the cognitive approach to consumer behavior – as many consumer researchers have – to the near exclusion of alternatives, is to overlook the rich variety of alternative explanations of human choice. The concentration on intellectual processing omits the role of the emotions, the influence of personality on choice, the direct effects of the environment, and many other insights into the nature of purchase and consumption. Although cognitive theories are important to contemporary psychology, so are the psychodynamism of Freud, the environmental shaping of behavior of Skinner, the study of motivation, lifestyle, social character, and self-image.

Recognizing this does not mean that the high-involvement cognitive approach is redundant – only that it is but one among many, and that it may refer directly to a rather narrow range of consumer decisions. But how can the various approaches, notably those assuming a highly involved versus a low-involved consumer, be reconciled? Where does each fit in understanding consumer choice in the marketing context?

In the book that introduced their model, Howard and Sheth (1969) noted that consumer decision making differs according to the strength of attitude toward the available brands in a product class. *Extensive problem solving* occurs when attitude strength is low, when the product class under consideration is poorly defined, and when consumers are unable to discriminate among the available brands. Consumers actively seek information in order to reduce their high brand ambiguity and engage in extensive deliberations before purchasing; in so doing they consider many brands before deciding which to buy. They are heavily dependent upon advertising, which is powerful in prompting purchases. Such consumer behavior is most likely to occur at the introductory stage of the product life cycle, though it may also be found at later stages among consumers who have only just discovered the brand (Howard 1989).

At a later stage, having tried some brands within that product class, consumers develop a moderately strong attitude toward brands. Although there is still some ambiguity about various brands' attributes and capabilities, and still some consequent search for information, choice criteria are shaping up, brand comprehension is increasing, and customers know a few brands well, favoring each about equally. This second stage in consumer decision making, *limited problem solving*, is most likely encountered at the growth stage of the product life cycle.

The third and final stage, *routine problem solving*, occurs when consumers have developed strong attitudes toward brands through experience with several. Brand ambiguity is low and buyers are able to discriminate among brands, showing strong preference for one (or possibly two) within a clearly defined evoked set. There is little or no external search for information and what does come their way is subject to selective attention and perception. Customers appear to buy on impulse, but this is only because they have well-developed predispositions toward the available brands. Routine problem solving is most probable at the maturity stage of the product life cycle.

Full understanding and practical use of the different modes of consumer decision making require a willingness to employ, as appropriate, different models, different frames of reference, and different concepts for each. The aggregate level of analysis employed by Ehrenberg and Goodhardt involves a more descriptive approach of the operation of whole markets rather than an explanatory approach based on individual decision making, which is the foundation of the comprehensive models. The aggregate-descriptive approach has also found numerous practical applications in such areas as market evaluation and new product development (Ehrenberg and Goodhardt 1979).

CONSUMER INNOVATORS AND INNOVATIVENESS

These analyses of consumer choice all imply that markets can be segmented temporally: that the earliest adopters of products can be separated from later adopters in ways that are practically useful to marketing mix management. Early identification of consumer innovators is of strategic importance in new product development, since it assists in the process of tailoring each element of the marketing mix to the requirements and behaviors of those buyers who initiate markets and without whom the social comparison that leads to diffusion would often not occur. New brands and products that do not appeal to this group are unlikely to find a mass market, and it has been argued that innovative buyers should be represented disproportionately in concept and product testing (Midgley 1977).

But what is an innovator? When most people hear the term 'innovator', they probably think of an inventor of a new machine or a person who does new and different things. In marketing and consumer psychology, the term refers to the earliest buyers of a new brand, service, product, store or other marketing offering. The fashion leader in clothing or the adventure traveler who yearns to go to the latest vacation spot are examples. The theoretical background for this theme in consumer behavior is that of the adoption and diffusion of innovations (Rogers 1983). This theory describes the spread (diffusion) of a new idea, practice, product or service over time through a social system. A new product type (such as the personal computer) or a practice (such as recycling) are examples. Diffusion theory is of particular importance for products in the introductory phase of the product life cycle because this body of knowledge describes the behavior of the earliest buyers of the new product.

An S-shaped curve (Figure 2.3) provides a good approximation of the diffusion history of an innovation. The new thing appears, is adopted by a few people, then by more people at a greater rate, until relatively fewer people remain to adopt and it is considered to have diffused successfully through the social system and is no longer new. Each person's individual decision to adopt or not to adopt represents the process of adoption or rejection of the innovation. The cumulative series of adoption decisions by the members of the social system form the diffusion curve.

If the relative time of adoption since introduction is measured as a deviation from the mean time of adoption for the whole system, this distribution follows roughly a normal

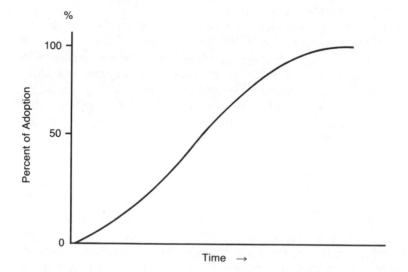

Figure 2.3 The S-shaped curve of innovation diffusion

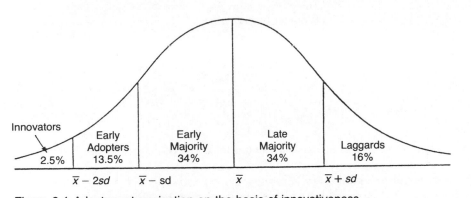

Figure 2.4 Adopter categorization on the basis of innovativeness
Source: Reprinted with the permission of The Free Press, a division of Macmillan, Inc. from *Diffusion of Innovations*, 3rd edn by E. M. Rogers. Copyright © 1962, 1971, 1983 by The Free Press.
Note: The innovativeness dimension, as measured by the time at which an individual adopts an innovation or innovations, is continuous. This variable, however, may be partitioned into five adopter categories by laying off standard deviations from the average time of adoption.

curve, the standard deviations of which can be used to distinguish the adopter groups. Figure 2.4 describes the distribution of adoption decisions about the mean time of adoption. Innovators may be taken, in theory, to consist of the first 2.5 percent of adopters, early adopters the next 13.5 percent, the early majority the next 34 percent, the late majority the next 34 percent, and laggards the last 16 percent.

The nature of consumer innovativeness has attracted much scholarly debate in marketing and has centered on two basic and interrelated questions: What is an innovation in marketing? What is innovativeness?

What is an innovation?

An innovation in marketing is something (a brand, product, idea, service, practice) that is perceived as new in the eyes of the members of a social system. Innovations may be technological changes or simply a new brand of a commodity. For marketing managers, this definition has two aspects, which need to be discussed to avoid confusion in determining whether something should be considered an 'innovation' or not. Because the central construct in marketing is the marketer/consumer exchange dyad, whether something is perceived as new or not may depend on who is viewing it. The following diagram (Figure 2.5) illustrates.

Cell 1 represents products in their maturity (such as Mello Yello or Persil) or decline (such as G.I. Joe): phases that are old (familiar) to the marketer as well as to the consumer, and therefore of little concern to innovators. These products may require constant changes in promotion to keep them profitable. If their sales are declining, they represent few profits for the firm unless they can be repositioned or reformulated to offer new value to the consumer.

Cell 2 contains products that are old in the eyes of the firm or agency sponsoring the innovation. These might be established brands or common products that the consumer

The product from the
consumer point of view

		old	new
		old	*new*
The product from the marketer or agency point of view	*old*	1	2
	new	3	4

Figure 2.5 Innovations viewed simultaneously from consumer and company perspectives

market finds new, novel or unfamiliar. This situation arises when a firm exports products to a country for the first time, or directs a marketing strategy to a new consumer segment such as the new cosmetics directed to men unfamiliar with them. In these situations, diffusion theory may be useful to explain consumer behavior and guide management action.

Cell 3 describes products that are old in consumers' eyes, but that may be new to the company. This difference in perception may lead to product failure when managers become collectively excited over their 'hot, new product' but customers greet the offering with a yawn. Managers sometimes live in constricted perceptual worlds in which minor product, packaging or promotional changes bulk large in their eyes. Not everybody gets as excited as the brand manager and his assistants over the new 'larger' size package or the new promotional scheme. Many products fail because they are simply 'me-too' – they offer no important consumer advantages in price or performance – even though their managers view them as earthshaking innovations. Diffusion theory offers few conceptual guides in this situation.

Cell 4 contains products that might be considered 'true' innovations because they are new to the company, probably technological advances, while simultaneously they are new to consumers, who haven't seen anything like them before. Pert Plus was such a product. Personal computers are a classic example. In this instance, the market may resist the new thing, requiring extensive effort by the firm to diffuse the new product. This is the classic new product/diffusion situation that the theory describes and in which consumer innovativeness may play a decisive role in the success of the new product.

What is consumer innovativeness?

Consumer innovativeness can be thought of as the tendency to buy new products in a particular product category soon after they appear in the market and relatively earlier than most other consumers in the market segment. Innovativeness is an unobservable, continuously distributed individual difference variable, comparable to any other consumer characteristic such as lifestyle, opinion leadership and involvement. Consumer innovativeness in part accounts for the timing of the decision to adopt an innovation. The more innovative the consumer, the more likely he/she is to buy early. Of course, many other factors influence individual adoption decisions. An income effect, for instance, can be seen where consumers with more disposable income tend to be early buyers. The marketing strategy introducing the new product also has an important impact on who the early buyers are.

Broad personality traits have been posited to impact consumption in a variety of ways. Within this context it has been shown that a broad or global personality trait described as a 'willingness to try new things' is associated with relative early purchase of new products (Goldsmith 1991; Hurt *et al.* 1977). Of more practical importance, however, is the fact that consumer innovativeness is domain specific. That is, consumers tend to be innovators within carefully delineated product categories: the movie buff who sees the latest movies first, the clothing fashion follower, the car enthusiast who owns the newest model, or the music innovator who must listen to the cutting edge in rock or pop music. These innovative consumers tend to be highly involved in their respective product categories and purchase more of the product category than do other consumers. They are very knowledgeable about the product area and make great use of specialty media in the product area, such as magazines and newsletters. Consumer innovators may be more inclined to take purchase risks and be more venturesome than later buyers.

Marketers would like to identify consumer innovators in a particular product class before introduction of the new product because they are most likely to be the product's first buyers. If this can be done successfully, the innovators can be treated as a target market. Promotion and distribution can be directed to the innovators to facilitate their purchase (adoption) of the product, thereby speeding its diffusion. For the marketer, the problem is how to measure product-specific innovativeness among consumer populations.

CHARACTERISTICS OF CONSUMER INNOVATORS

The marketing application of diffusion theory depends upon the ability of marketing managers to identify the various adopter groups – defined in terms of time since launch – and to tailor the marketing mix to their economic, social, psychological and behavioral characteristics. Research in a number of disciplines (from rural sociology to education, and from social anthropology to marketing) has shown a broad consistency in the general characteristics of innovators. Innovators frequently differ from later adopters in their

- socioeconomic status,
- social affiliations and behavior,
- personal traits,
- perceptions of new products, and
- purchase and consumption patterns.

Socioeconomic status

Numerous studies indicate that innovators have greater income and/or wealth than later adopters or the population as a whole. Standard of living and related characteristics such as education and literacy are positively related to the tendency to innovate. Numerous studies show that innovators differ from their social groups in occupational status, social class position, education and privilege. Innovators for touch-tone telephones, for instance, showed greater discretionary income and self-perception of wealth than non-innovators; they were less concerned about cost. However, while they were overprivileged within their own social class, they did not belong to a higher social class or have a higher income level than non-innovators (Robertson 1967b; Robertson, Zielinski and Ward 1984). Similar results are available for domestic appliances in general (Robertson and Kennedy 1969) and cars (Keggeris *et al.* 1970). Consumer innovators also tend to be upwardly mobile socially (Robertson 1971).

Social interaction and communication

Innovators in a wide range of contexts have greater or different mass-media exposure, contact with change agencies, group participation, interpersonal communication, opinion leadership, and 'cosmopoliteness' compared with others in the social system (Rogers 1983). Consumer innovators, for instance, prefer distinctly different television programs and magazines. They are also likely to show selective perception of advertisements for particular innovations that are of functional value to them, a purposeful approach to the innovation in question. Some of the earliest adopters of new products are also opinion leaders, communicating their 'finds' actively to other consumers (Rogers 1983; see also Gatignon and Robertson 1985; Robertson *et al.* 1984).

Personal traits and characteristics

The earliest adopters of new products are usually more experienced than others, more knowledgeable about the product field in question, have a more positive attitude toward change, show achievement motivation, educational aspirations, a pro-business orientation and empathy, and avoid mental rigidity. They are not noted for their satisfaction with life or with things as they are. Consumer innovators show a greater interest in or involvement with the product area to which the innovation belongs, have a positive approach to new ideas generally, a high perception of themselves as innovators, and aspire to upward social mobility for themselves and their children.

The attempt to link personality traits with innovativeness has proved more encouraging than most personality research in the marketing context but, as Chapter 6 will show, the results still have their subtleties and difficulties (Foxall and Goldsmith 1988; Kassarjian 1971; cf. Blake *et al.* 1973; Coney 1972; Jacoby 1971; Zaltman 1965). Nevertheless, innovative behavior has been related consistently if somewhat weakly with a number of personality traits, of which the most important is venturesomeness itself: the capacity to cope with high levels of risk and uncertainty, to show an inner-directed (self-contained and self-determined) approach to novel situations, and independence of mind and behavior (Midgley 1977: 56–64; Robertson 1971: 108). Research also shows that innovativeness is associated with self-monitoring – the tendency some individuals have to adapt to their social surroundings by observing and controlling their own behavior. This adaptability and flexibility apparently leads high self-monitors to try new things more often than low self-monitors (Goldsmith 1987).

Innovators are generally more willing than the population as a whole to experiment and try new products, and less likely than others to be influenced in their brand choice by small differences in price or product attributes. Venturesomeness probably discriminates innovators from non-innovators more readily than any other trait. Innovators are more willing to take risks, whether for consumer durables or fashion items (cf. Robertson 1967a; Baumgarten 1975; Midgley 1974). Innovators for grocery products and cars show a related trait, inner-directedness: their actions represent their personal values and standards rather than those common to other members of their social group (Donnelly 1970; Donnelly and Ivancevich 1974). The inner- (as opposed to the other-) directedness of the innovator corresponds to Midgley's view of the innovator's adoption decisions as occurring independently of those of other consumers. Innovators are likely to buy in spite of high levels of objective risk and to minimize the probable effects of perceived risk and uncertainty on their decisions and actions (Robertson 1971: 107).

Product perceptions and appraisal

Chapter 1 pointed out that the characteristics of a new product are closely connected with the speed with which it is likely to diffuse through the market. The characteristics noted were relative advantage, compatibility, complexity, observability and trialability (Rogers 1983). However, not only are these factors objectively associated with the speed of diffusion of new products: innovators perceive them differently from non-innovators. Innovators see more advantage, greater compatibility, less complexity, more conspicuous-ness and more opportunity for trial in a new product than do non-innovators (Ostlund 1974). There is mounting evidence that innovators for a range of product fields including packaged foods, solar energy systems, and hi-tech innovations can be identified by the extent to which they perceive a new product to be relatively advantageous, compatible, complex, conspicuous and divisible (Hirschman 1981; Labay and Kinnear 1981; Ostlund 1974).

Purchase and consumption behavior

The buying behavior of innovators and their patterns of product usage differ from those of other consumers in several ways, some straightforward and predictable from the nature of innovativeness itself, others less so. Several investigators have shown that the earliest adopters of new products and brands are heavy users of the product class: 'the innovator for a new kind of coffee is likely to be a heavy coffee drinker. The innovator for a new telephone product is likely to have a larger monthly telephone bill' (Robertson 1971: 100). Innovators for the touch-tone telephone were also more likely to adopt other domestic appliances: color TV, electric toothbrushes and electric carving knives (Robertson 1967b). Taylor, in a study of continuous innovations of fast-moving consumer products, found a strong relationship between usage rate and innovative trial: 'in 10 of 11 instances, those households that purchased more of the product class over the whole year tried the new products in the first quarter and their usage of the product class was substantially greater than that of later triers' (Taylor 1977: 106). Heavy users of computers and computing services tend also to be innovators (Danko and MacLachlan 1983; Dickerson and Gentry 1983; Peters and Venkatesan 1973). The same finding is apparent for food products and personal care items (Frank, Massy and Morrison 1964; Robertson and Gatignon 1985). Hence the attractiveness of innovators to marketers: not only do they initiate markets by communicating innovations to later adopters; they also consume a disproportionate volume of products they adopt, though they may show lower levels of brand loyalty than other consumers (Goldsmith and Hofacker 1991).

Robertson and Gatignon propose that innovativeness may be connected with product usage rate because of

> the greater knowledge and ability that heavy users have to evaluate new information. Heavy users have different knowledge structures – or ways to relate components of knowledge – such that improved predictions of outcomes can be made. The completeness and complexity of these information structures or schema determine the ability to mentally represent a problem, to isolate solution criteria, to identify decision strategies, and to evoke the products with the relevant attributes.
>
> (Robertson and Gatignon 1985: 86)

Continuity/discontinuity of innovations

The profile of the consumer innovator that emerges from this review is typically that of the first adopter of new domestic appliances: likely to be younger, with higher education, income and occupational status, usually involved to a greater degree in social activities, more likely to be an opinion leader for home appliances, more of a risk-taker, with a positive attitude toward innovation and probably already owning more domestic appliances to start with. Further, 'the innovator is a competent and self-assured person, intelligent and educated enough to set his/her own standards, and to evaluate innovations against these criteria' (Midgley 1977: 60). Taken together, the research findings point to consumer innovators who 'can comprehend the abstract implications of adopting major innovations', calculate and plan, and who 'have the financial resources to experiment. Above all else the innovators favor change and are willing to take risks, thus they are inner-directed and do not need the experience, attitudes and values of others to mould their decisions for them' (Midgley 1977: 60; see also Foxall 1984a; Robertson and Gatignon 1985; Robertson *et al.* 1984).

But, while all consumers may show innovativeness to some degree (Hirschman 1980; Midgley and Dowling 1978), most are first adopters for just one product class or, at most, for a small range of related product classes. Moreover, while the precise personal and behavioral characteristics of innovators need to be ascertained separately for each of these areas, there is some evidence that the dominant characteristics vary with the degree of continuity/discontinuity involved in the innovation. The ability to cope with risk, attraction to change and inner-directedness appear to be present in all consumers' personal profiles; however, different types of innovator can be distinguished based on their accompanying social, economic and psychological qualities.

- High educational levels, income and occupational status are relevant to the purchasing of the more discontinuous consumer durables such as TV satellite dishes, camcorders and the latest combined software for the home computer – with all the risks this entails and the levels of discretionary income it requires.
- But these innovator characteristics are less pertinent to fast-moving consumer product innovations such as grocery items, which are usually continuous: the lower the salience of price and other economic factors in the purchase decision and the greater the familiarity of buyers with the product class, the less likely it is that the educational, income and status considerations will apply.
- Fashion innovators have some characteristics in common with these other groups but exhibit more social integration, mobility and mass-media exposure, and show calculative planning and higher usage rates for the relevant product category (Midgley 1977: 60; Darden and Reynolds 1971; Goldsmith and Hofacker 1991; Midgley 1974).

MODELING INNOVATIVE ADOPTION

Models of the procedure in which individuals decide whether to try an innovation and, having tried it, whether to continue buying and using it, combine aspects of both the cognitive models and the ATR sequence. The best-known model of the innovation decision process (Rogers 1983), shown in Figure 2.6, depicts the process as five stages:

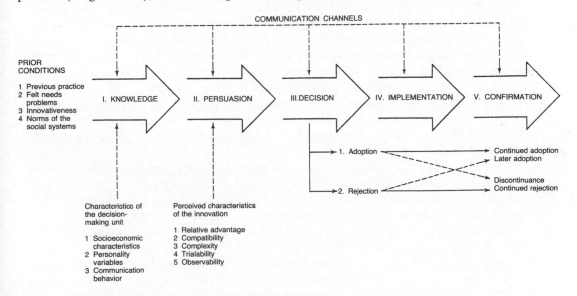

Figure 2.6 A model of stages in the innovation decision process
Source: Reprinted with the permission of The Free Press, a division of Macmillan, Inc. from *Diffusion of Innovations*, 3rd edn, by E. M. Rogers. Copyright © 1962, 1971, 1983 by The Free Press.
Note: The innovation decision process is the process through which an individual (or other decision-making unit) passes from first knowledge of an innovation, to forming an attitude toward the innovation, to a decision to adopt or reject, to implementation of the new idea, and to confirmation of this decision. Note that for the sake of simplicity we have not shown the consequences of the innovation in this diagram.

- knowledge,
- persuasion,
- decision,
- implementation, and
- confirmation.

Rogers (1983: 165) defines the innovation-decision process as 'the process through which an individual . . . passes from first knowledge of an innovation, to forming an attitude toward the innovation, to a decision to adopt or reject, to implementation of the new idea, and to confirmation of this decision'. The implication is that adopting or rejecting an innovation is an instance of high-involvement decision making which calls for the cognitive processing described in the cognitive information-processing models of consumer choice.

SUMMARY

This chapter presents the buying process as a sequence of interrelated cognitions and behaviors that marketers can use in the formation of their marketing strategies. Several models of consumer decision making are also presented as guides for further study and understanding of consumption. It is recognized that most consumer decisions do not follow an extended, detailed decision process, but instead can be characterized as low involvement. This means that little information is gathered prior to purchase, brand evaluation is chiefly accomplished through trial, and overt brand loyalty is rarely allocated to a single brand.

This chapter has sought to show how the facts of consumer behavior can be integrated into frameworks or models that are of use in marketing management. Chapter 1 presented some of this information in relation to the product life cycle but the remainder of the book is intended to elucidate the models of consumer choice presented in Chapter 2.

The ATR model also captures the far more prevalent low-involvement, low-commitment mode of consumer behavior in which social influence (e.g., word of mouth) or corporate influence (e.g., brand advertising) leads first and foremost to the awareness and curiosity that provokes trial. Trial and its outcomes, the consumers' actual experience of the product in use, then emerge as the principal influence on the rate of repurchase, if any. Although the model is clearly relevant to fast-moving consumer goods, it also summarizes many of the procedures inherent in durables purchasing.

The remainder of the book presents the major themes in the analysis of consumer behavior, integrating them to elucidate the modes of purchasing and consumption we have briefly discussed in this chapter, and indicating their relevance to the marketing considerations raised in Chapter 1.

Chapters 3, 4 and 5 are founded upon the underlying model of a consumer cognitively engaged in information processing. These chapters are relevant to both the comprehensive theories of a highly involved consumer engaged in extensive problem solving and the concept of the less involved routine problem-solver inherent in the ATR representation. In both cases, consumers have formed beliefs, attitudes and intentions based either on active rational consideration of the options before them, or on their prior behavior with and evaluation of familiar product classes and the brands that constitute them. Chapter 3 provides an overview of consumers' perceptual processes, the procedures that inaugurate their reception, handling and interpretation of information. Chapter 4 deals in greater detail with that cognitive process, presenting and discussing learning and memory. It also deals with a rather different form of learning, which is not usually incorporated in the cognitive models except incidentally: the learning that occurs as a result of the consumer's direct contact with the environment. The psychological outcomes of information processing that shape consumer purchasing and consumption – attitudes and intentions – are the subject of Chapter 5.

The next two chapters consider the personal role of the consumer in purchase and consumption. Chapter 6 is concerned with the ways in which personality variables may affect purchasing irrespective of information processes, and the ways in which the cognitive style of the consumer affects the manner of cognitive decision making and problem solving. Chapter 7 discusses the motivations of consumers: the social and psychological, as well as economic and cultural influences that encourage – and which at times appear to compel – shopping, buying and using products and services.

The last two chapters consider consumer behavior in the context of its social and physical environments. Chapter 8 discusses the way in which pre-purchase (search and evaluation) and purchase behavior is shaped by such aspects of the retail environment as in-store displays of merchandise and crowding, while Chapter 9 is concerned with the effect of social groups, including the family, and of the social structure, including social stratification and culture, on consumers' decision making and consumption.

Part II

The cognitive consumer

Chapter 3

Perceptual processes

WHAT IS PERCEPTION?

Describing how consumers make choices is only one step toward an understanding of consumer behavior. We must also gain insight into how consumers obtain and use information to reach their goals. Consumers become aware of and learn about brands through packages, promotions, advertisements and conversations with other people. Brand awareness is clearly a prerequisite of buying, but naturally it cannot of itself guarantee sales. Many people are well aware of Guinness advertisements, for example, and consume them avidly without ever thinking of drinking beer. Moreover, after consumers become aware of brands, their buying decisions are guided by their perceptions or impressions of brands formed from the information they get about brand characteristics. Thus, the study of perception is one part of the study of the largely unconscious processes through which information in the external environment is attended to, transformed into beliefs, stored in memory, and acted upon by consumers.

Effective marketing management rests on two fundamentals.

- First, consumers act on their perceptions which stem principally from the information they receive.
- Second, managers need to understand the nature of the perceptions their customers and potential customers have of themselves, their social world, and the products available to them.

Our review of consumer behavior, therefore, shifts its focus now to consumer cognition: the activities involved in perceiving, thinking, reflecting and understanding. As with so many of the terms encountered in the behavioral sciences, perception is used rather vaguely in everyday discourse but must be understood more precisely if it is to be useful in explaining aspects of human behavior. This does not mean that we have to construct a definition of great scientific weight in order to appreciate its relevance to the study of consumer behavior, however. Consider the following interpretation.

Harrell (1986: 66) understands perception to mean 'the process of recognizing, selecting, organizing, and interpreting stimuli in order to make sense of the world around us'. Perception of goods and services depends in part on the stimuli to which consumers are exposed and in part on the way these stimuli are given meaning by consumers. This latter process is sometimes called perceptual encoding. Our different perceptions of products can account for different attitudes and behaviors toward products. These ideas will be helpful when we discuss the importance of perception for marketing management, where the interest is in attracting the consumer's attention and communicating some key information about a product.

Two facets of perception are of special interest. First, people become aware of their environment through the five senses and therefore sensation is the process with which perception begins. But perception is not synonymous with sensation, despite their clear interconnectedness. It is true that some writers have presented perception basically in terms of the five senses, as does the following paradigm put forward by Young (1961):

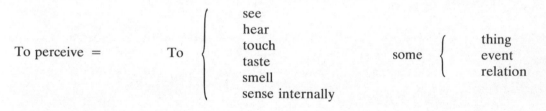

Equally important, and this is the second facet, is the process of interpretation which depends on the socio-psychological meanings the individual attaches to the object perceived (the stimulus). These socio-psychological meanings are greatly influenced by the motives that direct behavior. Hence, the perceptual process is very selective, so that the consumers pay attention to and interpret stimuli that reinforce and enhance their views of their world, of themselves, and of the goods and services that they buy. Because motives manifest themselves in a wide variety of ways among different consumers, perceptions of reality differ from individual to individual as each person interprets physical and social stimuli so that they are harmoniously accommodated within his overall world-view. This is accomplished by the individual reconstructing what he perceives so that it does not conflict with his basic attitudes, personality, motives or aspirations, or perhaps by modifying these slightly to allow the overall impression to be harmonious. The basic principles at work here are that consumers pay attention to stimuli deemed relevant to their existing needs, wants, beliefs and attitudes. Once attended to, the information derived from the stimuli is interpreted and stored in memory so as to reinforce and enhance existing attitudes and behaviors.

Many examples of the operation of perceptual processes in marketing can be cited. Not only is foil wrapping an attention-getting packaging material, the use of foil enhances the brands it surrounds, endowing them with prestige or status and adding value in the eyes of the consumer (Higgins 1984). A yellow hue in the skin of a chicken signifies health, succulence and freshness to many consumers. In order to give his chickens this yellow skin, thus making them stand out in the grocery displays and leading consumers to evaluate his chickens favorably compared with their less yellow competitors, Frank Perdue feeds his chickens lots of marigold petals and corn (Copulsky and Marton 1977). Such sensory features as color, design, typography and visual images are used by consumers to decide what a brand is, what it says about its user, and what it is worth. The prestige or status of a brand, whether it is 'old-fashioned' or 'modern', or whether it is top or bottom of the line, is often determined by the way in which the product is packaged and merchandised (Moran 1980). The image consumers have of a brand, in other words, is often derived from their perception of the brand formed from relatively minor stimulus cues. These images, however, may form the basis of brand choice, brand loyalty or new product trial.

The selective nature of perception and attention

Each and every consumer in our economic system is daily bombarded with many hundreds of messages, each of which tries to inform, persuade, convince, teach or change the individual in some way. Some of these messages come from sources the consumer trusts implicitly; some are rejected without further thought; but the majority of messages contain a mixture of obvious truth and doubtful claims that would require time, effort and possibly expense to prove or refute. Clearly no one has the time to evaluate every message that comes his or her way, or even to give a portion of attention to all that do so. One way of coping with the constant bombardment of information and persuasion with which the individual has to contend is through selection of what is perceived. As was apparent when we discussed the nature of interpreting stimuli in the process of perception, much of this selection is automatic, as new perceptions are made to fit comfortably with existing cognitions.

A famous study of selective perception was reported by Hastorf and Cantril (1954), who interviewed students from Princeton and Dartmouth colleges who had been shown a film of a controversial football match that had taken place between the two college teams. Newspaper reports of the game pointed out that there had been considerable amounts of rough play by both sides but that Dartmouth had contributed more to this than Princeton. Having watched the film of the game, the students were asked to say how many fouls each team had committed. On average, the Dartmouth students attributed about as many fouls to each team (4.3 to their own team and 4.4 to the other) while Princeton students, on average, attributed far more fouls to their opponent's team than to their own (9.8 compared with 4.2). Clearly, perception depends on viewpoint: selective perception means that, to some extent at least, people have the ability to see and hear what they choose to see and hear, to 'screen out' messages they do not wish to attend to, be influenced by, or even consider.

Which messages are attended to and allowed to penetrate or 'get through' to conscious awareness are determined by many factors. A large body of research shows that one set of factors resides in the stimuli themselves. Consumers are more likely to pay attention to cues in the environment that exhibit certain characteristics. Advertising messages, for instance, which are novel or unusual attract attention, as do those that contrast in some way with the rest of the information surrounding them. Other attention-getting stimulus factors include the size of message, its placement in the environment, whether it is in color, how loud or vibrant it is, and whether it moves. Obviously, advertisers would like their messages to be observed in the least distracting circumstances possible.

A second factor relevant to whether messages are noticed can be described as 'response opportunity factors' (Mackenzie 1986: 174–5). The extent to which consumers are being distracted by other stimuli, and the amount of repetition of the primary message, also affect the amount of attention given to a message.

Finally, characteristics of the message recipient influence attention. These include how much information a consumer desires to receive, his or her values, motives and attitudes, as well as social situation, current interests and preoccupations. As we have seen, messages which are in tune with what the individual already believes stand a much better chance of gaining attention, being perceived, and actually remembered than those that are at odds with the individual's preoccupations or merely tangential to his or her interests and needs. The latter are likely to be condemned without a hearing.

Suggestions and expectations play a decisive part in determining whether an individual perceives a stimulus and the ways in which it is interpreted, if at all. Maier (1965: 23) shows that there is considerable variation in the perceptions of objects and figures depending on the suggestions that shape the observer's expectations. The following figure, for instance, can be seen as two X's, or as an upright V superimposed on an inverted V.

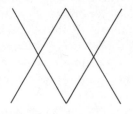

If the suggestion is made that the figure is a W on top of an M, it may be seen as such. Maier also suggests that it can be perceived as a diamond with extended sides. The fact that the context within which perception takes place vitally affects the process of perception is, of course, of crucial importance to the consumer researcher and marketing executive. It means that the firm sells as many different products as it has potential buyers, and this is the basis for some forms of market segmentation. This possibility contains within it, however, the danger of product proliferation and 'false segmentation' if the segments are not sufficiently large to support profitable production which exploits economies of scale. Selective perception also has implications for other areas of the marketing mix, notably advertising.

PERCEPTION AND CONSUMER BEHAVIOR

Fundamental to understanding the role of consumers' perceptual processes in their purchase and consumption behaviors is the question of how consumers perceive themselves.

After discussing this, we turn to consumers' perception of each of the marketing mix elements.

Consumers' self-perceptions

Consumer researchers' interest in self-image psychology stems from the belief that consumers choose products that are consistent with their perceptions of themselves and reject those that are incongruous with them (Sirgy 1980,1982). Since purchased products also contribute to the development of the buyer's self-image, his selection of products and brands may, if this hypothesis is generally valid, be seen as an effort to maintain consonance and avoid or reduce dissonance.

Advertising agencies sometimes use self-image theory to guide their creation of commercials that portray brands as a natural part of everyday life, as an extension of the consumer's self. They may even use ethnographic methods to study real consumers and their purchases in natural settings to determine how the personalities of products and brands match those of their target users (Miller 1990).

Two self-concepts have been employed extensively in consumer research: (a) *actual self-image*, which refers to the entire way in which the individual sees himself, his evaluations and description of himself, and (b) *ideal self-image*, which is the individual's perception of what he should aspire to become (e.g., Green *et al.* 1969; Hughes and Naert 1970; Grubb and Stern 1971; Hughes and Guerrero 1971). Recently, however, the individual's *social self-concept*, the image he or she would like others to have of him or herself, has received research attention (Malhotra 1988; Sirgy 1980).

Malhotra defines self-concept as

> the totality of the individuals' thoughts and feelings having reference to themselves as subjects as well as objects. Hence, self-concept includes (a) the self as knower, or subject, or I, i.e., the process of active experiencing; and (b) the self as known, or object, or me, i.e., the content of experiencing. Furthermore, the ideal self (the person as I would really like to be), actual self (the person that I believe I actually am), and social self (the person as I believe others see me) are . . . important components of this multi-dimensional construct.
>
> (Malhotra 1988: 7)

Table 3.1 shows how these aspects of self-concept have been conceptualized and treated in various social scientific traditions.

Several studies have demonstrated the general tendency of consumers to select brands that are broadly in accordance with their self-perceptions and with their subjective images of brands (Dolich 1969). In the case of cars (a product area to which early researchers paid particular attention), consumers have been classified as 'cautious conservatives' and 'confident explorers' on the basis of responses to self-image tests. Each of these groups exhibited clear car preferences: the former ('cautious conservatives') for small cars, which were perceived as convenient and inexpensive to run; the latter ('confident explorers') for larger cars, which were seen as expressive of their buyers' outgoing, even dominant

Table 3.1 A summary of the various approaches to self-concept

Approach/theorist	Definition of self-concept	Explicit/implicit treatment of		
		Ideal self	Actual self	Social self
1 Self as a concept				
James (1907)	All that we call our own, and with whom and with which we share a bond of identity	Self-enhancement, Self-esteem, Level of aspiration	Me, Spiritual me Material me	Social me
Allport (1955)	Proprium – all the regions of our life that we regard as peculiarly ours	Ego enhancement, Propriate striving	Self-image	Extended self
2 Symbolic interactionism				
Cooley (1902)	Everything an individual designates as his own and to which the individual refers with the personal pronouns 'I', 'me', and 'myself'	Implicitly in self-feelings	I, me, myself	Looking-glass self, Social self
Mead (1934)	Self-concept is a social structure arising out of social experience	Implicitly in self-realization	I, me	Generalized other
3 Neo-Freudian				
Sullivan (1953)	Self-system – an organization of educative experience	Implicit in reward contingencies	Good me, Bad me, Not me	Significant other
4 Organismic				
Lecky (1961)	Organized conceptual system of an individual's thoughts about himself	Self-esteem	Conceptual system	Implicit in adaptation to outer world
5 Phenomenological				
Snygg and Combs (1949)	Phenomenal self – everything the individual refers to with the words, I, me and mine	Enhancement of the phenomenal self	Preservation of phenomenal self	Implicit in the individual's atmosphere
Rogers (1951)	Consistent conceptual pattern of perceptions of characteristics and relationships of the I or the me, together with values attached to these concepts	Self-enhancement	Self-maintenance	The organism grows by becoming more socialized

Approach/theorist	Definition of self-concept	Explicit/implicit treatment of		
		Ideal self	Actual self	Social self
6 Cognitive				
Sarbin (1952)	The self is a cognitive structure, it includes substructures	Implicit in continual and progressive change of self	I, me, mine	Social self
7 Current				
Burns (1979)	Self-concept is an organization of self attitudes	Ideal self	Cognized self	Other self
Epstein (1980)	A self-theory of what the individual is like	Optimize self, Self-esteem, Enhancement of self-system	Maintenance of self-system	Influence of significant others
Rosenberg (1979)	The totality of the individual's thoughts and feelings with reference to himself as an object	Desired self	Extant self	Presenting self

Source: Malhotra, N. K. (1988) 'Self-concept and product choice: an integrated perspective'. Journal of Economic Psychology, 9, 8–9. Reproduced by kind permission of Elsevier Science Publishers BV, and N.K. Malhotra.

personalities. Marketers can use to good advantage the fact that products not only convey information about consumers' self-images, but also play an active role in forming these images. Witness the success Pontiac has had in boosting car sales by marketing 'sporty and expressive cars'. Research told them that 'flashy cars make middle-aged women feel younger. The result: a commercial that shows a teenager persuading his mother to buy a sporty red Sunbird' (Mitchell 1986).

Owners of different cars appear to have differing perceptions of car brands, and also appear to select cars that are in line with their self-image (Birdwell 1968). In addition, car owners may perceive themselves as being similar to other owners of the same brand of car (Grubb and Hupp 1968).

Even the early researchers were active, however, in broadening the product base of their work. An investigation of beer consumption showed that beer drinkers had very different self-perceptions from those of non-drinkers (basically, the former saw themselves as more confident, extrovert and sociable) (Grubb 1965). Moreover, a study by Landon (1974) of consumer preferences for a wide range of products (from beer to color television, from art prints to snow skis) confirmed that consumer choices correlate highly with either self-image or ideal image. Consequently, the overall conclusion from these studies is of considerable marketing significance. The product positions, promotional strategies, brand names and so forth of consumer goods will be more appealing to consumer market segments if they are perceived as congruent with these consumers' self-images or ideal images.

Another study (Giges 1987), suggests that different levels in self-esteem, the individual's overall self-evaluation, may be linked to differences in buyer behavior. Consumers who think highly of themselves tend to spend more for products that make them feel good:

entertainment, alcoholic beverages and beauty-enhancers. Frequent purchasers of wine, beer and coolers who have high esteem outnumber those with low self-esteem by about 2 to 1. On the other hand, nearly 92 percent of low self-esteem consumers said they bought frozen dinners, while only 78 percent of high self-esteem consumers claimed to buy them.

Other researchers have continued to widen the scope of self-image consumer research by investigating a variety of products: 'the results, though weak, have been generally supportive of the hypothesis that consumers prefer, intend to buy or use brands/products which are more congruent with their self-concepts' (Malhotra 1988: 5–6). Moreover, the matching of self-image to goods and services embraces not only product attributes but promotional, distributive and pricing elements of the marketing mix. Advertising portrays ideal behavior patterns for consumers, suggesting that buyers of particular products and brands may attain their ideal selves as a result (Pollay 1986). Advertising that appeals positively to consumers' self-images has been shown to be more effective than that which does not (De Sarbo and Harshman 1985); that which contradicts audience members' self-concepts is particularly irritating (Aaker and Bruzzone 1985). A variety of retail outlets has also been investigated with respect to consumers' self-concepts and, once again, the expected matching occurs (Belch 1982; Belch and Landon 1977; Stern *et al.* 1977).

Against this, it must be admitted that some studies have produced results contradictory of the general pattern (e.g., Schewe and Dillon 1978; for a valuable and instructive review, see Sirgy 1982). However, there is reason to believe that improvements in the theoretical and methodological bases of empirical work are overcoming some of the problems of earlier research. Few investigations, for instance, have found the expected differences between actual, ideal and social self-concepts. The reconceptualization of self-concept as a multi-dimensional construct has, however, shown that these distinctions are valid and potentially capable of being incorporated in marketing strategies based on segmentation of consumers' image-based preferences. In a study of consumers' preferred house types, Malhotra (1988) found that some 60 percent of respondents preferred houses consistent with their ideal self-concepts; 22 percent preferred houses congruent with their actual self; and 18 percent preferred houses consistent with their social self.

Many researchers have omitted to consider the mediating effects on self-concept and behavior of other personality factors such as cognitive style and cognitive complexity. As we have seen, more complex information processors are likely to learn quickly, comprehend advertising messages that are open to multiple interpretations, and show greater recall. In a study which incorporated these considerations, Malhotra (1988) indeed found that consumers scoring high on cognitive complexity were more adept than low scorers in matching their preferences with their self-concepts; the reason may be the ability of cognitively complex consumers to form clear images of both themselves and the available product choices.

Perceived risk

Another important feature of consumer perceptions and their impact on decisions involves the amount of risk that consumers perceive to be present in the product purchase decision. This concept should be distinguished from the objective risk present when a consumer buys a product. The concern here is with how much risk the consumer perceives or feels is being run. As with all perceptions, this depends on how the consumer interprets the product information provided. Perceived risk is usually described as the function of two factors. The first is the amount of *uncertainty* present in the information a consumer has about a product. Lack of information or knowledge may heighten the perception of risk. The second factor is the extent of the *consequences of purchase*. Obviously, products that can be purchased with little information, or for which a poor product choice has few negative outcomes, will probably be perceived as low-risk purchases. Where much information is needed, or lacking, or desired, perceived risk may increase. Where the consequences of a bad choice are severe, their perceived risk may increase as well (Bauer 1960; Cox 1967a).

Consumer researchers have described several types of perceived risk associated with purchasing behavior. These may be present in any combination and in different degrees for any given purchase (Gemunden 1985).

- *Functional or performance risk* occurs when the product chosen might not perform as desired and thus not deliver the benefits promised.
- Where the loss of money is an important consideration, *financial risk* is said to be high.
- *Physical risk* refers to possible harm coming to the consumer as a result of purchase.
- *Psychological risk* broadly describes instances where product consumption may harm the consumer's self-esteem or perceptions of self.
- Consumers run *social risk* when a product choice is not approved of by others, resulting in social embarrassment or rejection.
- *Time risk* results when the passage of time reduces the want satisfying ability of the product, such as when a product rapidly becomes obsolete (Ross 1975).

The amount of risk consumers perceive is a function of many variables, and consumers have many options when it comes to reducing the amount of risk they perceive associated with product purchase. Briefly, perceived risk may increase as a function of characteristics of the product itself, such as price, length of time the product needs to be retained, switching costs, additional products or services needed to be consumed along with the product. Risk also depends on characteristics of the consumer: the greater the resources the consumer has at his disposal, the more willing and able the consumer is to gather and use information; and the more experience the consumer has with the product class, the lower the perceived risk. Finally, external forces influence the amount of risk perceived in a given purchase. As more information is made easily available to consumers, and they are given opportunities to reduce the consequences of choice, the lower the perceived risk.

Obviously, for marketing managers, efforts to reduce the risk perceived in the purchase of a given brand should lead to a greater probability that the brand will be chosen. Managers need to examine carefully the purchase of their product from the consumer's point of view, determine which type(s) of risk are most important, and then design strategies to reduce the risk in the eyes of the consumer. Typical risk-reduction techniques are the free sample, warranties, guarantees, coupons, money-back offers, test drives, personal service, detailed usage instructions, and endorsements from change agents (Pinson and Roberto 1988: 301–2). The manager should not limit him- or herself to these tried and true strategies, however; effective managerial use of risk-reduction strategies should stem from a thorough understanding of the principles of perceived risk and a sensitivity to the presence of risk in the mind of the consumer.

CONSUMER PERCEPTIONS OF THE MARKETING MIX

Perception and communication

It has been estimated that some 90 percent of the stimuli that individuals perceive come to them through the agency of sight; much of the rest comes via hearing. It is therefore no surprise to find that advertisements rely heavily on visual and auditory stimuli. But loud noises, bright colors and large advertisements do not, of themselves, guarantee that the consumer will give his or her attention to the message being broadcast by the advertiser. The use of haunting melodies, pastel shades, regional accents, and careful adjustment of advertisement size in relation to total page or poster size all affect perception and, depending on the product being advertised, may do a better job than more aggressive or standardized methods.

Further, the selective nature of perception restricts the effects of any given advertisement no matter how prominently it is positioned or whatever sensory stimuli it incorporates. Consumers' motivations may play a key role in the allocation of attention: greater attention will be paid to stimuli for which the consumer already has a need or is interested in. Someone who is currently thinking about buying a house is likely to respond to all the advertisements placed by building firms in his local newspaper, giving them his undivided attention; if he does not plan to buy a new car for another year, he cannot be expected to give car advertisements the same consideration. Another reader, who is about to change his car but is momentarily uninterested in the housing market, may well show the reverse behavior. Perhaps neither notices the advertisements for a new supermarket or those for shoes.

Because consumers' perceptions of advertisements are not necessarily identical with those of the advertiser, it is imperative that consumers' reactions to messages be monitored. The audience's response to a marketing message may be quite different from that which the marketing management of the advertising firm assumed, and may render months or even years of marketing planning obsolete in the time required to show the advertisement. The phrase 'You're never alone with a Strand', and the cigarette advertisements of which it was part, have become a classic example of this but it must be borne in mind that all messages are to some extent distorted and misunderstood by some section of the market, simply as a result of consumers' filtering the messages they receive. As Drayton puts it:

> The message broadcast by the marketer, if it penetrates the perceptual filter at all, will be modified by the forces of perceptual interpretation to conform to the individual's expectations. Knowing how the consumer perceives his world and the place of advertising messages within it has become part of the marketing task.
>
> (Drayton 1976: 2)

All elements of the marketing mix communicate something about the firm to the consumer, of course, and it is not enough to get the advertisement 'right' while paying insufficient attention to the factors that complement or detract from it. Pack sizes, pack shapes and packaging materials may all affect sales through influencing the consumer's perception of the firm's overall market offering. Again there is scope for differences in perception between managers and consumers (McClure and Ryans 1968).

Gestalt approaches to perception

Gestalt psychology stresses the fact that perception of a stimulus takes place within a known context and that the individual's reaction is thus crucially affected by his general world-view. (The German word 'Gestalt' means 'whole' or 'entirety'). Stimuli never occur in isolation from others (unless, perhaps, under experimental conditions when there is still scope for the individual's interpretation to be affected by the context provided by previous experience and memories). In marketing, this fact acts as a deterrent to the temptation to judge the consumer's whole image of product, brand or store as simply the sum of its various components.

There are two important ways in which this approach to perception can be used to understand consumer behavior. The first, 'closure', is by far the more vital. In closure, the individual tends to complete information (usually sentences or figures) which are presented to him only partially. It is well demonstrated in the Schweppes advertisements which included the phrase 'Schhhh . . . you know who'. A more recent example is provided by advertisements for KLM which contained no reference to the airline's identity other than a list of the letters of the alphabet which *omitted* the three consecutive letters that make up its name. As long as the procedure does not confuse the consumer or contain ambiguous or esoteric knowledge, it probably serves the purpose of making the potential buyer think rather longer than usual about the product's brand name and thereby facilitates recall of it. If, however, the type of closure employed is less obvious than the above examples, the result may well be failure (Schweppes's follow-up campaign based on the 'weppe' – an 'essential ingredient' of the company's drinks – had nowhere near the same appeal and seems not to have been widely noticed).

The other application of the Gestalt phenomenon in marketing refers to the tendency of people to perceive proximate objects or symbols as definite patterns. Examples of proximity are:

```
          x   x   x   x   x   x
        x   x   x   x   x   x
      x   x   x   x   x   x
    x   x   x   x   x   x
  x   x   x   x   x   x
```

and

```
          c   f   i
        b   e   h
      a   d   g
```

The first is seen as a series of diagonal lines rather than a pattern of horizontal or vertical ones; the second is perceived as three three-letter patterns but they are abc, def, ghi, rather than cfi, beh and adg. Recognition that symbols are perceived according to their position within a larger pattern can have implications for store layout, advertisement design and packaging. The principle of proximity, while it is of analytical interest, demonstrates well the tendency of some behavioral scientists to elaborate and add sophistication to marketing phenomena which are adequate on a commonsense level for the needs of practitioners.

Product and brand perception

Interesting studies have been made of the ways in which consumers perceive the products they buy and the brands they regularly choose. In particular, attention has been focused on the ways in which branding and brand perceptions affect the consumer's perceptions of product characteristics and attributes. Some of the tests that have been carried out throw considerable light on the process in which consumers perceive products. For example, Allison and Uhl (1964: 36–9) conducted an experiment to discover whether blindfolded beer drinkers were capable of distinguishing types and brands of beer. They also wished to determine the effect of brand identification on consumers' reactions to and evaluations of beers. They concluded that: 'Participants in general did not appear to be able to discern the taste differences among the various brands, but apparently labels and their associations did influence their evaluations.'

These findings indicate that customers' perceptions of products derive from marketing effort such as brand images and brand differentiation in addition to the physical characteristics of the product alone. Further, it can be concluded that in some cases those product attributes which are marketing based may be the consumer's only guide to want satisfaction. Thus all of the factors that impinge on the construction of a brand image must be examined in order to ascertain their effects on consumers' perception of the firm's marketing mix. It is necessary in this context to underline what has already been said about differences in product perception between consumers and sellers; even in packaging there can be considerable variations. A recent investigation of the reasons for product failure shows that in most cases it is the product itself or its package which is at fault and misunderstandings regarding consumers' perceptions are undoubtedly responsible for many of these failures (Foxall 1984a).

Brand image

Brand *image* refers to the organized set of perceptions consumers have formed about the brand. You might say that a brand image is the sum of all the perceptions consumers have about the brand. Brand images are important because consumers use these mental representations to distinguish one brand from another and as the basis for their purchasing behaviors. In marketing and consumer behavior, perceptions are reality, so that brand images are of primary concern to marketers. Brand images are formed as consumers receive information from the media, from other consumers, and from personal experience with brands. A brand's image is a mental representation that the brand evokes in the consumer's mind as the combined result of marketing and advertising strategies, the influence of opinion leaders and other social communication, and the brand's performance. Brand images thus are quite complex, consisting of several dimensions: personality, connotations, advantages, users and situations.

A brand's *personality* describes what it is like – what impression it makes on the consumer. Is it fashionable, lively, conservative, reliable, fun, effective, or what? Guess jeans, for example, are fashionable and sexy, but not rugged or expensive. Calvin Klein Jeans, on the other hand, are sophisticated, chic, and suggest money in the pocket. Brand personalities are created chiefly by advertising, naming and packaging. A black package, for instance, identifies the brand as sophisticated, while a pastel package signifies the brand is feminine or delicate, and green implies a favorable link with the environment.

A brand's *connotations*, or what the brand makes the consumer think of, also forms part of its image. What does the brand suggest? Kool cigarettes have traditionally suggested the menthol taste, reinforced by both the name and advertising that featured the brand side by side with snow and running water. More recent Kool ads have used cartoon penguins to suggest a hip or with-it message to potential smokers (Dagnoli 1989).

The brand's *advantages* are the specific benefits it delivers as it is consumed. What does it do for me? These are consumer evaluative judgments of the brand's performance characteristics that differentiate it from other brands. Since the direct benefits of a brand to the consumer are of primary importance, we see many firms use this brand aspect as the chief means of creating and enhancing image. Volvo cars are safer than many other cars because of specific design features that are illustrated in advertising. Mercedes are chiefly conservative status symbols, but BMWs are trendy symbols of youthful success. Sometimes brand names feature the key benefit(s) of the brand and contribute to its image: Easy-Off oven cleaner, Carpet Fresh carpet cleaner, Close-Up toothpaste.

Another part of a brand's image may be the distinctive type of *user* associated with the brand's consumption. Some brands are strongly associated with a unique user profile. Usually this is carefully cultivated by the marketer because of the twin promises that (a) using the brand acts as a symbol of what kind of person you are, or (b) you can become more like a desirable consumer type by using the brand. Thus, brands are sometimes strongly identified with user types, such as the rugged, independent Marlboro cowboy or the Players gang of sophisticated, urban swingers. Barkely is smoked by an attractive, urbane gentleman, and Virginia Slims by independent, modern, young women. Advertising featuring clearly identifiable consumer prototypes is usually trying to create a brand image this way.

Finally, some brands are identified with certain *usage situations*. Their consumption either occurs more frequently at certain times of the year or day, or the marketers would like to encourage brand use of specific times, places or circumstances. Ads strongly suggest that Miller beer is consumed by heavy-drinking, blue-collar men after work. Lowenbrau is presented as the weekend beer of light-drinking, white-collar men and women. Champagne is presented as a festive drink, especially around Christmas and New Year. When guests come over, it's time to bring out the Chivas Regal.

Image analysis

There are as many product positions as there are brands to fill them. In conceptualizing markets for competing brands, it can be useful to think of each product's position in terms of a multidimensional image of that brand, similar to that shown by the image analysis in Figure 3.2. Image analysis based on such measurements allows marketing managers to compare and contrast their brands with competitors in a quantitative way. Focus groups, previous research findings, depth interviews and intuition all have been used to determine the managerially relevant dimensions of commonplace consumer products such as jeans. In new empirical research, a random sample of consumers from the target segment is generally asked to rate each competing brand along a number of dimensions and the mean scores are plotted. Consumers also rate their ideal brand on these dimensions. The marketer might choose to position the brand as the one most appropriate for a certain situation, the one that gives the most value for the money, or the one most likely to bestow status on the user.

```
┌──────────────────────────────────────────────────────────────┐
│        Fashionable -- -- -- -- -- --  Not-fashionable          │
│          Expensive -- -- -- -- -- --  Inexpensive              │
│               Sexy -- -- -- -- -- --  Dumpy                    │
│               Dull -- -- -- -- -- --  Exciting                 │
│          Well made -- -- -- -- -- --  Poorly made              │
│   Worn by swingers -- -- -- -- -- --  Not worn by swingers     │
│   Not worn casually -- -- -- -- -- --  Worn casually           │
│         Prestigious -- -- -- -- -- --  Not prestigious         │
└──────────────────────────────────────────────────────────────┘
```

Figure 3.1 Image analysis of jeans

Since managers use the marketing mix to position the brand, they must choose exactly the right combination of the four Ps needed to give the brand the desired position. Lowering the price, offering promotions, and running ads that stress what a good value the brand is, will most likely give a brand the image as the low-cost/bargain price alternative. Raising the price, limiting the distribution, focusing few ads in select media, and forbidding retailers from discounting, will result in the brand having a prestigious image in consumers' minds. Successfully accomplishing both tasks of conceptualizing the brand's position and developing the most effective marketing mix to achieve it are aided by the research approach termed perceptual mapping. Discussing this procedure not only explains the concept of positioning further, it is also an informative insight into consumer psychology and how understanding this aids the marketer.

If we ask consumers to evaluate and compare a set of brands along a single dimension, say relative prestige, we would get a hierarchy of brands ranging from the least to the most prestigious with many intermediate brands in between. Each consumer might arrange the brands in a different order, depending on his or her perception of each brand's prestige, and there would be an arrangement of brands representing the average perceptions across

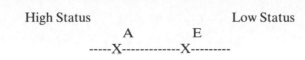

Figure 3.2 A unidimensional map of brands of jeans

a target segment. Figure 3.2 presents a unidimensional array of brands of jeans, which compares brands A and E on the basis of the degree of status they are perceived to confer.

If a market is very simple, if the brands are evaluated on only one feature, such a unidimensional arrangement of brands would suffice as a positioning analysis. In most markets, however, brand images are more complex; the brands exist perceptually in a multidimensional product space as they are arranged in the consumers' minds along several dimensions at once. The multidimensional measurement of the product space for a set of brands is generated by a family of statistical techniques called multidimensional scaling (MDS) (Churchill 1991: 448–64).

The data input to these computer programs is generated by asking samples of consumers either to compare pairs of competing brands with one another for preference or similarity (non-metric MDS) or by rating them (metric MDS). The output generated by the MDS program is a multidimensional perceptual map that shows the brands in their perceived space. A hypothetical example is shown in Figure 3.3, which compares brands of jeans. In theory, the number of dimensions of the perceptual space can be larger than two or even three, but in reality, since it is difficult for humans to perceive relationships among the brands in more than two or three dimensions at the most, perceptual maps usually are limited to these types (Wind 1981; Wind *et al.* 1981). The researcher's job is to work with managers to identify the axes of the map – the dimensions of the perceptual space being described – which the computer program cannot label. In the example shown, it appears to the managers that status and quality are the two dimensions that consumers use to compare these brands of jeans. The map then shows that, while Brand B jeans are perceived to be of high quality (durability), they appear to lack status in the eyes of jeans consumers. Changes in advertising or promotion may be needed to give the brand a more prestigious image in the minds of consumers. Many insights into a brand's image among a target segment and its relationships to other brands can be drawn from examining these maps.

Marketers of both mature brands and stores can use both image analysis and perceptual mapping to gain great insight into how well their brands compare with other brands and how consumers view their brands. Perceptual maps may suggest new marketing opportunities, perhaps through the development of a brand closer to consumers' 'ideal' positioning, or an existing brand might be repositioned to achieve the same purpose. Less dramatically, changes and improvements in marketing strategies can be stimulated by this information. Advertising can be created to change perceptions of specific features of brands to bring them closer to ideal, desired features. A marketer may even choose to reposition a brand, changing its position in consumers' minds. Repositioning is often stimulated by declining market share or a serious attack from another firm's brand. Recently, for example, General Motors' Oldsmobile division decided that lagging sales necessitated a major marketing strategy change to reposition the brand from its traditional image as a

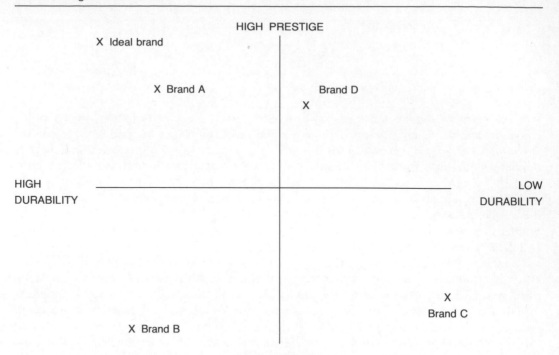

Figure 3.3 A multidimensional perceptual map of the jeans market

quality vehicle for older, conservative buyers to a 'contemporary, hi-tech product and image . . . with the theme the new generation of Oldsmobile – this is not your father's Oldsmobile' (Serafin 1988; Treece 1989). The challenge was to appeal to younger buyers without alienating the older customer base.

Price perception

Perception has implications too for another element in the marketing mix, namely price. There is considerable evidence that for many products and services, consumers judge product/service quality by price, a practice which has implications not only for marketing management but for such aspects of economic and social policy as the distribution of income.

Offered two similar versions of the same product, differing only in price, some consumers choose the more expensive item. Such behavior may be irrational in terms of economics but is easily explicable in the context of an affluent society in which discretionary income runs at high levels and social status is judged by levels of expenditure and conspicuous consumption. It is also explained in individual terms by the fact that most children are socialized into linking not only quantity, but also quality, with price. Naturally this phenomenon is not capable of being extended to all products and services; its very nature tends to make it exclusive to those items that confer status or that reinforce the individual's sense of ambition or achievement. Its domain can be established only through empirical testing and it remains an intriguing possibility for marketing differentiation.

Buyers' subjective perceptions of prices (the price-quality relationship) are by no means fully understood (Monroe 1973). Many consumers have strong notions of the expected or normal price level for a product but, within a range either side of this level, price changes do not usually affect willingness to buy. The lower end of this range is marked by a price below which consumers are suspicious of the quality of the item; the higher end, by a price above which the product is competitively uneconomical (Gabor 1988; Monroe 1973; Zeithaml 1982). Not only are there limits to such price insensitivity: the phenomenon appears to hold only in the absence of other informational cues by which quality can be judged (Etgar and Malhotra 1981). It is clear, none the less, that if price and demand are directly or positively related, the importance of pricing as a component of the marketing mix is greatly enhanced.

Another facet of consumers' perceptions of prices is the question of so-called 'psychological pricing'. In the United States, as many as four-fifths of food products may have prices ending in 9 or 5, while in Britain the use of prices ending in 9 pence or 99 pence is widespread. The reasoning behind such pricing strategies is that consumers are likely to perceive a bargain if the price ends in an odd number; 'odd-pricing' is extensively used in cut-price sales promotions to increase the feeling that a price has been drastically reduced. Despite the popularity of this method of fixing prices in some product areas (ladies' shoes, for instance), there is a lack of experimental evidence for its value in augmenting consumers' susceptibilities to buy. Especially where consumers attempt to compare prices and quantities from product to product or brand to brand, the practice of 'price psychology' may serve only to confuse the would-be buyer, or its effect may be neutralized as consumers automatically 'round up' figures to facilitate comparisons.

A related area, though one which is not strictly a perceptual phenomenon, involves consumers' consciousness of prices. There is some evidence that price awareness is affected by socioeconomic background. Studies of British housewives have found that middle-class consumers were more ready to suggest prices for the products they had purchased than were their working-class counterparts. The latter tended to be more accurate in their estimates of such prices, however, giving the impression that price consciousness is inversely related to social class. But, while price awareness is on the whole low, price-aware consumers are apparent and identifiable: they tend to be of very high or very low incomes, well educated, single, in full-time employment, relatively highly exposed to advertising, and multistore shoppers who use shopping lists (Pinson and Roberto 1988: 309). Price awareness among consumers is generally low, though it increases over time for products priced on the low side and decreases for higher priced products (Assael 1987; Gabor 1988; Williams 1981).

The issue of psychological pricing is a difficult one for the manager. In many businesses a body of experience or folk wisdom has been built up that guides pricing decisions. Systematic study of the effects of price differences on consumer reactions may be a more effective way of developing guidelines for pricing decisions. New techniques such as 'scanner' or 'single source' data will allow managers to determine more precisely the effects of price difference on sales and profits.

Store perception

Various facets of a store or other business contribute to its image as projected by management and, more importantly perhaps, as perceived by its customers. Berry (1969) suggests that there are five major components of store image, namely location, design, product assortment, services and personnel, each of which contributes to the consumer's overall perception of the place in which he or she buys. But the manner in which consumers perceive the totality of the business enterprise derives from far more than just the physical attributes of the organization. Indeed, the entire range of intangible factors that are at work is so wide that it is unlikely that a customer's general image of a store can be traced back with certainty to any specific factors. The precise influences of advertising, interpersonal communication, experience and so on that determine store perception are too complex and too closely interrelated to be accurately defined let alone measured with any great degree of exactness.

Studies of shopper perceptions, for example, suggest that Wal-Mart shoppers rate Wal-Mart higher and spend more money there than similar K-Mart shoppers. Why would such similar retail outlets engender such different perceptions and results? Some experts have suggested that the reason may lie in such seemingly minor differences as the fact that Wal-Mart employees wear vests, while K-Mart employees don't, or in the fact that Wal-Mart bags shopper purchases in brown paper bags and K-Mart uses plastic (Schwadel 1989).

Customers' perceptions of stores are vitally affected by consumers' own self-perceptions and motives. Stone (1954) isolated four types of store selection motive depending on whether buyers were primarily economic (that is, price conscious and with limited spending power), ethical (shopping where they thought they ought to shop), personalizing (selecting stores for the service and personal attention provided) or apathetic (choosing stores that were convenient but which had no other major characteristics to make them stand out). It is also clear from research that consumers' self-images influence the places in which they shop. Thus, while wives of professional men usually buy in the same store as each other, few of them are likely to choose any stores in common with lower-class women (Davies 1976). Such results as these emphasize also the effects of peer groupings and social position on store selection and perception.

Geographers and planners have provided considerable data on the spatial aspects of consumers' store perceptions, and a variety of models of consumer learning behavior and attitudes has been put forward (Davies 1976). While none of these has proved capable of explaining more than a handful of the dimensions involved in this area of consumer behavior, it has been clearly demonstrated that housewives are able to distinguish between stores that are friendly versus unfriendly, honest versus dishonest, modern versus old-fashioned, etc. It has further been shown that store perceptions vary from class to class (higher-status shoppers are more likely to rate supermarkets as lacking in friendliness) and that age impinges on housewives' images of greengrocers (younger women thought they were more dirty than did older consumers) (Davies 1976; Dawson 1980). This whole field is showing signs of promise but is beset by methodological and conceptual problems; as such it suggests a fruitful area of study for an interdisciplinary team of researchers, behavioral scientists as well as geographers, since each discipline brings essential perspectives to the analysis of consumer behavior which are likely to be neglected by others. We return to the subject of consumers' in-store behavior in Chapter 8.

SUBLIMINAL PERCEPTION

Subliminal advertising

Perception that takes place below the threshold of sound, vision, or other sensual mode is known as subliminal perception. This phenomenon has suggested to some observers the idea of subliminal advertising (Packard 1957). This technique would expose extremely weak or short advertising messages in the context of other media, such as the insertion of rapidly flashed messages to buy a product into a movie or television show. The idea is that because consumers are unaware of the presence of the ads, they can be influenced by the message. A frequently cited example of subliminal advertising involves James Vicary, an American junior executive, who claimed in the late 1950s to have insinuated advertising messages into normal movie performances and to have caused thereby a 17 percent increase in sales of Coca Cola and an increase of 58 percent in popcorn sales in the movie Rouse foyer.

The public consternation that ensued is hardly surprising, but the fact that subsequent replications of Vicary's experiments failed to produce comparable results is less widely known. It has even been suggested as an alternative explanation that the positioning of popcorn and Coke in the foyer during the six-week period of the tests led to the increase in sales. While subliminal perception may be possible, it does not appear to operate in favor of those who would like to manipulate others. The only people likely to be influenced to buy the product in question are those who would no doubt purchase it anyway; moreover the vast majority of people do not perceive subliminal messages at all. 'The whole idea of insinuating into the mind an idea which runs contrary to its basic trends is absurd' (Brown 1963: 189). The mechanism that protects the individual from mental overload and that results in selective perception also appears to operate here: attempts to circumvent the mechanism through subliminal advertising appear to pose little threat to the independence of the consumer.

Use of subliminal advertising might well have quite deleterious consequences for the manager since consumers may misunderstand stimuli that are presented at levels below the normal thresholds of sensory experience. Barthol and Goldstein (1959), in a review of the topic, point out that the message 'Drink Coca-Cola', subliminally projected, could be read as 'Drink Pepsi Cola' or 'Drink Cocoa' or even 'Drive Safely'. They conclude that consumers are safe, since 'we are staunchly protected by our insufficient nervous systems, our prejudices, our lack of attention, and the inalienable right to completely misunderstand, misinterpret and ignore what we don't see clearly' (Barthol and Goldstein 1959: 35).

An extensive review of subliminal advertising has been conducted by T. E. Moore (1982). Although there is some evidence that subliminal advertising may, under closely regulated conditions, induce affective responses and arouse basic physiological drives, the effect is weak, the experimental studies that attest to it are open to charges of methodological impurity, and the putative results hardly form the basis of a coherent marketing strategy in which unattended stimuli could influence whole market segments. Perceptual thresholds differ from person to person with the effect that

> there is no particular stimulus intensity or duration that can guarantee subliminality for all viewers. In order to preclude detection by those with relatively low thresholds, the stimulus would have to be so weak that it would not reach viewers with higher thresholds at all. Lack of control over position and distance from the screen would further complicate matters. Finally, without elaborate precautions, supraliminal material (i.e., the firm or commercial in progress) would almost certainly wash out any potential effects of a subliminal stimulus.
>
> (T. E. Moore 1982: 41)

Furthermore, there is voluminous evidence, rigorously garnered through experimental research, to the effect that stronger rather than weaker stimuli invoke the more behavioral change in individuals (T. E. Moore 1982: 47). The notion that marketing managers should employ the weak approach to persuasive influence inherent in subliminal advertising, when techniques both more intense and more subtle are available to them, is a counter-productive proposition for practical marketers. An even more strongly worded denunciation of subliminal stimuli as a serious topic in marketing and advertising can be found in Pratkanis (1991). In any case, the practice is specifically prohibited in many countries (Harrell 1986: 94).

Subaudible perception

The attempt to present message stimuli so weak that they fall below consumers' sound thresholds (e.g., verbal statements included subaudibly in radio advertisements) appears doomed to failure. Low-volume messages are easily masked by the audible material in which they are ensconced, while the delivery of subaudible verbal material at greatly accelerated speeds render the message undetectable as well as incomprehensible (T. E. Moore 1982). Similar claims to those made about the assumed potency of subliminal advertising are now often directed at messages on gramophone records that are allegedly recorded backwards in order to influence listeners at an unconscious level. Vokey and Read conclude on the basis of a large volume of experimental research, that such 'backmasking' has no discernible effect on behavior. Moreover, in practice, backward messages appear to be more illusory than real:

> In summary, despite large effects in tasks requiring discrimination on the basis of physical parameters of backwards speech, we could find no evidence that subjects are influenced either consciously or unconsciously by the semantic content of backward messages. On the issue of the alleged presence of these messages, our results suggest that people's perception of these messages is most likely a function of active construction on the part of listeners.
>
> (Vokey and Read 1985: 1237)

Embeds

Interest in subliminal perception in the context of marketing has been rekindled during the last decade as a result of claims that the public is frequently exposed to messages in the form of words 'embedded' into the pictorial fabric of advertising copy. The implication is that although readers cannot consciously detect these stimuli, they are nevertheless influenced by them to purchase the advertised products or brands (Key 1973, 1980). It is alleged, for instance, that embeds that contain sexual imagery have been included in advertisements for products such as swimsuits, skin-care cream, women's magazines, and cracker biscuits. In some cases, the word 'sex' has allegedly been incorporated in camouflaged form in the background of advertisements. In others, sexually suggestive poses and images have been used in ways that hide them from the casual reader (Key 1970).

However, Vokey and Read (1985) argue that alleged embeds are often impossible to detect in practice. Their laboratory experiments have demonstrated, moreover, that even when embeds are present in visual material, they do not affect recall behavior. In one experiment, subjects were shown equal numbers of three types of holiday photographs: one type were the straightforward, untouched slides; the second type had the word 'sex' embedded three or four times on each slide; the third type contained embedded nonsense syllables in the places where the second type contained the word 'sex'. No subjects noticed the word 'sex' on the slides before it was brought to their attention. Half the respondents were immediately retested by being shown the slides again and asked whether they had seen each one previously. The other half undertook this second test two days later in order to investigate the view that subliminally received information requires an elapse of time to become effective. The results show that sex-embedding did not increase the rate of recognition of the slides on the second exposure. Nor did the time lapse affect the results: indeed, the accuracy of recognition was reduced by the two-day interval (Vokey and Read 1985: 1232).

SUMMARY

Perception, which refers to the reception and interpretation of external stimuli by an individual, begins with the process of sensation and is a selective mental operation. Without attention being given to a stimulus, little perception will take place. People give their attention largely to those things that are novel, interesting, or from which they derive satisfaction of needs and wants. Consumers react to advertisements, products, packages and so on according to their motives, attitudes and social situation; moreover each individual's perception of these marketing mix elements is unique to him or her.

Consumers perceive several types of risk in the purchase of many products. Managers should take active steps to reduce this perceived risk as a normal part of any marketing strategy. Subliminal and Gestalt models of perception were also discussed in this chapter and were found to have interesting but limited applications to marketing. Perceptions of stores (store images), prices, brands and advertising messages may vary significantly from one part of a company's market to another. Consumer behavior is a process of learning of which perception is only the beginning. Thus we need to follow this discussion of perception with a description of how consumers learn and the implications of consumer learning for marketing strategies.

Chapter 4

Cognitive and behavioral learning

WHAT IS LEARNING?

Learning is conceptually related to perception. Both involve the individual consumer's responses to environmental and psycho-social stimuli; both can be explained theoretically in terms of either a stimulus–response or a cognitive paradigm; both processes are intrinsically connected with and shaped by the individual's attitudes, personality and motives; finally, both perception and learning are important in explaining several aspects of consumer behavior and hence are of practical concern to marketing management. Consumers store information in memory in the form of associations: for instance, a core construct such as a brand name may be connected or linked with a variety of other constructs such as the attributes of the brand (its price, color, size, and the benefits it confers) as well as how the consumer feels about it (its quality, how it compares with similar brands, the emotions it evokes). These associations are important to marketers because they are the information base used by consumers when making purchase and use decisions.

Most of the information consumers have stored in memory regarding goods and services (what they know, think or feel about brands) comes from the process of learning. This information frequently forms the basis for their behavior. Thus consumer researchers talk about how consumer perceptions and attitudes influence their actions, and marketers are concerned with what consumers think and feel about their brands because these thoughts and feelings are precursors to purchase and consumption. Although consumer learning takes many forms, the principal means by which marketers communicate with consumers is through advertising. Consequently, much of the discussion of learning involves advertising effects. The present chapter discusses the many ways in which learning can take place and what marketers can do to promote positive learning about their brands.

The concept of learning is a broad one that has been defined in a variety of ways. These different perspectives can be confusing if they are not distinguished from each other. The most basic distinction in learning theory is between the cognitive and behaviorist approaches. Cognitive learning theory views learning as chiefly a conscious mental activity, whilst behavioral approaches describe learning as largely unconscious changes in overt and verbal behaviors. The following diagram illustrates the broad learning types and their sub-categories.

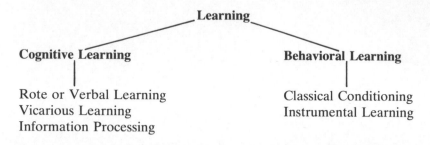

This chapter is concerned, first, with the learning that takes place as a result of marketers' efforts to influence consumers through the promotion component of the marketing mix: personal selling, sales promotion, and especially advertising. The focus will be upon how information gets from the external communication environment into the long-term memory of consumers where it is available for use in consumer decision making. We shall try to describe the many ways in which this kind of learning can take place. Second, the chapter reviews the ways in which learning occurs in the form of changes in consumer behavior as a result of the consumer's experience.

COGNITIVE LEARNING

If learning is defined as changes that take place within the content or organization of long-term memory, we have a perspective on consumer behavior that promises to explain much of what we observe in the marketplace as well as suggesting a variety of ways for marketers to influence consumers. First of all, we must ask: What do consumers learn? The answer is that much of our participation in the marketplace involves learning. From other people, chiefly parents, friends and co-workers, consumers learn values, skills, behaviors, tastes, preferences and the meanings of products and brands. From the marketer and advertiser, the consumer learns the names, features, facts and impressions about brands which, in turn, influence action. Consequently, the marketer must ask: What do I want my customers to learn about my product? And, perhaps more importantly: What do my customers learn about my product? Will the consumer learn positive things about the product that might lead him to buy it? Will he or she be satisfied with the product and want to buy it again, or learn to avoid it? In essence, this learning perspective forms the heart of the marketing concept and represents one of the major challenges to marketers in competitive environments in which other marketers strive to teach consumers to prefer their brands.

Rote learning: memory through repetition

Perhaps the simplest form of learning in the marketplace occurs when consumers are repeatedly exposed to information such as brand names, slogans, jingles or claims, which they simply memorize without paying much attention. That is, this information is stored in memory just as it is received with little conscious thought (cf. the discussion of low-involvement learning in Chapter 2). When this information is visual, the form of learning is termed *iconic rote memory*, referring to the memorization of things seen. When what is memorized is aural in nature, *echoic rote memory* takes place. Consumers memorize information they hear repeatedly. In addition to simply being stored in memory, these learned bits or chunks of information may become associated with other chunks of information in the mind, forming weak beliefs and feelings about brands. This type of learning is sometimes also called incidental learning and is an example of Krugman's low-involvement learning.

For instance, consumers may form the weakly held belief that a particular brand is desirable or effective because the spokesperson in the ads repeats this claim over and over; positive associations are created by the choice of words used in the message, by the impressions consumers have of the spokesperson, the music used in the ad, the colors or settings of the ad, and so forth. Thus, when questioned, one consumer claimed to prefer Budweiser beer because it was the 'King of Beers', repeating the brand's slogan heard many times before. Of course, this was not the underlying reason for brand preference, but because this information is the most easily available in memory, it was offered as justification.

Such weakly held beliefs and associations stored in memory over time may form the basis for brand choice when purchase is made. Marketers thus should be careful to repeat brand names and slogans as often as possible, given their finite promotional budgets (see Krugman 1965). This partially explains the simplicity of many brand names and the efforts made to create names that evoke positive associations in the consumer's mind. This effect can be facilitated by using brand names that incorporate the principal benefit the product promises to deliver to the customer (Easy-Off oven cleaner, or Close Up toothpaste), or which have intrinsically positive associations (Joy dishwashing detergent, Satin cigarettes), or which make the name easy to remember (rhyming or alliteration in slogans facilitates memorization: 'For all you do, this Bud's for you'; 'I was flat till I went fluffy' (for Pert shampoo).

Learning vicariously: modeling and imitation

Also called observational learning, this form of learning occurs when consumers imitate the behavior of others. Grounded in social learning theory (Bandura 1977), vicarious learning describes the way in which consumers learn patterns of behavior by watching others behave and then applying these lessons to their own lives. A variety of consumer behaviors, such as shopping, interacting with sales clerks, brand selection and consumption, can be modeled for consumers who pattern their future behavior on the examples observed. Marketers frequently attempt to influence consumers through advertising featuring models of how they would like consumers to behave with regard to their products. Consumers also learn by imitating other people in their natural environment, and this influence on consumer behavior will be discussed further in Chapter 9.

Information processing

Formal learning refers to the instruction of consumers by other people. This type of learning most often takes place in face-to-face interactions with others, in which the consumer is given specific information about what to think and do. Formal learning takes place frequently within the family setting and forms part of the process of socialization by which children are given the skills, knowledge, beliefs and preferences of their social environments. Formal learning can also take place between consumers and salespersons who instruct them in the mysteries of a product category. Marketers try to use the formal learning approach in advertising by developing didactic ads that impart specific instructions about the brand to the audience.

Reasoning takes place when consumers take information they have about a brand and deduce their own conclusions regarding the brand's suitability for purchase and use. This may involve integration of new information with existing knowledge already stored in memory, or the evaluation of a brand's attributes against standards used by the consumer as criteria (often called the evaluative criteria) to determine brand suitability.

Formal learning and reasoning are two forms of learning about products that imply a heavy investment of time and cognitive energy by the consumer. In this way they differ from rote learning mechanisms, which take place on the surface of awareness and require little effort by the consumer. These similar perspectives on cognitive learning can be integrated into a more complex view of how consumers learn called 'information processing', which encompasses a wide range of cognitive activities.

In general, information processing is a generic term used to describe the series of stages or steps by which information is encountered in the external world, attended to by the consumer, interpreted, understood and stored in memory for future use in making buying decisions. We have already sketched out this area of consumer study in our discussions of perception. In fact, perceptual processes are usually thought of as a subset of the larger information processing model. Figure 4.1 presents a version of this paradigm.

Exposure

Exposure to information in the environment refers to the fact that in order for the consumers to receive information, one or more of the receptor organs – eyes, nose, ears, skin – must be in physical contact with some stimulus containing the information. We see the ads in pictures, hear the sound tracks, voices and noises. We read text and listen to other consumers. We smell and touch products. All these are ways in which the messages contained in external stimuli are available for consumers to learn. If the customer is not first exposed to market information, he or she cannot possibly learn it and use it. Two facts about the process by which information gets from the environment into memory are

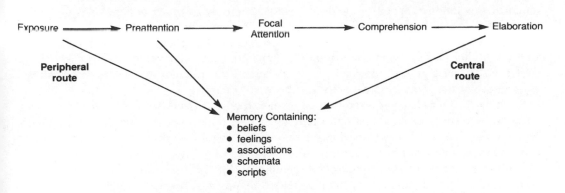

Figure 4.1 A model of consumer information processing
Source: After Greenwald, A. G. and C. Levitt (1984) 'Audience involvement in advertising: four levels', *Journal of Consumer Research*, 11, 581–92.

important to bear in mind. First, consumers are exposed only to a small subset of the possible messages directed toward them. Second, consumers are limited by the built-in capabilities of their sense organs and brain structures to processing only small amounts of the information available to them at any one time. These two limitations on the flow of information into consumer memory are highly relevant to marketers' efforts to persuade consumers of the superiority of individual brands.

Consumers are exposed to information in the environment on both a voluntary and an involuntary basis. Sometimes consumers actively seek out information from a variety of sources, so that they can make decisions using what they learn. Much of the time, however, consumers are exposed to market information in the form of advertisements, promotions, packages or sales pitches, whether they intend to or not. Consumers are very selective with regard to the information to which they voluntarily expose themselves. They pick and choose which magazines and newspapers to read, which TV and radio programs to watch and listen to, which stores they shop in, and so forth. Even the patterns of travel followed by consumers are selective in that they do not go everywhere, only to a narrow set of preselected residential, work and play destinations. Hence, it is very important for marketers to understand these patterns of voluntary exposure of the market segments they wish to communicate with. Audience demographics, psychographics and buying habits are the principal means by which the media describe the listeners, watchers and readers of their products. Marketers try to match up these audience profiles with the characteristics of their target segments, seeking to find the most efficient media vehicles to reach their customers. The effectiveness of specific media vehicles in reaching consumers is evaluated by research into media reach and circulation.

Preattention

In psychological terms, attention refers to the amount of mental effort or cognitive capacity allocated by an individual to the stimulus environment or task at hand. This attentional capacity is finite, and the human mind is so constructed that it attempts to conserve as much of this limited capacity as possible, allocating only as much energy as is needed to accomplish the tasks at hand in the most efficient manner possible. In short, human attention is selectively allocated, leaving consumers not explicitly aware of most of the stimuli in their information environment. Thus, the lowest level of awareness can be described as preattention, in which the mind uses little capacity to process information, while most of the processing capacity is otherwise occupied.

Little research has been devoted to the persuasion of consumers at this shallow level. Some researchers have suggested that information can be transmitted to memory through the repetition of simple messages and images that do not require large amounts of information-processing capacity for assimilation. A 'mere exposure' hypothesis has been posited whereby positive feelings or heightened recognition for some stimulus, say a brand name, can be engendered simply through repeated exposures, even though the consumer pays little conscious attention to it (Zajonc and Markus 1982). The extent to which consumers have learned from advertisements even at this low level of processing can be assessed through measurement of consumer recognition of ads to which they have been exposed.

Focal attention

Since attention is only partially under the voluntary control of the individual, much marketing and advertising effort is devoted to gaining focal attention. Focal attention may be defined as the mind's ability to process information, to decipher the message and transmit at least part of the information contained therein to memory. Part of the story of focal attention is the voluntary, effort-filled activity involved when consumers seek out product-related information, 'pay attention' to advertisements, or otherwise bring their ability to process information to bear upon some aspect of the marketplace. Usually this voluntary allocation of attention is impelled by the need to attain some goal, or is driven by longstanding involvement with the product area. Hence, the consumer who feels that clothes are an important part of life seeks out clothing-related information by attending to clothing ads, talking to sales people and others about clothes, and spends time inspecting clothes in the store. Voluntary attention is very selective; consequently, marketers devote time and money to reaching the involved consumer with messages communicating brand superiority information.

In addition, attention can be attracted by environmental stimuli. This involuntary attention is important to marketers because if they are successful in attracting attention to their messages, the information contained therein is more likely to enter memory than if they rely on some weaker forces such as mere exposure to achieve this goal. Hence, a wide variety of techniques is employed to create focal attention in consumers. The use of humor, fear, visual imagery, sexual imagery, unusual stimuli and so forth in advertising attracts attention which can then be focused on the message contained in the ad. The advertiser hopes that once focal attention is engaged, the brand message will be stored in memory for future use. Celebrity spokespersons, real or fabricated in the media, are used at least in part to attract attention, although the glut of actors hawking products in recent years has tended to diminish this effect to some extent (Alsop 1985). Marketers measure the amount of focal attention that has been allocated to ads by the extent to which consumers can recall the ads with and without clues to which ads are in question.

Comprehension

Once a message, such as an advertisement, has been attended to and its features (the characteristics of the way the message is presented) noted, the information contained within the message, its content, must be deciphered by the consumer. This is the process of comprehension, in which the mind retrieves information from memory and uses it to assign meaning to the elements of message content, forming new representations which themselves can be stored in memory. Comprehension is the process by which the consumer understands what the message says. Many factors play a role in the comprehension of advertising messages:

- existing expertise in the product area,
- product involvement,
- expectations consumers have of what they will learn, and
- individual differences across consumers.

Marketers are interested in how consumers respond to their messages because they feel that future behavior is affected by the quality and quantity of the information consumers store in memory upon message reception. By being attentive to these factors and their effect on consumers' cognitive responses, marketers themselves learn how consumers respond to their messages. The principal types of cognitive responses are:

- support arguments when the consumer accepts the message content,
- counter arguments when rejecting message content,
- source bolstering, and
- source derogation, which refers to positive and negative thought about the message context (the presentation of the message).

Like the stages in information processing that precede comprehension, comprehension of the message itself is highly selective. Consumers may comprehend and thus respond to messages in a wide variety of ways.

Elaboration

Elaboration is the final stage of information processing, and refers to the creation within memory of complex networks of ideas and feelings about products, based upon the messages that marketers transmit to consumers. The new information may be extensively integrated with prior information to form a cognitive structure within memory. Cognitive structures termed 'schemata' represent the total integrated network of information, feelings, and associated ideas consumers have about products, brands, services, stores, etc. (Lynch and Srull 1982). Product-related schematas contain not only information but plans for action, intentions, and instructions for future behavior.

A special type of schema, called a script, is a stereotyped event sequence, describing what a consumer should do in a particular consumption situation. For example, the series of steps followed by the typical consumer upon entering a fast-food outlet – ordering food, finding a seat, etc. – is a script contained in the memories of many consumers. Since much consumption behavior is guided by schemata and scripts, these cognitive structures are coming under increasing attention by consumer researchers.

The organization and systematization of knowledge occurs in the consumer's *long-term memory store*, which contains information for periods of several minutes to many years. It is from this source that the consumer's internal search for information is generated when a novel stimulus (say, an advertising message) provokes curiosity. Long-term memory also influences the consumer's external search for information. Much information is filtered out, however, before it reaches the long-term memory. For just a brief period of time, information passes from the senses to the consumer's *short-term memory store* where, if it is not acted upon in ways that ensure its longer-term storage, it is lost within a minute. Moreover, only a few items or chunks of information can be retained within short-term memory at all (Miller 1956).

Four functions of memory increase the likelihood that information will be transferred from the short-term to the long-term store and thus retained for future use. The first is *rehearsal*: by mentally repeating information, the individual increases the chance that the material will be linked to other stored information and thereby retained. Second is *encoding*: the process in which information is symbolically or verbally represented so that it can be more easily stored, associated with other data, and retrieved. The third function of memory, *storage*, includes the operations described above as elaboration, the organization of information. Finally, *retrieval* is the process in which information is returned from the long-term memory to short-term memory so that it can be used in making evaluations and decisions. (For a description of memory processes and the evidence for the information processing approach, see Gordon 1989.)

An area of concern for marketers is the fact that recent studies have shown that a great deal of the information consumers are exposed to is miscomprehended (Jacoby and Hoyer 1982). These studies suggest that the effectiveness of advertising is more strongly linked to the power of the copy, to the media selected, or to the timing of the ads than to the sheer amount of money spent. The need to ensure that advertising messages are simple (encouraging rehearsal and encoding) is indicated here. The repeated use of easily perceived brand names, advertising jingles and packaging design also encourages storage and retrieval. Much depends on the cognitive complexity of the audience, its ability to handle complicated concepts and structures, and thus on its intellectual level. Another factor is the degree of involvement felt by consumers with both the advertising and the product field, a theme to which we shall soon return.

First, another topic of perennial concern – the measurement of advertising effectiveness – requires brief mention (before we consider it more fully in the next chapter). Marketers use a variety of techniques, including day-after-recall (DAR scores), recognition tests and copy tests to determine whether their advertising expenditures are justified. The information processing model can act as a guide to understanding the effects of advertising in the following way. Since each stage of the process is highly selective and forms a discrete unit of analysis, tests performed at each stage can potentially pinpoint reasons for advertising success or failure. Studies of ad reach and circulation, for instance, may indicate that many members of the target market are not being exposed to the ads themselves, so that failure to expose consumers to the ads explains lack of success. Recall and recognition tests may disclose failure to attract attention, and recall and copy tests may reveal miscomprehension. Studies of cognitive response give insight into the ways consumers react to the specific features of an ad message or mode of presentation. This information helps managers and copywriters to tailor the ad to make it as effective as possible. All in all, information processing forms one of the most interesting and important areas of marketing research because of the obvious impact of consumer learning on consumer behavior.

Consumer involvement and expertise

A great deal of attention has been focused in recent years on the concept of involvement in consumer and marketing research. This stems from a growing awareness that the concept of involvement in one form or another plays an important role in the operation of almost every major concept used to explain consumer behavior. For instance, involvement may affect or mediate attitude formation, brand loyalty, consumer satisfaction, perceived risk, or repetition in advertising (Kassarjian and Robertson 1981). In spite of the acknowledged importance of the involvement concept, however, there is as yet no universally agreed definition of what 'involvement' means. Several distinct ideas have been formulated, each with its own area of application and implications for marketers.

First to announce the concept of involvement was Krugman (1965), who (as we noted in Chapter 2) argued that when exposed to the mass media, consumers either lacked personal involvement (the most common reaction) or they manifested a high degree of involvement, defined not as attention, interest or excitement, but as 'the number of conscious 'bridging experiences', connections, or personal references per minute that the viewer makes between his own life and the stimulus'. Krugman's theory can be characterized as 'involvement' with advertising messages or 'communication involvement', and forms a part of the general theory of information processing. In the high-involvement state, consumers pay attention to and evaluate the arguments of the messages they receive and form attitudes toward the advertised brands based on their evaluation of the information received. Thus Krugman's high-involvement situation describes the information-processing approach to consumer learning with all its complexities.

In the low-involvement mode, consumers process very little of the information received, but repeated exposures to messages in this state will leave a basic perceptual structure for the advertised brand, enough for consumers to act upon by purchase and use. For the low-involved consumer, final attitudes toward the brand are formed through personal experience with the product after, rather than prior to, purchase. Low-involvement learning thus takes place as a result of repetition leading to the rote memorization of simple information. This process is described by learning psychologists as latent learning (learning in the absence of relevant motivation) or incidental learning (learning without intention to learn). Much learning in the marketing environment takes place this way and is important to success. Analogously, some portion of product-relevant word-of-mouth communication is informal and incidental; vague information and attitudes toward products are spread from one person to another via casual conversations and incidental learning.

A. A. Mitchell (1979) offers an alternative view of involvement that takes the personal importance component of Krugman's theory, but gives it different emphasis. According to Mitchell, involvement is a state variable describing internal individual differences among consumers. The involved state is conceived of as having both 'intensity' (the level of arousal, interest or drive toward the topic) and 'direction' (the level of generality of the topic). Consequently, to discuss the involvement of a consumer with some topic, one must specify the level of concern manifest as well as whether it is with the product category, a particular brand, or purchase for a particular reason.

These different views are synthesized and extended by Houston and Rothschild (1978), for whom involvement is essentially the personal relevance of a product to the consumer. This involvement may take three forms. The first is *situational involvement* and occurs when the situation elicits a great deal of involvement among consumers for the period of the situation. For instance, consumers may feel little continuing involvement with their clothing until some situation arises in which clothing is important. Consequently, the consumers may devote an unusual amount of thought, time and money to purchasing the right clothing for the situation, only, to reduce these levels once the situation has past.

Contrast this with the consumer for whom clothing is a constant topic of thought and attention. Such consumers may be said to manifest *enduring involvement*. This broad category of involvement is distinct from situational involvement because of its persistence and because its origins lie in more deep-seated motivations (Antil 1984). Consumers may be said to exhibit enduring involvement in the form of 'ego involvement' when the product area is important (personally relevant) to his or her lifestyle or self-concept. A second source of enduring involvement arises when the product area is seen by consumers as an important way they can express their values or other strongly held beliefs. Such a reaction produced in consumers by products may be called 'commitment' to the product because purchase or use (avoidance) of the product expresses closely held values, as when consumers seek out and use phosphate-free detergent so as not to harm the environment. Thus 'enduring involvement' in the product area may differentiate consumers from one another and explain a great deal of their manifest behavior.

Finally, situational and enduring involvement combine to produce *response involvement*, defined as 'the complexity or extensiveness of cognitive and behavioral processes characterizing the overall consumer decision process' (Houston and Rothschild 1978: 185). Response involvement describes the effort consumers make to attend to and respond to product-relevant information in the communication environment. Thus, it incorporates Krugman's type of involvement and is marked by more or less complex information search, information processing, and decision evaluation.

A Situational involvement – involvement as a process
    1 Communication involvement (Krugman)
    2 Situational involvement (Houston and Rothschild)
    3 Response involvement (Houston and Rothschild)

B Enduring involvement – involvement as a state
    1 Ego involvement (Antil, Mitchell)
    2 Commitment (Antil, Mitchell)

Figure 4.2 Types of involvement

All forms of the involvement construct are characterized by similar features. In high-involvement situations, consumers actively search for and are attentive to information; they compare brands feature by feature and they use complex decision strategies. Low-involvement situations are routine purchases for consumers, little information is assimilated or employed, and simple decision strategies are used. Figure 4.2 shows the types of involvement.

Closely related to the concept of consumer involvement are two similar constructs: familiarity and expertise (Alba and Hutchinson 1987). *Familiarity* with products comes from the number of product-related experiences accumulated by the consumer; it may affect the way in which consumers react to product-relevant information, marketing strategies and new brands. Marketers should evaluate the familiarity of consumers with the product area prior to designing strategies targeted to specific markets.

Expertise is the ability to perform product-related tasks successfully. Expertise increases as familiarity increases and has at least five dimensions.

- *The amount of cognitive effort* expended to process information. As expertise increases, the amount of cognitive effort needed to process product-relevant information decreases. In fact, as expertise becomes optimal, many information-processing tasks become automatic for the consumer, and schemata or scripts become very detailed.
- *Cognitive structure* This means that expert consumers have more detailed knowledge, more associations, for the product in memory; they have a more highly refined set of categories used to evaluate the product.
- *Analysis* Expert consumers have access to and use much more information in evaluating a product than do novice consumers. They also use analytic processing (using rules to evaluate many features, sometimes called 'bottom-up processing') to form the evaluations. Novices use 'top-down' or holistic processing in which evaluations are based on simple rules of thumb.
- *Elaboration or number of associations stimulated* by a product-relevant message. Expert consumers tend to form more and richer associations than do novice consumers. They recall more information about messages and are more likely to draw conclusions and make comparisons rapidly.

- *Enhanced ability to recall or recognize* relevant messages because of the greater retention of information in memory.

Taken together, these dimensions of expertise have important implications for marketers who wish to communicate effectively with their customers.

Elaboration likelihood

The Elaboration Likelihood Model (ELM) was developed by Petty *et al.* (1983) to bring the concept of the motivational state described by enduring involvement to bear upon the question of the persuasiveness of advertising. The basic question is this: How does advertising persuade, given the differences in both ability and motivation to process information which characterize mass media audiences?

Consumers who display high enduring involvement in a product area are more likely to pay attention to a message than consumers who lack this level of involvement. Their message involvement is thus a consequence of their enduring involvement. Their attention will be focused upon the message argument (the claims for brand superiority) and they will process more of the information contained in the message. They are more likely to experience more cognitive responses to the message. If they are persuaded by the message, it will be a function of how convincing they found the message arguments. This process of persuasion is termed in the ELM the *central route to persuasion*. Figure 4.1 shows this as the route from elaboration to memory.

For consumers less involved in the product category, the message will hold no intrinsic interest. Their attention, however, may be attracted by some feature of how the message is presented rather than by the message argument itself. That is, the attention-getting components of the message or the creativity with which the ad is executed may attract their attention so that they will focus low levels of their information-processing capacity upon these features of the message. This does not mean that the message may not be persuasive. Using less cognitive effort, these consumers may use some heuristic such as 'buy the most familiar' and purchase the advertised product simply as a result of becoming familiar with the product through the ad. They also may develop positive feelings about the product because of the music, color, or attractiveness of the spokesperson without really evaluating the product itself. This form of persuasion is termed by the ELM as the *peripheral route to persuasion*. This is shown in Figure 4.1 as the direct route from exposure to memory.

Obviously, the ELM explains some of the bewildering complexity with which the topic of persuasion confronts researchers by combining characteristics of the audience (high and low involvement) with those of the message (argument versus presentation). For the manager, the ELM suggests that an understanding of the involvement levels of the target market can guide the development of persuasive advertising.

BEHAVIORAL LEARNING

So far, we have depicted consumer behavior as a problem-solving and decision-making sequence, the outcome of which is determined by the buyer's intellectual functioning and rational processing of information. Like the comprehensive models of consumer behavior, we have portrayed the consumer as a receiver and handler of information who extensively searches for and evaluates the available options, deriving from this procedure the attitudes and intentions that determine such purchase behaviors as brand or store choice and repeat buying. Marketer-dominated persuasive communications have been credited with initiating and influencing this sequence, the advertising message producing within its recipient a series of psychological effects which culminates in purchase of the advertised brand (Atkin 1984). Moreover, choice has been understood as a mental process initiated by the consumer's awareness of a multiplicity of options, the internal conflict thus generated is reduced by cognitive evaluation of the possibilities available, reasoned consideration of the costs and benefits each entails, and finally decision making (Hansen 1976). We turn now to consider the kinds of stimuli that can impinge on consumer behavior and the learning by experience to which they lead.

Learning associations: classical conditioning

While the rote memory form of learning suggests that simple consumer beliefs about products can be formed through repeated exposure to information about those products, consumers also learn to form more sophisticated beliefs through a process of association called classical or respondent conditioning. Originally identified by Ivan Pavlov, a Russian physiologist, classical conditioning describes a largely unconscious process through which humans, as well as other animals, acquire both information and feelings about stimuli.

Pavlov observed that the dogs in his laboratory salivated not only when they were given food but whenever they heard the footsteps of the assistants who brought the food to them. Through the experimentation suggested by this, he established that the dogs would salivate in the absence of food when a bell was rung, as long as the bell had previously been sounded on many occasions just as the food was presented. He explained the dogs' behavior by claiming that they had come to associate the arrival of the food with the ringing of the bell.

The presentation of food is a stimulus which elicits the salivatory response naturally or spontaneously, i.e., in the absence of conditioning. The food is known as an unconditioned stimulus (UCS), the salivation as an unconditioned response (UR). The constant pairing of food with the ringing of the bell results in the ringing sound taking on some of the characteristics of the unconditioned stimulus. In the end, the sound of the bell becomes a conditioned stimulus (CS), able to elicit, on its own, the salivatory response, now known as a conditioned response (CR).

The psychology of conditioned reflexes became popular during the early decades of this century among American behavioral scientists who reacted against the extensive use by psychologists of introspection as a means of gaining information from human subjects. John Watson, the 'founding father of American behaviorism', did much of the early work to establish a school of psychology which purported to be objective, denying the mental causation of behavior and concentrating fully on the environmental influences which shaped observed responses. After leaving academic life, Watson became an executive with the J. Walter Thompson advertising agency where he sought to apply the thinking behind classical (Pavlovian) conditioning to attempt to persuade consumers to buy (Cohen 1979).

After some years of neglect, classical conditioning is once again attracting the interest of marketing and consumer researchers (McSweeney and Bierley 1984; Nord and Peter 1980). The basic process is as follows. A stimulus either well understood or viewed favorably produces a response in the consumer: for example, feelings of pride are elicited upon seeing the nation's flag; feelings of warmth and love arise upon seeing a baby. In these examples, the flag or baby is termed the unconditioned stimulus, and the feelings they evoke are the unconditioned response. Pairing or associating some other neutral stimulus, called the conditioned stimulus (such as a brand name) with the unconditioned stimulus will, over time, cause the consumer to feel the same feeling when only the brand name is encountered. In other words, the consumer unconsciously learns to associate the original unconditioned feelings with the new stimulus, so that after repeated pairings the conditioned stimulus alone produces the feelings which have now become a conditioned response. This form of learning is best accomplished when the conditioned stimulus appears prior to the unconditioned stimulus (giving it predictive value as a signal of what is to follow), when the conditioned stimulus is presented very close in time and space to the unconditioned stimulus, and when the pairings occur frequently.

It has been suggested, for instance, that the background music in many television advertisements acts as an unconditioned stimulus that elicits the unconditioned emotional responses likely to result in the purchase of the advertised brand. Through the constant pairing of the music with the product, it is argued, the product encountered say on the supermarket shelves or in a showroom may act as a conditioned stimulus which elicits the pleasant emotions and positive attitudes that make purchase more probable. Gorn (1982) showed that background music (UCS) played during the decision process could be associated with a colored pen (CS). In his experiment, 200 students heard the music while watching an advertisement for a cheap pen. Half the students heard popular music which had been judged favorably by a panel as pleasant and 'liked' music (the ad seen by these subjects featured a beige-colored pen). The other hundred students heard classical Indian music, judged unfavorably (and saw a light blue pen). All 200 subjects were later asked to choose either a beige or a light blue pen: 79 percent chose the color associated with the 'liked' music. In debriefing, most attributed their choice to their color preference and only one mentioned the music. Replication using a rather different experimental design has failed, however, to confirm the result (Allen and Madden 1985).

The classical conditioning model explains why consumers learn to associate certain beliefs and feelings with certain brands, and many consumer preferences are learned this way. In addition, further principles of classical conditioning explain other marketing phenomena. Stimuli similar in characteristics to original conditioned stimulus may elicit responses identical to the responses elicited by that stimulus. According to this principle of *stimulus generalization*, similar stimuli produce similar responses. Once the original association of response to stimulus is learned, it can be generalized to other stimuli through association and repetition, so long as the stimuli are similar to the original stimulus. This principle forms the basis for the family branding strategy where a company puts the same brand name on a variety of often unrelated products (e.g., Kraft cheese and salad dressing), and consumers react equally positively to each new product so long as the brand name as a whole continues to elicit positive reaction.

Stimulus discrimination, on the other hand, refers to the fact that people also learn to make different responses to similar stimuli, discriminating among them. Thus consumers form strong brand preferences for essentially identical products by learning to discriminate between them. Some marketers encourage stimulus generalization (usually making their brand look and sound like a competitor's), hoping that the consumer's feelings for the competitor's brand will be generalized to their own brand. Other marketers strive to make their brand distinctive, so that consumers will discriminate and associate positive feelings only with their brand. (There is, however, a down side to this: poor consumption experiences or dissatisfaction with one product bearing a brand name may transfer these negative feelings to other products bearing the same brand name.)

Learning instrumentally: operant conditioning

The instrumental learning approach relates behavior – or, more accurately, the rate at which it is performed – to the consequences similar responding has produced in the past. A response that acts upon the environment to produce consequences is known as an operant response (Skinner 1953). Consequences that increase the rate at which a response is performed in similar circumstances are known as reinforcers; those which reduce its rate of performance, as punishers. Behavior is ultimately explained in terms of the individual's learning history: the kinds of responses he or she has performed and their reinforcing and punishing consequences. But there is another class of stimuli which can help in the prediction and control of behavior. These are antecedent or pre-behavioral stimuli. Unlike the UCS and CS of classical conditioning, they do not elicit reflexive responses but simply signal the availability of reinforcement (or punishment) if a particular response is performed.

At its simplest, the operant or instrumental conditioning framework consists of Antecedent stimuli (A), Behavior (B) and its Consequences (C). The framework may be depicted as

$$A : B : C$$

where A means elements of the physical or social setting that set the occasion for or signal certain outcomes (C) (rewarding or punishing) that are likely to follow from the performance of a particular behavior (B). The colons indicate that A does not automatically lead to B, nor B to C, but that the relationships involved are probabilistic (Blackman 1980).

More technically, the reinforcers (known as reinforcing stimuli) are depicted symbolically as SR; behavior is termed a response (R); and the antecedent elements of the situation are known as discriminative stimuli (SD) because the individual learns to discriminate behaviorally in their presence by performing a response that will either result in reinforcement or avoid punishment. Hence the operant learning framework is usually shown as

$$SD \ \rightarrow \ R \ \rightarrow \ SR$$

Everyday instances of this 'three-term contingency' abound. For example, a discriminative stimulus (say, a familiar armchair) signals the availability of particular reinforcements (rest, comfort, physical relaxation) which are contingent upon the performance of a specific response (sitting appropriately in the chair). Positive reinforcement occurs when the reinforcer is accepted (physically, not by mental assent) by the individual. A thirsty person's drinking is positively reinforcing because the probability of such behavior being repeated in similar circumstances thereafter is increased. The drink is not reinforcing because of any of its intrinsic qualities (e.g., flavor) but because of its effect on the rate of response, the sole dependent variable in operant research. Much consumer choice is explicable in these terms, including brand choice and store patronage; for example, a store logo can be a discriminative stimulus for pleasant service, this reinforcer being contingent upon entering the shop and speaking to an assistant. Similarly, a brand name of a food item may signal reinforcing flavors which are consequent upon consuming the product (Foxall 1990).

Negative reinforcement occurs when the behavioral response which is strengthened operates on the environment to remove or avoid a consequence. For example, a customer is likely to walk past a store where her complaints have met with abusive outbursts. Walking past and shopping elsewhere avoid such aversive consequences and are said to be negatively reinforced; i.e., their rate of repetition is increased by avoidance/escape rather than by approach.

Primary reinforcers are unconditioned or unlearned: food is reinforcing to a hungry animal automatically and not as a result of learning. *Secondary* reinforcers are learned or conditioned: while they initially exerted no reinforcing effects on behavior, their repeated pairing with a primary reinforcer resulted (via one or other form of conditioning) in their exerting a reinforcing effect in their own right.

The multidimensional theory of consumer motivation described in Chapter 7 is based in large part on the operation of instrumental learning. It argues that consumer behaviors (SR) that are reinforced in terms of the attainment of physical, social, symbolic, cognitive, hedonic and experiential goals, are likely to be repeated. Thus, consumers learn through experience which products and brands to buy because they best provide the benefits consumers seek.

Not all behavior is rewarded or reinforced, however. Some consequences of behavior are neutral: they do not affect the rate at which similar responses are repeated. And some behavior is said to be 'punished' by its consequences: it is followed by an aversive rather than positive consequences and, as a result, is less likely to occur again. Thus

$$SD \rightarrow R \rightarrow SA$$

where SA is an aversive stimulus. (The removal of a positive stimulus has the same effect on behavior.) For example, the purchase of a brand which has aversive consequences – e.g., frowns from the neighbor with whom one is shopping – is punished by that consequence. The removal of a benefit previously paired with a purchased brand – e.g., a bonus sample of a related product as part of a short-term promotion – is a punisher when repurchase of the brand is reduced once the promotion is withdrawn (Hintzman 1978).

A response which is no longer reinforced, either positively or negatively, tends to extinguish, i.e., not to be emitted anymore by the individual. The removal of the reinforcer, in this case, is not contingent upon the response and, therefore, neither punishment nor negative reinforcement is involved. For example, suppose a movie is scary and exciting. Consumers are likely to queue up in droves to see the sequel when it is released. But what if the sequel and subsequent movies in the series are boring? Fewer and fewer consumers attend (SR). The product no longer provides the experiential benefits (signalled by the advertising) (SD) that consumers have learned to expect. The response behavior (R) is quickly extinguished.

More complex behaviors

Chaining

Discriminative stimuli, via constant pairing with a primary or secondary reinforcing stimulus, become conditioned reinforcers in their own right. The radical behaviorist explains complex behaviors in terms of sequences of three-term contingencies in which each discriminative stimulus not only signals the availability of a further reinforcement contingent upon the performance of an operant behavior, but reinforces the preceding operant. For example, shopping at a supermarket may entail (a) writing out a shopping list, (b) leaving home, (c) driving and parking, (d) entering the store, (e) selecting the required items, (f) taking them to the checkout, and (g) paying for them. Only the last of these is obviously reinforced (by the receipt of the primary reinforcers purchased). However, the behaviorist explanation of the sequence of actions suggests that each response, by being paid with the conditioned reinforcers, becomes a conditioned reinforcer in its own right, with the exception of the initial response which becomes a discriminative stimulus (it has no prior response to reinforce). Thus, whilst only the final response in the sequence appears to be reinforced, the preceding action (taking the goods to the checkout) becomes a discriminative stimulus for the reinforcement of that final response. Taking the goods to the checkout, through pairing with immediately antecedent actions such as brand selection, becomes a reinforcer, too. The chain of events is, therefore, analyzed in reverse order. Chaining indicates why, in human learning, reinforcement often appears to be delayed (Skinner 1953: 224).

Shaping

Complex new behaviors do not generally appear spontaneously. Sometimes a final response may be explained as appearing after preceding acts which, taken together, constitute a chain of successive approximations of the terminal behavior, each reinforced in turn. This process, 'shaping', is not a matter of forming a habit, which implies that an existing response is frequently repeated, but of learning a new terminal response through performing a sequence of prior actions that build toward it. For instance, before doing all of his or her monthly grocery shopping at a one-stop hypermarket, the buyer may emit a series of behaviors that approximate this final response, e.g., visiting the store, browsing, doing a proportion of shopping there, each of which is differentially reinforced and which make the final response the more probable.

Discrimination and generalization

A response that is reinforced in the presence of one stimulus but not another is said to be differentially reinforced. The individual who behaves differently according to the controlling antecedent stimulus is said to have made a discrimination, and this accounts for the situation-specific nature of many actions. Store choice, for example, may be explained in terms of the discriminations that the consumer has learned as a result of differential reinforcement in various shops, or because of different patterns of availability of products or brands.

Reinforcement refers not simply to the strengthening of the precise response of which it is a consequence: reinforcement of one response may strengthen other responses that belong to the same class as the original operant. The circumstances in which the other responses are emitted will generally resemble (i.e., contain the same discriminative stimuli as) those in which the original response was reinforced. Thus, an individual's purchasing one food product in a given store may, if reinforced, be followed by his buying a range of similar products there. This process is response generalization. Another example is the trial purchase of a product marketed under the same brand name (the controlling stimulus) as previously purchased items whose purchase has been positively reinforced. The consumer's behavior in each case amounts to performing a similar operant in the context of a given setting which marks the availability of contingent reinforcement and can be explained in terms of the controlling discriminative stimulus. A response which has been reinforced in one situation may generalize to other similar (but not identical) situations – a process known as stimulus generalization – as when a consumer buys a brand in a given store and subsequently purchases it from similar outlets. (Note the same terminology is employed here as in classical conditioning, but in a rather different context.)

Schedules of reinforcement

Schedules of reinforcement influence the rate at which behaviors are learned and extinguished (Ferster and Skinner 1957). When a response is reinforced every time it occurs (a schedule of continuous reinforcement), activities are quickly learned but they also extinguish rapidly when reinforcement ceases. Physical responses such as turning on a switch to obtain light are learned in this way. Complex responses such as those involved in playing chess are similarly best learned when reinforcement is continuous. Reinforcement may also be intermittent, being given at fixed or variable intervals of time or in fixed or variable ratios to responses. When reinforcement occurs less than every time the response is emitted, the rate of extinction is very slow.

Intermittent schedules depend on time (interval schedules) or the performance of a number of responses (ratio schedules) before reinforcement. Under fixed interval (FI) schedules, reinforcement is given every time a specific interval of time has elapsed for a response made after that interval, regardless of the number of responses made. Under fixed ratio (FR) schedules, reinforcement is given when a specific number of responses has been performed, regardless of the time taken. A schedule parameter of 100 means that every 100th response is reinforced. Variable interval (VI), like FI, schedules make reinforcement dependent upon the performance of a single response after an interval of time, but the time that must elapse varies from reinforcement to reinforcement. Variable ratio (VR) schedules are such that a different number of responses is required for each succeeding reinforcement. The rate of response under variable schedules is typically steady and continual, and VR schedules tend to result in a higher response rate than VI schedules (Foxall 1992).

Consumer choice behavior

An operant analysis of consumer choice might begin, like a cognitive account, with an external stimulus such as an advertising message or word-of-mouth communication. But the extent to which this stimulus controlled behavior would depend, in the operant interpretation, upon the individual's reinforcement history, i.e., whether the purchase/consumption response advocated had come under stimulus control as a result of prior reinforcement of similar responses in the presence of the discriminative stimulus. An operant analysis would concentrate upon observable responses and their environmental influences. Cognitive notions like sensation and perception would be superfluous to describe the way in which consumers learned to discriminate behaviorally as their responses came under the stimulus control of verbal behaviors; speech would also be described in terms of symbolic verbal responses under stimulus and reinforcement control and thinking as a series of cover tacting responses. Affective responses would similarly be described as 'self-descriptive tacting responses under the reinforcement control of the verbal community'. Thus, the presentation of a positive reinforcer leads to responses that are described as 'joyful'; the removal of such a reinforcer leads to responses that are 'depressing'. The presentation of a negative reinforcer leads to responses that are called 'fearful', whilst the removal of such a reinforcer offer 'relief' (Hillner 1984: 159).

The marketing mix

At its simplest, consumer behavior in the context of marketing entails three stages; the initial presentation of novel discriminative stimuli (say, in an advertisement for a new brand in an existing product class), which indicate what reinforcements will be forthcoming as a consequence of specified purchase and consumption responses. A subset of current users of the product class will try the new brand, assuming its availability and that its price does not make it prohibitive for all buyers. As a result of the performance of the brand during the trial stage, purchase and consumption will be reinforced or punished by their consequences, i.e, the probability of their being repeated will increase or decline depending upon how the consumer is rewarded or punished by the functioning of the item and/or the behavior of others who show approval or disapproval. This portrayal of the consumer-buying process resembles Ehrenberg's Awareness–Trial–Reinforcement Model, though it denies any explanatory role to internal causes such as awareness, curiosity and dissonance (Ehrenberg 1974). Within this framework, the action of each element of the marketing mix can be understood by means of the three-term contingency.

Product

Products and services contain numerous elements (attributes or features), each of which is a discriminative stimulus that signals reinforcement conditional upon purchase and consumption responses. Trial and repeat purchase do not depend upon the consumer's reaching a conviction of the efficacy of an advertised brand before he or she buys, the final stage in a sequence of mental states through which prolonged persuasive messages have propelled him or her (Lavidge and Steiner 1961). Instead, these behaviors result initially from the consumer's previous experience with similar brands and advertisements (more or less credible message sources), and, once the new brand has been tried, from the direct consequences of using it. Thereafter, purchase and use may come under stimulus control, requiring only a logo, brand name or point-of-sale advertisement to increase the probability of a sale and subsequent consumption. The non-product elements of the mix shape and maintain purchasing, particularly at the first and third stages of the process.

Promotion

Advertising and other marketer-dominated messages portray discriminative stimuli in the form of rules, suggestions, norms, promises, prompts and other verbal and non-verbal descriptions of the contingencies of reinforcement. The messages signal reinforcements (described in terms of the attributes of the advertised brands and their benefits-in-use) and show how they depend upon the consumer's performance of specific responses that other elements of the marketing mix facilitate. The implication is that the beneficial consequences depicted can be obtained only when certain procedures which culminate in brand selection are followed, and the advertisement may indicate how easily these necessary responses which shape this final choice can be executed: 'Your local shop can . . .'; 'Our friendly representative will . . .'; 'Just clip the coupon and . . .'.

Sales promotions are deals which offer the buyer some additional benefit ('money off' or '20 percent more' or 'a free gift') that can be obtained by performing specified responses. They may, as in free samples, encourage trial so that the consequences of use will reinforce that response and shape behavior until the brand is incorporated into the consumer's repertoire. They may offer greater value for money, which rewards the buyer for purchase and use of the promoted brand through the provision of more reinforcers. They can require the performance of a series of responses which involve the repeated purchase of the promoted brand before the additional reinforcer becomes available. Such promotional methods include shaping and chaining as the final response is produced and maintained through a series of individually reinforced approximations: sampling, coupon redemption, competitions and collectable items all play a part (Peter and Nord 1982; Rothschild and Gaidis 1981). The effectiveness of sales promotion methods lies in their capacity to offer reinforcements on intermittent (fixed and variable interval and ratio) schedules in addition to those provided by the purchase and use of the brand itself: i.e., promotional deals reinforce every nth purchase or reward only a proportion of purchasers (Nord and Peter 1980).

Distribution

Distribution strategies also entail the careful management of discriminative stimuli contained in store layouts, store locations and retail images, which are positioned to reduce the time and effort required to make a purchase response. Merchandising techniques aimed at selling particular brands or pack sizes involve the physical presentation of the antecedent stimuli in ways that encourage unplanned or 'impulse' purchasing, the buying of complementary products, and greater overall purchase volume. Store location research is similarly directed toward the physical maximization of traffic flow and sales. Store images comprise a range of discriminative stimuli which show how reinforcements are conditional upon shopping at a given store; these stimuli make up what is usually described as store 'atmosphere' or 'ambience', but can be analyzed in terms of quality, price, locale, sales assistants' behavior and service (Berry 1969). Store managers segment their markets on the basis of consumers' learned differential responses to these stimuli and reinforce them accordingly (Berry and Kunkel 1968).

Price

Finally, price information is frequently a discriminative stimulus for the aversive consequences of buying: the surrender of a valuable general reinforcer, money. While purchasing is a response that is reinforced by the acquisition of primary and secondary reinforcers, it is simultaneously punished by the forfeit of ability to obtain other reinforcers (Alhadeff 1982). Nevertheless, a segment of many consumer markets employs price within limits as an indicator of quality and/or performance: even the surrender of money is, for this group, a source of positive reinforcement derived from the superior appearance or performance of the item bought and the admiring comments or glances that result from conspicuous consumption.

SUMMARY

Learning broadly refers to the way consumer behavior is affected by information and experience. The results of learning are changes in consumer memory structures and overt behaviors. Learning may take place in a variety of ways, all of which have important lessons for marketers.

Rote memory refers to learning of verbal material through repetition. Classical conditioning refers to learning associations by repeated pairing of different stimuli. Vicarious learning takes place when consumers copy the observed behavior of others. Instrumental learning describes the process of reinforcement of behavior by positive and negative consequence. Cognitive learning occurs when consumers are given specific instructions to follow in order to deduce which behaviors they should perform based on information. Information processing is a form of cognitive learning also stressing the role of information. It refers to a multistaged process by which consumers pay attention to information-laden stimuli in their environment, such as advertisements and promotions, and use this information to make decisions about which products and brands to purchase.

The type of learning that takes place may be a function of several factors: familiarity, expertise and involvement. Involvement refers to the investment of time, energy, thought and feelings a consumer makes in a product or brand. Because high-involvement learning differs profoundly from low-involvement learning, marketers and advertisers need to be aware of the level of involvement manifested by their target consumers in the relevant product category and must use this information appropriately in devising marketing strategies. The elaboration likelihood model explicitly links information processing and involvement, showing that level of involvement directly affects the types of information processing occurring as consumers are exposed to advertising.

All forms of learning may apply to a given consumer purchase decision. Moreover, some consumers may buy a brand through one learning process (such as vicarious learning), while other consumers buy the same brand after going through another learning process (viewing an advertisement and then trying the product). Different learning processes may lead to contradictory outcomes, as when a brand is bought after a positive recommendation from a neighbor (information processing), but is avoided in the future after a bad experience (instrumental conditioning).

Chapter 5

Attitudes and behavior

THE MEANING OF ATTITUDE

The concept of attitude occupies a central position in both social psychology and consumer behavior studies. Researchers interested in consumer theory ascribe great importance to the role of attitudes in explaining consumer behavior, and applied researchers make extensive use of attitudes to predict behavior and to evaluate advertising. Attitudes form an important part of consumer theory and marketing practice because they are felt to be the crucial link between what consumers think about products and what they buy in the marketplace. In the current context, attitudes are essentially the affective or evaluative reaction consumers have toward elements of marketing strategies and the brands these strategies are designed to promote. The theory of attitudes includes, in addition to the affective reactions, both beliefs about the attributes of products as well as intentions to behave toward them. Measuring and understanding consumer attitudes allow marketers to develop the products consumers want, promote these products effectively, and evaluate their efforts at promotion.

An attitude is generally understood to refer to a predisposition to respond in a consistent manner to a stimulus, i.e., a tendency to act or behave in some predictable way. Attitudes are usually represented as being positive or negative, favorable or unfavorable to an object, idea or other entity; indeed, Hughes (1971: 9) defines attitude as an 'individual's favorable or unfavorable inclination toward an attribute of an object'. In the marketing context, consumers hold attitudes toward brands, products, companies, stores or advertisements; consumer attitudes are their liking or disliking of these stimuli. Attitudes are learned or acquired rather than inborn; they are formed as a result of personal experience, reasoning or information, the communicated experience of others (Lutz 1991; Fishbein 1975).

Attitudes are, indeed, a major outcome of the various types of learning discussed in Chapter 4.

Behavioral scientists do not universally agree as to the components or elements of attitudes. Some argue that attitudes have three elements termed beliefs, affects and intentions, respectively. The cognitive element concerns knowing and believing ('I think Coca-Cola tastes best'), the affective element denotes liking or disliking ('I like Coca-Cola'), and the conative or behavioral intentions element ('I always buy Coca-Cola') is the part corresponding most clearly to attitude as we have defined it (a predisposition to behave).

This multidimensional theory of attitudes is opposed by those who restrict 'attitude' to refer only to the affective element, so that they use the term 'attitude' as a unidimensional concept meaning only feelings of liking or disliking. Using the term this way, however, presents several difficulties. The various dimensions of attitude may not always correlate with each other, even in the same individual. Since it is easier to measure the cognitive and affective elements, there is a tendency to discover what the consumer thinks about a product while overlooking his overt behavior in the marketplace. It is therefore necessary to check whether attitude tests do in fact measure the conative or behavioral dimension of consumer behavior; otherwise they are of very limited use as predictors of buying choice. We follow the multidimensional model because a large body of research supports this view and the different elements are of use to marketing managers. First, however, we discuss the functions attitudes perform as mediators between the individual and his or her environment.

Attitude functions

The functions of attitudes have been described by several psychologists and sociologists. Lutz (1991) points out that attitudes assist in the organization of psychological and behavioral activities. Maier (1965) states that attitudes determine meanings (by providing a context for the interpretation of new information), reconcile contradictions (by helping individuals to evaluate each other's opinions), organize facts (as in the process of selective perception), and select facts. Katz (1960) attributes four functions to attitudes:

- *the adjustment function*, in which the individual assesses the utility of objects for the attainment of his goals,
- *the ego-defensive function*, in which the individual uses attitudes to protect his self-image by emphasizing his place in his social world,
- *the value-expressive function*, by which the individual expresses his central values and self to others, and
- *the knowledge function*, by which the individual constructs the meaning of his world, or gives explanation to both physical and metaphysical phenomena.

These descriptions of functions suggest many diverse uses of attitudes for humans (consumers). Another way to view the functional issue is to take the position that all the above functional descriptions are similar, in that they describe a basic purpose of attitudes, only they view attitudes in different motivational contexts and hence suggest that there are different types of functions. The alternative view is that attitudes serve one basic function, that of social adaptation (Kahle 1984). This means that attitudes, like other social cognitions such as values, are useful to human functioning because they help us acquire useful information, assimilate new information, and efficiently direct our behavior; in short, to adapt to our environment so that we may best live and survive. Attitudes are a type of cognition that is useful because they organize and abstract a variety of experiences and informational inputs, thereby facilitating adaptation:

> Attitudes are adaptation abstractions, or generalizations, about functioning in the environment . . . that are expressed as predispositions to evaluate an object, concept, or symbol. This abstraction process emerges continuously from the assimilation, accommodation, and organization of environmental information by individuals, in order to promote interchanges between the individual and the environment that, from the individual's perspective, are favorable to preservation and optimal functioning.
>
> (Kahle 1984: 5)

The reason that there appear to be so many attitude functions is that humans have different motives; as objects are perceived to satisfy these motives, the mind forms attitudes toward them that simultaneously assess their characteristics (beliefs), evaluate them favorably or unfavorably (affect), and register a predisposition to respond to it (intention) in the most economical way possible so that this object can be used or avoided in the satisfaction of our many needs. The adjustive, social, value-expressive, ego-defensive, and other functions are simply the operation of this attitude mechanism in various motive areas. For marketing purposes, then, attitudes are of great importance because they represent how consumers assess and react to advertisements, brands, products, stores and so on, as they seek to satisfy their many needs through consumption. In this light, attitudes can be viewed as explainers and predictors of a wide variety of marketplace behavior.

THE MEASUREMENT OF ATTITUDES

Testing or measuring attitudes provides the bulk of marketing research work as traditionally conceived. Despite recent advances into other areas, this task retains an important position in consumer studies. This section deals with several characteristic types of attitude measurement used extensively in marketing and the related field of behavioral research (Hughes 1971).

Rating scales

Researchers frequently use simple rating scales to measure consumer beliefs, feelings or evaluations of products, brands, stores and services. A rating scale usually asks a respondent to indicate what he/she thinks of or feels about a brand by marking a position on some continuum or series of ordered categories that describe what he/she thinks or feels,

Table 5.1 Rating scales

Fox jeans are:

expensive _____ cheap

How expensive do you
think Fox jeans are?

expensive   cheap
[ ]   [ ]   [ ]   [ ]   [ ]   [ ]

thereby providing a single-item indicator of attitude. Such scales are used to measure behavioral intentions and self-reports of behaviors as well. Table 5.1 shows examples of graphic and itemized rating scales.

Likert: summed ratings

One of the most commonly used attitude measures was developed by Rensis Likert (1932) as a convenient measure suitable to survey research. A Likert Scale consists of a series of statements about an object, providing a multi-item measure. The respondent is asked to indicate his/her level of agreement on a scale of choices by rating each statement: strongly agree, agree, neutral, disagree or strongly disagree. For instance, the example in Table 5.2 illustrates the measurement of consumer attitudes toward a brand of jeans using a Likert Scale.

Quantifying the scaling element in the Likert method is accomplished by attaching the numbers 1 to 5 to the responses; an individual's attitude may thus be scored by summing his/her measurement, but it must be stressed that a score 2x is not indicative of an attitude twice as strong as that represented by a score of x. Attitude items are often reverse worded so as to avoid potential 'halo' bias that could arise if all items are worded in one direction and to check that respondents are really reading the attitude items.

Table 5.2 Example of Likert Scales

Encircle one of the symbols following each statement. SA stands for 'Strongly Agree', A stands for 'Agree', ? for 'Uncertain', D for 'Disagree', and SD for 'Strongly Disagree'.

I like Fox jeans.	SA	A	?	D	SD
I think Fox jeans are classy.	SA	A	?	D	SD
*Fox jeans are uncomfortable.	SA	A	?	D	SD

Indicate the extent to which you agree with each of the following statements by placing a tick under the appropriate number; 1 means 'Strongly Agree', 2 means 'Agree', 3 means 'Don't Know', 4 means 'Disagree' and 5 means 'Strongly Disagree'.

	1	2	3	4	5
*Fox jeans are a good buy.					
*I think Fox jeans are sexy.					
Fox jeans are expensive.					

Note: * Indicates item is reverse scored

Table 5.3 Osgood's Semantic Differential

	Fox jeans							
	1	*2*	*3*	*4*	*5*	*6*	*7*	
old-fashioned	____ :	____ :	____ :	____ :	____ :	____ :	____	modern
*valuable	____ :	____ :	____ :	____ :	____ :	____ :	____	worthless
*cheap	____ :	____ :	____ :	____ :	____ :	____ :	____	expensive
*beneficial	____ :	____ :	____ :	____ :	____ :	____ :	____	not beneficial
useless	____ :	____ :	____ :	____ :	____ :	____ :	____	useful
*matters to me	____ :	____ :	____ :	____ :	____ :	____ :	____	doesn't matter
*significant	____ :	____ :	____ :	____ :	____ :	____ :	____	insignificant

Note: * Indicates item is reverse scored

Osgood: The Semantic Differential

The method of measuring attitudes devised by Osgood, Suci and Tannenbaum (1957), known as the Semantic Differential, is designed to elicit subtle nuances of meaning which respondents attach to words or concepts and which are not normally identified by other methods. Pairs of antonyms are separated by seven spaces and the respondent is required to indicate by ticking in a space the extent to which he/she thinks the bipolar adjectives describe the object. Use of semantic differential scales allows the marketing researcher to discover differences in attitude between different groups of consumers or in the same group about different products. An example is shown in Table 5.3.

Crespi: Stapel Scale

The Stapel Scale (Crespi 1961) is a simplified version of the Semantic Differential, making it useful in situations where the former might not be appropriate, as with poorly educated respondents or in a telephone interview. The Stapel Scale consists of a single adjective describing the brand and from six to ten numbered scale points, the respondent is asked to circle to indicate beliefs or attitudes. Table 5.4 shows the Stapel Scale in use.

ATTITUDE–BEHAVIOR CONSISTENCY

Attitudes and behavior

Attitudes both affect and are affected by behavior. In seeking ways in which behavior can be predicted from attitudes, it is tempting to represent the relationship of attitudes and behavior as a one-way association, thus

Attitudes → Behavior

Table 5.4 Crespi's Stapel Scale

	Fox jeans	
3	3	3
2	2	2
1	1	1
expensive	modern	useful
−1	−1	−1
−2	−2	−2
−3	−3	−3

But it is clear that, if attitudes are themselves influenced by past behavior, the relationship must be more complicated; it is usually represented as a two-way process. This representation also incorporates the multidimensional model of attitudes and makes explicit the sequence with which this model describes the relationships among the attitude components:

Information
Reason   } Beliefs → Affect → Intentions → Behavior
Experience

   Much of the work of consumer researchers specializing in attitude studies has been based on trying to elucidate the relationships among these different constructs. A recent review of a body of evidence (Sheppard, Hartwick and Warshaw 1988) suggests that within carefully described constraints, the model does a good job of explaining and predicting behavior. The theory, models and measurement of attitudes are all interrelated, so that understanding and using the construct depends in large part on understanding how the concept of attitudes is operationalized or measured in consumer research. We shall return to the issue of attitude–behavior consistency, therefore, after considering further how attitudes have been conceptualized and measured.
   A crucial test of the entire information-processing model is whether its cognitive outcomes – attitudes and intentions – are consistent with its behavioral outcomes which, in the present context, include purchasing and consumption of products and brands. The assumption, once accepted uncritically in both social psychology and marketing, of direct correspondence between an individual's general attitude toward an object and his or her specific behavior with respect to that object is not justified by the empirical evidence. Wicker (1969: 52) points out that 'product-moment correlation coefficient relating to two kinds of response are rarely above 0.30 and are often near zero . . . Only rarely can as much as 10 percent of the variance in overt behavioral measures be accounted for by attitudinal data.'
   Both social psychology and marketing are also founded on the expectation that changes in behavior are likely to follow changes in attitudes and that strategies of persuasive communication (advertising or sales promotion) can be built upon this. Again, at the level of general attitudes toward an object, the empirical evidence fails to support this taken-for-granted proposition:

What little evidence there is to support any relationship between attitudes and behavior comes from studies showing that a person tends to bring his attitude into line with his behavior rather than from studies demonstrating that behavior is a function of attitude.

(Fishbein 1973)

As would be predicted by Festinger's (1957) view that humans strive toward the reduction of dissonance, individuals appear to be under strong pressure to reconcile their attitudes with their divergent actions by modifying the former (see also Bem 1972).

The evidence against attitude–behavior consistency was never as one-sided as the conclusions of the reviewers suggested, but the empirical findings indicate, none the less, that the simplistic assumption that 'attitudes cause behaviors' is an inadequate summary of the scientific results. For one thing, the statement ignores the other determinants of behavior such as personality traits, self-images, motives, past behavior, and the social and physical setting in which the action occurs. Of itself, the expectation that 'attitudes cause behaviors' is no more meaningful or useful than the insight that 'eating leads to obesity'. Attitude research has over the last twenty years increasingly reflected the view that our knowledge must be made more precise, capable of specifying how and when a quantified change in one variable (attitude) is likely to be followed by a quantified change in another (behavior).

The Theory of Reasoned Action

One of the most systematic and widely used approaches to attitude conceptualization and measurement in marketing has been developed by Martin Fishbein and Icek Ajzen (Fishbein and Ajzen 1975; Ajzen and Fishbein 1980). Their Theory of Reasoned Action places attitudes within a sequence of linked cognitive constructs: beliefs, attitudes, intentions and behavior. Their model also includes the social aspects of attitude formation.

Moreover, the approach implicit in the Theory of Reasoned Action (Fishbein and Ajzen 1975) has proved especially attractive in respect of the problem of attitude–behavior consistency. The model actually predicts behavioral intentions rather than behavior, but it is assumed that under the right conditions, intentions will approximate behavior itself. Behavioral intentions are portrayed as a function of two other factors:

- the respondent's *attitude* toward behaving in a prescribed manner, and
- his or her *subjective norm*, i.e., the respondent's beliefs about other people's evaluations of his or her acting in this way, weighted by his or her motivation to comply with what they think.

Any other influences that might influence behavioral intention are assumed to feed into these. The approach is valuable for its abandonment of the notion of direct correspondence between global attitudes and specific behaviors, its reliance on the very precise concept of 'attitude toward the act', and its introduction of the subjective norms to represent extra-attitudinal (social) influences. Each construct is measured separately and used to predict the subsequent construct. Figure 5.1 summarizes the theory and Table 5.5 shows the measures.

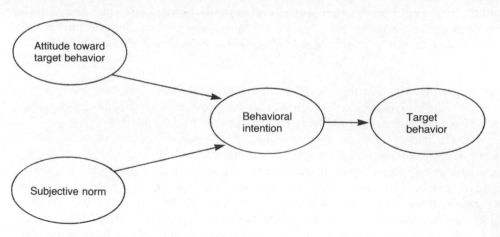

Figure 5.1 The Theory of Reasoned Action
Source: Derived from Fishbein, M. and I. Ajzen (1975) *Belief, Attitude, Intention, and Behavior: An Introduction to Theory and Research*, Reading, MA: Addison-Wesley.

Other work carried out during the last several years (Ajzen and Fishbein 1977) throws light upon the relationship between measures of attitude and measures of behavior and upon the legitimacy of using one as a predictor of the other. The overwhelming conclusion to emerge is the impossibility of making accurate predictions of behavioral choices on the basis of respondents' stated attitudes or intentions, except under the most closely specified conditions. If high correlations of attitude/intention and behavior measures are to be obtained, those measures must correspond exactly in four respects. Not only must the object which is the target of the enquiry be clearly stated: so must the action which he or she is to imagine performing with respect to that target object. Similarly, the time and the context must be detailed.

Hence it is not sufficient to measure global attitude toward an object (e.g., a consumer's appraisal of frozen vegetables) in order to predict whether he or she will purchase Bird's Eye frozen peas on the next shopping trip. Rather, the consumer's evaluation of the consequences of say buying that brand in a supermarket on the next shopping trip would need to be accurately and specifically recorded in order to predict his or her target behavior.

Fishbein and others who have used this model have presented empirical evidence to show that high correlations (of the order of 0.8 or 0.9) can be obtained between the measure of behavioral intention and that of subsequent, corresponding behavior. However, such correlations can be obtained only under conditions that are 'maximally conducive'. We have encountered several of these conditions – measuring attitude toward the act, for instance, and correspondence between measure in terms of target, action, time and context – but given these provisions, the most important of the conditions is that the expression of a behavioral intention must be the immediate antecedent of an opportunity to behave in the intended fashion (Fishbein 1973). The longer the period of time between intention and attitude, the lower will be the correlation, and the less accurate will be predictions of behavior based on the measure of attitude or intention. Obviously, the longer this interval, the greater the possibility that new situations will emerge bringing in their wake new

Table 5.5 The Theory of Reasoned Action: concepts and their measurement

The Theory of Reasoned Action is represented by the formula:

$$B \cong BI = (W_1)(A_{act}) + (W_2)(SN)$$

Each part of the formula is measured separately and combined.

B = a specific consumer behavior such as brand choice,

might be measured as an actual choice from a selection of brands, the results of a diary of product purchases, or the records of purchase recorded by a supermarket scanner.

BI = behavioral intentions, what the consumer intends to do,

might be measured by asking a question such as:

The next time you go shopping, how likely are you to buy Fox jeans?
extremely likely   1   2   3   4   5   6   7   extremely unlikely

A_{act} = consumer's attitude toward performing behavior B,

is a complex variable derived from the formula: $A_{act} = \Sigma\, b_i\, e_i$, where

    b = belief, the subjective probability that performing the behavior results in consequence i
    e = evaluation, or the subjective feeling of goodness or badness of consequence i
    n = number of relevant behavioral beliefs

The b's might be measured with a scale like this:

Wearing Fox jeans will make me sexy.

very likely   ____ : ____ : ____ : ____ : ____ : ____ : ____ very unlikely
              +3   +2   +1   0   −1   −2   −3

And the e's might be measured this way:

If jeans make you sexy, that is . . .
very good   ____ : ____ : ____ : ____ : ____ : ____ : ____ very bad
           +3   +2   +1   0   −1   −2   −3

SN = subjective norm, or the influence of important people on the decision,

is also a complex variable derived from the formula: $SN = \Sigma\, NB_j\, MC_j$, where

  NB = normative beliefs, regarding a consumer's belief that the jth person or group expects them to perform or not perform the behavior

  MC = the consumer's motivation to comply or not comply with the expectations of the jth person or group

    j = the number of relevant other persons or groups

NB might be measured like this:

My friends think I should buy Fox jeans.

extremely likely 1   2   3   4   5   6   7   extremely unlikely

And MC might be measured by this scale:

Generally, I do what my friends think I should do:

all the time   ____ : ____ : ____ : ____ : ____ : ____ : ____ never
             +3   +2   +1   0   −1   −2   −3

W_1 and W_2 = empirically determined weights reflecting the relative influence of each factor on BI. These are ordinarily determined using regression analysis.

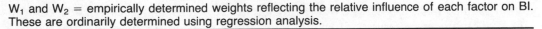

consumer goals, new opportunities to pursue alternative intentions, new demands on time and money, and blocking the achievement of the original behavioral intention (Foxall 1984b; Harrell and Bennett 1974; Ryan and Bonfield 1975, 1980; Wilson *et al.* 1975).

MARKETING IMPLICATIONS

In the case of brands in established, steady-state markets (i.e., where sales are on a steady if small upward trend from year to year), consumers' intentions to buy any brand that they have previously purchased are closely related to their future purchase behavior. That is, a consumer who has used and is satisfied with a brand is likely to predict that he or she will try it again on a future purchase occasion and is very likely to follow this up with actual purchase of the brand – not necessarily on every subsequent purchase occasion, for few consumers are as loyal as that, but from time to time (Ehrenberg and Goodhardt 1979). Intentions are a function of past usage and its consequences, such that

$$I = k\sqrt{U}$$

where I = Intention to repurchase the brand; U = past usage; and k is a constant which varies from market to market (Ehrenberg 1972). In this instance, attitude research is important to marketers not because it predicts what brands consumers will buy, but because it can explain why they buy the brands they do. This information is valuable to managers who want to know how their brands are perceived by consumers and need guidelines for changing or promoting their brands.

Moreover, in new product marketing, measures of attitudes toward and intentions to buy projected new products may be useful guides to product development. Especially when the new product is a fairly close substitute for existing items, consumers may be capable of predicting whether they would at least try the new brand. Unexpected situations that intervene between market research and the launch of the product may not affect the rate of trial if unexpected, unfavorable circumstances that prevent intending purchasers from actually trying the innovation are roughly balanced out by unexpected, favorable circumstances that prompt or enable others to make a purchase.

However, up to 80 percent of new consumer products fail at the point of consumer acceptance (Clancy and Shulman 1991; Foxall 1984a). Both new products that differ extensively from existing market offerings ('radical' or 'discontinuous' innovations) and those that differ but little ('incremental' or 'continuous') have high failure rates despite the efforts of many companies to anticipate demand by carrying out considerable pre-launch market research, frequently called new product development (NPD).

The NPD process

New product development is more effective when it takes the form of a formal process rather than ad hoc procedures governed by intuition or 'gut feel' (Rockwell and Particelli 1982). The process comprises a definite sequence of planned activities, each of which is intended to reduce uncertainty and enable a decision about proceeding to the next stage to be made. Typically, the stages have been represented as exploration (the search for ideas and opportunities), screening (the elimination of ideas that are unlikely to succeed), business analysis (concept testing and financial appraisal), development (of the physical product or the service and the rest of the marketing mix), testing (in the marketplace) and commercialization. Not all new products go through all of these stages; those that do may not necessarily follow so orderly a sequence. NPD involves many more information-gathering stages than six, but the major purpose is the same. Each phase begins with the formulation of the firm's information requirements and ends when a go/no-go/or hold ('wait and see') decision can be made (Cooper 1976).

Concept testing and beyond

The first time new product ideas are subjected to evaluation by potential consumers is often in concept testing: the idea for a new product or a reformulated/repositioned brand is put verbally to a sample of typical buyers and users (Worcester and Downham 1978). Concept testing is intended as a check on whether customers understand, like and value the idea. It is also extensively used as a method of assessing whether they would be likely to purchase the resulting product. The relevant data take the form of respondents' evaluations of the concept (attitude or affect) and their verbally stated purchase intentions using self-report scaling methods like those illustrated earlier in this chapter. When these data are employed to predict future consumer behavior in the marketplace, the implication is that they are capable of yielding valid forecasts of the main dependent variables that define sales, i.e., consumers' rates of trial, repeat buying, adopting and purchase frequency (Tauber 1977). How accurate is concept testing for this purpose? There are some dramatic examples of the wrong decision being taken in spite of respondents' positive reactions to concepts and correct decisions being taken despite their profound lack of enthusiasm (Sands 1980). More formal studies, notably those reported by Tauber, strongly suggest that concept testing cannot predict even trial behavior with precision, let alone the repeat buying that determines market share. Tauber writes:

> What makes a product successful is obtaining enough committed adopters who will use the product frequently enough over time. . . . The implicit assumption of concept testing and product testing is that attitudes and intentions expressed during a pre-market situation will relate to later adoption behavior. This assumption is fallacious.
>
> (Tauber 1981: 176)

The data in Table 5.6 reflect consumers' intentions to buy (expressed during concept testing) and their perceptions and behavior (gauged twenty-five weeks after the beginning of advertising for the new brand). Awareness is clearly related to some extent to purchase intention, and both probably reflect interest in the product class. Of those who became aware, the prior expression of definite purchase intention, was associated with trial. But significant amounts of trial also came from the other respondents who were less sure they would buy or convinced they would not. Moreover, among triers, the expression at concept

Table 5.6 Purchase intention at concept stage and reported interview behavior

Purchase intent at concept	Proportion aware (week 25) %	Proportion tried of those aware %	Repeat of total sales from each group %	%
Definitely buy	71	31	25	52
Probably	60	16	30	43
Might/might not	54	17	22	56
Probably not	52	8	8	50
Definitely not	38	10	15	40

Source: Tauber, E. (1981) 'Utilization of concept testing for new-product forecasting: traditional versus multiattribute approaches', in Y. Wind, V. Mahajan and R. N. Cardozo (eds) *New-Product Forecasting*, Lexington, MA: Lexington Books, 173–85. Reproduced with the permission of Lexington Books, an imprint of Macmillan, Inc. Copyright © 1981 by Lexington Books.

stage of a purchase intention, positive or negative, weak or strong or noncommittal, appears not to affect the probability of repeat purchase.

Tauber indicts tests that rely on the assumption that measures of attitude and intention, in the absence of experience with the product, can predict behavioral choices:

> Concept tests and product tests do not work. Take a look at their history. Most marketers are aware of the high failure rate of new consumer products. Yet the A. C. Nielsen Company, in a study of the introduction of many new products, concluded that for products that survived the first eight months, test markets were a good prediction (correct 75 percent) of national introductory results. So when do all of these failures happen? Obviously, they occur at the test market stage. Thus the track record of pretest-market screening is poor. And what are the techniques generally used for this screening? – Concept testing and product testing. The limitations of concept and product tests as predictors of subsequent sales are borne out by empirical investigations and literature surveys (W. L. Moore 1982). Furthermore, they are generally of value only in the case of continuous products where consumers are well aware of standard attributes and functions; for discontinuous innovations they are unlikely even to predict trial.
>
> (Tauber 1981: 182)

However, simply knowing that these techniques have severe limitations in the prediction of consumer choice is not enough. Unless market researchers and new product managers appreciate why these limitations exist, they cannot critically review their NPD procedures with a view to reconceptualizing or improving them. The required understanding demands an appraisal of the role of attitude and intentions measurement in consumer research.

Reassessing attitude data in NPD

The foregoing discussion highlights the fallacy of expecting verbally stated attitudes and intention to predict future brand choice before the item has even appeared on the market.

Concept tests can, at best, do no more than help forecast whether anyone will try the product. They are no more useful in predictive terms than that, and do not always perform 'at best' – as the examples of a new lipstain, instant potato and instant dried milk show only too well (Iuso 1975). However, the greater the extent to which a measure of past (or preferably) current behavior can be used to predict future behavior, the more accurate will be the forecasts (Bagozzi 1981, 1982). Bentler and Speckart (1981) put forward a model shown in Figure 5.2, which augments Fishbein's approach by positing direct links between (a) prior behavior and target behavior and (b) attitude and target behavior. This model has been tested by Fredericks and Dossett (1983), who found that information about prior behavior certainly increased the predictability of target behavior but the inclusion of attitude variables did not. Furthermore, the use of prior behavior to explain target behavior tended to demote behavioral intentions: 'In essence, once prior behavior is included in the model, the effects of intention become nonsignificant' (Fredericks and Dossett 1983: 509).

Tauber's (1977) examination of several sales forecasting methods designed to be used prior to test marketing confirms these findings in the context of consumer behavior. Two methods – regression models employing historical data and laboratory test models – are of benefit in predicting trial and repeat purchase for relatively continuous items, e.g., a new brand in an established convenience food product class which requires little if any change in consumer behavior. Of the two, the laboratory approach performs better and relies on measures of present buying behavior in addition to attitude and intentions measures. The most promising means of predicting future repeat buying with a degree of accuracy that makes the effort managerially worthwhile are sales-wave experiments. This approach relies on consumers' current behavior to predict future choice. Specifically, the customer is given

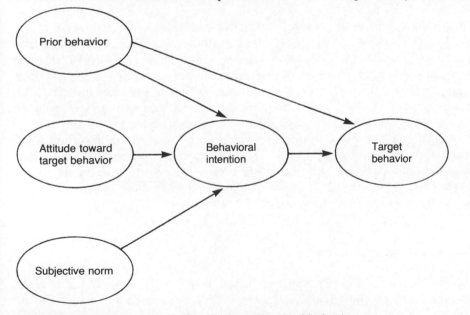

Figure 5.2 Modified model of attitudes, intentions and behavior
Source: Derived from Bentler, P. M. and G. Speckart (1981) 'Attitudes "cause" behaviors: a structural equations analysis', *Journal of Personality and Social Psychology*, 40, 226–38.

the opportunity of purchasing the new brand on several occasions (typically up to six), at a reduced price, in the expectation that post-wear-out level of adoption will become apparent and measurable. Thus evidence may be gained about the likelihood of the consumer including the new brand in his or her repertoire of similar brands and of buying it from time to time. Relatively continuous products with features that set them apart from existing brands appear particularly amenable to prediction by this method.

The general conclusion must be that, given the present state of knowledge, forecasts made on the basis of tests that occur early in the NPD process are unlikely to yield worthwhile predictions of purchase choice. Only later, when measures of overt behavior are available, can future behavior be predicted with useful accuracy. Such measures are costly and they come too late to abort many projects that will not fulfill the financial objectives set for them. But for the present at least, these limitations must be accepted as facts of life; they tell us much about the nature of marketing intelligence and its legitimate use in marketing decision making. The tendency over recent years has been to assume that quantitative techniques can make up for the basic inadequacies of the data that link attitudes/intentions and behavior. Some market research organizations still promise that the concept testing they undertake can consistently provide accurate predictions of new brand performance. But the evidence, theoretical and practical, suggests that such predictions can only be made much later in the NPD on the basis of behavioral rather than attitudinal measures (Clancy and Shulman 1991).

PERSUASION: GENERAL CONSIDERATIONS IN ATTITUDE CHANGE

The study of attitudes includes the study of communication and the evaluation of the effectiveness of marketing communications. Because attitudes are thought to play such an important role in shaping consumer behavior, a great deal of marketing effort is directed to forming or changing attitudes by means of product promotion, including sales promotion and advertising. An important goal of marketing strategy is persuasion. For our purposes, we can define persuasion as the use of communication to change attitudes in order to change behavior. Although attitude change remains an inexact science and provides an imperfect technology to influence consumer behavior, a large body of findings from social psychology provides many helpful suggestions regarding the principles of attitude change through communication. Basically, the persuasion process consists of a sequence of two broad factors that determine the impact of the communication: the message source and its channel, and the message itself and its receiver.

Message source and channel

The source of the communication refers to the characteristics of the communicator of the message. Message sources may be the advertiser, the spokesperson in the advertisement, or a sales person. The three most studied source characteristics are credibility, attractiveness and power. Credibility includes expertise, objectivity and trustworthiness. That there is a direct connection between the credibility of a message's source and the amount of attitude change the message produces may appear to be a commonsense proposition. Thus, marketers and advertisers feature highly credible sources in their ads, such as doctors, nurses and pharmacists for health-related products, and actresses for make-up and clothing: areas in which they are presumed to be experts.

If these 'experts' endorse a product, their opinion appears more trustworthy. In view of the fact that many consumers tend to discount much of what persuasive advertising claims, the use of a credible source may be crucial in gaining the audience's attention and in ensuring that selective perception does not cause the message to be screened before it is even considered. It is also important that such sources not be used indiscriminately. The credibility of the source should be matched up with the features of the product. Sources who are not credible or who are not appropriate for a given product will not be likely to persuade consumers. For example, the matching of ex-Beatle, Ringo Starr, with Sun Country Wine Coolers was not successful because he did not appeal to the Cooler's young demographic target segment (Stroud 1988: 75).

The channel is the means by which a message is transmitted from the source to the receiver. Channels of communication include the (informal) non-marketer-dominated interpersonal communications (word of mouth), and (formal) marketer-dominated mass media and personal selling. The channels used for advertising are usually divided into either print or electronic media. The former includes newspapers and magazines, and the latter consists of radio, television and the other electronic media available to marketers today (video cassettes and theater commercials are examples). The issue of importance to changing consumer attitudes arises from the fact that identical messages may be received differently by consumers, depending on the channel used to transmit the message. This channel effect needs to be taken into account when designing an advertising strategy.

The idea that consumers of the mass media are passive recipients of whatever they read, listen to and watch is frequently encountered. It goes hand in hand with the views that the mass media 'inoculate' each audience member with precisely the same message, and that the formal channels of communication are immensely powerful. It has become apparent from empirical investigations that 'people come to the media, as to other messages, seeking what they want, not what the media intend them to have' (Schram and Roberts 1971: 51). People retain considerable choice over the media offerings to which they expose themselves. Moreover, because they are distant from the source of messages reaching them through mass channels, they rely greatly on their immediate social groups for a context within which to interpret messages received via the formal communications system.

The 'two-step flow of communications hypothesis' postulates that the effects of mass-media communications are not felt directly by the majority of the people. Rather, messages from the mass media are picked up by a relatively few influential individuals (known as *opinion leaders*) who, in turn, disseminate information to the rest of their informal social groups by word of mouth or interpersonal communication. As Lazarsfeld *et al.* (1944: 151) succinctly put it: 'ideas often flow from radio and print to the opinion leaders and from them to the less active sections of the population'. Informal communication, word of mouth, may be much more influential than formal or mass communication. The communications process is, in practice, far more complicated than the two-step hypothesis allows. In addition to the specialized roles of formal and informal communication channels, there is much interaction between opinion leaders themselves, and there is a two-way flow of information from opinion leaders to followers and back. Further, the audience is far more active, seeking out information from both formal and informal sources, which are not necessarily in competition with each other. In actively seeking information about products and services, the consumer audience uses three sources in a kind of optimal balance. These are:

- *manufacturer-dominated* channels (the mass media and the marketing mix),
- *consumer-dominated* channels (word of mouth), and
- *neutral* channels such as consumer reports, *Which?* and the editorial matter in magazines and newspapers, which describes and evaluates products and services.

Each has its peculiar advantages and disadvantages for the consumer. The first is cheap but biased, the second is more reliable but may not be readily available, and the third is trustworthy but expensive. The consumer satisfies the need for information by using all three in a complementary fashion (Cox 1963). This approach places much emphasis on the complementary interaction of the various communication sources as well as on the information seeking of the goal-oriented, involved consumer.

The message and its recipient

The message represents what the marketer wants to say to the consumer. It is the specific information that the marketer believes will change the consumer's attitude encoded into symbolic form in order for communication to take place as the consumer decodes the message and processes the key information. Researchers have described many elements of the message and the way it is presented. Of concern to marketers are the types of presentation, fear appeals and humor appeals, as well as the order in which information appears in the message.

A recurrent theme in attitude research is the role that fear plays in persuading people to alter their opinions and behavior. Fearful messages explain to the consumer that harmful consequences will result if the consumer does not use the product or buy the brand. A considerable body of research findings show that fear appeals may be effective in persuading message receivers to change their attitudes (Sternthal and Craig 1982). Fear appeals usually parallel the types of benefits consumers seek from the products they buy. Hence, for toothpaste, a fear appeal might stress the risk of tooth decay or gum disease if the brand is not purchased and used. Many personal care products stress the negative social consequences of not using deodorants. Life insurance appeals frequently challenge the listener to think about the consequence to his/her family of not having enough life insurance. Growing health concerns among American consumers have led food marketers and advertisers to increase the number of health claims for such foods as Campbell Soup and Kellogg cereals (Alsop 1987a).

Humor may attract attention, increase memorability, overcome sales resistance, and increase the persuasiveness of advertising messages (Scott, Klein and Bryant 1990). Many classic advertising campaigns of the past, such as those for Volkswagen and Alka-Seltzer, relied on humor to attract consumers' attention; they made the ads memorable, and led them to develop a positive evaluation of the product (Sternthal and Craig 1973). Recent carpet advertisements featuring amusing children and actor Don Reckless as the carpet itself, have been credited with creating new interest in carpet and in promoting brand preference unique to this product category (Alsop 1987b).

In the case of both fear and humor, each technique must be used carefully because the arousing ability of each appeal could cause consumers to focus most of their attention on the fearful or humorous elements and consequently ignore the brand being advertised. In addition, these appeals should be matched to the products they are trying to sell so that the appeals should be appropriate to the benefits the products deliver. A mismatch between the advertising appeal and the product benefit eliminates the potential persuasiveness of fear and humor advertising appeals.

Another consideration in the content and structuring of advertising messages is that of the one-sided/two-sided appeal. Should persuasive messages include elements that are unfavorable to the product or service that is being marketed? On the face of it, there might appear to be no case for presenting potentially damaging information to any audience, no matter how sophisticated and educated it may be, for any amount of damage to the company's image or its brand images must surely result in lost sales and reduced profit. Despite such natural misgivings, there is fairly conclusive evidence that, within a specified context, two-sided appeals (those which incorporate arguments for and against the product or brand) may be more effective than one-sided appeals (Hovland *et al.* 1948).

The constraints on this technique are threefold:

- the market or segment receiving the message must be currently unconvinced of the article's attractiveness (i.e., consumers who are at present not buying the brand and those whose current attitudes make them unlikely to do so in the near future are ideal targets for two-sided appeals);
- those most persuaded by the two-sided appeal tend to be highly educated (thus the academic practice of presenting both sides of an argument seems to appeal to those who have received large amounts of formal education); and
- the technique is advisable where there is a likelihood that the audience will find out about the less attractive (or even unattractive) side of the product anyway.

Much of the early work supporting the two-sided message thesis was carried out in the context of messages which, although they were persuasive, were of a non-commercial origin. There is now additional evidence that for a limited range of products (for example, kitchen ranges, cars and polishes) the two-sided appeal is superior to the one-sided message (Faison 1961).

A question that arises in the context of the two-sided appeal is: In what order should the messages be presented so that the positive one has the greatest impact? Even in the case of one-sided appeals, it is natural to wonder whether the strongest arguments should be presented first or later, in order to have maximum impact on an audience. There is no decisive answer to either question. The research findings to date are inconsistent, some resulting in the advocacy of primacy (the first argument is the most effective), some in favor of recency (the latest or last message is most effective). Many pieces of research suggest, however, that order of presentation makes no difference to the overall message's impact.

Engel *et al.* (1973: 337–8) point out that commonsense is also contradictory: if the strongest appeal comes first it may well arouse attention on a large scale, but the weakness of succeeding messages may only detract from the general communication's effectiveness. More recently, Engel *et al.* (1990: 384) conclude that it is currently impossible to predict which effect will appear in a specific ad.

Yet another message consideration in persuasive communication is that of repetition or the frequency with which the message must be received before it has any effect. A convincing body of evidence supports the generalization that repeating persuasive messages increases consumer awareness of the message and is likely to lead to increased attitude change (see Belch 1982 for a brief review of this evidence). It is well known, however, that the rate at which memory decays is very great, and that an audience's retention of the information presented in a single advertisement cannot be taken for granted for long. Awareness of advertised brand names among an audience has also been shown to decay at a fast rate, even after several repetitions of the message have been employed to establish it. Even when a maximum level of awareness is achieved, some repetition is necessary to maintain this; if advertising campaigns for some products are suspended and subsequently revived, a disproportionate amount of advertising may be necessary before previous levels of awareness are obtained again. This does not mean that all campaigns must be continuous; the rate at which consumers learn increases when there are carefully regulated periods of rest from time to time in the receipt of the messages.

Receiver characteristics refer to distinguishing characteristics of consumer markets, which may affect their responses to marketers' attempts at persuasion. The amount of existing knowledge, strength with which attitudes are held, levels of income and education, lifestyle and personality differences are just some of the characteristics of consumers that can potentially affect the way they interpret and react to advertising. Hence, marketers must be knowledgeable about their target markets and tailor their persuasive messages to specific groups of consumers by incorporating into the message features of the receiver market. For instance, experts in a product area are likely to process product-related information differently than non-experts and to remember it differently as well (Alba and Hutchinson 1987).

Cognitive dissonance

Cognitive dissonance is a condition reflecting a tendency toward mental unease which occurs when an individual holds two attitudes, ideas, beliefs (or other cognitions) that are not in harmony with each other (Festinger 1957). In this situation, the person tries to reduce dissonance – perhaps by dropping a cognition, perhaps by strengthening one – in an effort to make beliefs and attitudes consistent. Dissonance may thus be a factor in motivation because it leads the individual to change an opinion, attitudes or behavior in order to reach a state of 'consonance' or harmony.

Perhaps the best-known application of dissonance theory in the context of consumer behavior concerns the post-decisional doubt expressed by purchasers of new cars (Engel 1963). The existence of dissonance among such customers was deduced from their tendency to seek further information about the model just bought, despite having previously considered several alternatives. Engel questioned some of the conclusions of others in this area. He suggests that dissonance may result only from price factors and explains increased ad awareness after purchase in terms of the buyer's increased perception of the car's attributes once he has it at home in the garage or has driven it for a while. Recent car buyers may well need reassurance that their decisions were sound and this can be achieved through advertising messages aimed specifically at them. Indeed, without such follow-up they may be more likely to select different brands in future, or even trade in their recent purchase early.

Cognitive dissonance has also been evoked to explain consumers' reactions to the prices charged for new products when they are introduced to the market. Doob *et al.* (1969) conducted experiments with five products (mouthwash, toothpaste, aluminum foil, light bulbs and cookies) to test the notion that consumers who pay a high initial price for an item are more likely to make repeat purchases than those who pay a low introductory price. They explain their results, which generally support this hypothesis, in terms of dissonance theory: 'the more effort . . . a person exerts to attain a goal, the more dissonance is aroused if the goal is less valuable than expected'. Dissonance is reduced as the individual increases his liking for a goal, and therefore it is thought that the higher the price paid by the consumer, the greater is the tendency to like the brand and become loyal to it. Hence, in the long term, sales may be higher following a relatively high introductory price.

STRATEGIES OF PERSUASION

On the basis of the preceding analysis, we draw attention to two broad strategies of persuasion which are used by marketing managers. The first involves changing elements identified by the Theory of Reasoned Action; the second, methods of utilizing interpersonal communication among consumers.

Modifying attitudes and subjective norms

The models of attitude discussed above suggest a variety of strategies for changing consumer behavior by modifying attitudes or subjective norms. These are briefly listed below:

- Link or associate the brand with key goals consumers have; that is, show that the brand provides the benefits that consumers seek: 'Fox jeans will make you sexy!'
- Change consumer beliefs (the b's in the Fishbein model) about a brand so that they see that your brand is superior to other brands in providing key benefits: 'Fox jeans are the least expensive you can buy'.
- Change consumer beliefs about competing brands: 'Brand X jeans are more expensive than Fox jeans'.
- Change the evaluations (the e's in the model) so that a product attribute is seen as a good thing to have. Thus the marketer might stress that an attribute on which his brand is strong is actually more important than consumers thought: 'The best jeans you can buy are the least expensive jeans.'

- Add a new belief combination to the brand. Thus products are constantly 'new and improved' to enhance their attractiveness and competitiveness: 'Fox jeans have been prewashed with a special process to make them better.'
- Change normative beliefs (NB) by suggesting that important others believe that the consumer should buy the brand: 'Your friends all think that Fox jeans are the ones to buy.'
- Change the motivation to comply (MC) by suggesting that the consumer should bow to the wishes of others and buy the brand: 'You will win friends if you buy Fox jeans.'
- Add a new subjective normative component (SN) to the decision process: 'Co-workers will think you know your clothes if you wear Fox jeans.'

These strategies of behavior change presume that the consumer is relatively involved in the message, that is, he or she is actively interested in what the ad has to say and is paying attention to the arguments in the message. This situation, however, does not describe how most consumers interact with advertising most of the time. Many studies confirm that, of the vast number of advertising impressions to which consumers are exposed during the course of a normal day, very few receive enough active processing to be stored in memory.

Most consumers, most of the time, are passive, not active, viewers of advertising. In this low-involvement state, many of the attitude-change strategies described above would not be likely to be effective because they all presuppose some active information processing. Hence, for the low-involvement situation some other attitude-change strategies can be suggested. One of these is to increase consumer involvement with the ad prior to initiating one of the other strategies by featuring attention-getting devices such as loud noises, bright colors, movement or striking images.

Another strategy is to link the brand to some topic consumers are already highly involved with, that is, pairing the brand with people, events, ideas or situations that consumers already find involving. An example might be the use of children in ads to (a) attract attention and (b) cause the consumer to associate children with the brand. Celebrities also can be associated with brands, creating higher levels of arousal for the brand than normal.

Influencing interpersonal communication

Marketers and advertisers frequently make use of reference group appeals in advertisements (see also Chapter 9). These ads feature people representing the advertised brand or the reference group itself. The people in the ad either talk among themselves or talk directly to the consumer, telling him or her that the brand should be purchased because it will promote group membership or group identification, or because it is the right choice to make based on the group's superior knowledge. Such ads may feature either 'typical consumers' or ordinary people as well as celebrities, depending on the type of group (membership or aspirational) involved.

A related use of reference group appeals in advertising is that of opinion leaders to promote a brand. People in business frequently subscribe to the belief that 'A satisfied customer is your best sales person'. This is because the individual consumer who spreads word-of-mouth information about a product is seen by other consumers as high in credibility and trustworthiness. Their credibility is, in fact, likely to be higher than that of sales pitches or impersonal, paid advertising because they have experienced the product first hand and have no apparent vested interests in the product's success. In addition, use of other people as sources of product information is a way to reduce the risk associated with product purchase.

While the influence of opinion leaders is potentially important to any product, this social phenomenon occurs most often for products that are

- visible because socially consumed,
- distinctive and identified with personal values,
- new and unfamiliar, and
- likely to be perceived as risky.

Further, opinion leadership has been shown to be product specific rather than a general characteristic. There is some overlap in opinion leadership across related product categories, so that the person whose advice is frequently sought in matters of clothing and fashion may also be asked to give information about cosmetics and perfume. But this individual's influence is not likely to extend to lawnmowers and books.

What are opinion leaders like? While a large body of research has tried to answer this question (Chan and Misra 1990), only a few generalizations can be offered, chiefly owing to the product-specific nature of the phenomenon. What opinion leaders have in common, regardless of the product category, are:

- greater involvement with the product,
- more familiarity and expertise with the product, and
- more extensive exposure to the mass media in general and, particularly, where the product in question is concerned.

Several personality and demographic characteristics have been suggested as contributing to opinion leadership, including lower dogmatism and higher public individuation. This means that opinion leaders may differ from non-leaders in being more open-minded and more inclined to act and feel different from others (Chan and Misra 1990). For the product marketer, however, these generalizations may be less useful than detailed studies of the specific product category for which they are responsible. For example, Goldsmith *et al.* (1987) have shown that both black and white women are more likely to be fashion opinion leaders than men.

In practice, marketers most often make use of opinion leadership in marketing strategies when they seek to influence the opinion leaders for a product directly through special communications in the media, direct marketing to them, and by means of offers of special incentives such as free samples, coupons, prizes and discounts. These efforts are made in the hope that the opinion leaders will, in their turn, spread positive word of mouth about the marketer's brand. A second way in which marketers use opinion leadership is in advertising that allows consumers apparently to eavesdrop on the conversations of other consumers and thereby participate vicariously in the process of social communication.

These efforts may be particularly important for the marketers of new products who wish to reach the product innovators.

While several early attempts to measure opinion leadership as an individual difference variable similar to lifestyle or personality were difficult and expensive, simple-to-use self-report measures have now been developed (Childers 1986; King and Summers 1970; Goldsmith and Desborde 1991). These more recent measures possess high reliability and validity and are appropriate for the survey techniques widely used by marketing research. Another method of identifying opinion leaders uses commercially available mailing lists, the purchase of which places the marketer within easy reach of consumers who have revealed through prior purchase or media usage that they are likely to serve as opinion leaders for other consumers by virtue of their interest or expertise in a product area.

With this information, marketers have available several strategies for using opinion leaders to improve sales of an existing product or to enhance those of a new one. For instance, a marketer of a new type of tennis ball could purchase a list of all the tennis pros in the country and mail each of them a free sample for their trial, encouraging them to tell other players about the new product. In fact, professionals in many areas – physicians and farmers, for example – frequently receive product samples, coupons, deals and other promotions intended to prompt them to spread positive word of mouth about the product.

Rather than focusing on existing opinion leaders, another strategy invites the marketer to try to create opinion leaders for a product through sampling or other product usage and relying on these customers to spread the product's fame by word of mouth (Mancuso 1969). Also, marketers and advertisers use many gimmicks to stimulate positive word of mouth in the social network independently of opinion leaders by prompting consumers to talk about brands among themselves. The use of balloons, contests, outrageous publicity, and so on, while seemingly a waste of time, may in fact stimulate a great deal of product-related conversation among consumers and thereby increase sales. Usually, however, such stratagems provide only short-term sales boosts. Finally, as noted above, one of the principal types of advertisement features consumers talking to other consumers about the product while the audience listens in; such vicarious substitutes work well when consumers are socially isolated and give an impression of community. This type of advertisement is particularly useful when disclosure that one uses the product might lead to embarrassment. Sanitary towels, denture cleaners and contraceptives are products for which genuine dialogue between consumers may not easily take place. The advertisement permits consumers to make comparisons among brands and to consider product features that would not come up during everyday conversation.

Measuring attitude change: advertising effectiveness

Attitude formation, attitude change, and the practical matter of measuring these phenomena are usually viewed within the context of persuasive communication. Marketers are interested in knowing how effective their attempts at persuasive communication are in convincing consumers to buy their brands. This straightforward, practical concern is deceptively complicated in the real business world because so many uncontrolled variables interact to influence both the effect of advertising and the sales of products. Consequently, the topic of measuring the effectiveness of persuasive communications (advertising) is very complex, both in theory and in the real world (Driver and Foxall 1984).

Basically, marketers use some form of attitude measurement such as the ones discussed above to measure attitudes both before (pre-tests) and following (post-tests) persuasive messages. Differences in attitude 'scores' then represent changes in attitude attributable to the messages. Such controlled experiments are called 'copy tests' in advertising research. (Many other features of the ads, such as spokesperson attractiveness, message and overall emotional reaction are measured via copy tests as well.)

Other measures of advertising effectiveness thought to reflect changes in consumer attitudes are based on the memory consumers retain of the ads. There are difficulties, unfortunately, involved in the measurement of retention. The only basic way of doing this is by asking direct questions about the advertisements and brand names consumers have recently encountered, though there are several variations in practice in the way this can be done. When no cues are given to the respondent (a method known as the unaided recall technique), he is expected to describe all the advertisements he has seen within the last seven days and perhaps, depending on the interests of the researcher, to say where he saw them. This makes it difficult for the respondent to place his perception of advertisements in any frame of reference and the rate of recall is lowest using this method.

In a different approach, subjects may be asked a more specific question, such as to recall advertisements for a given product or product range (e.g., cigarettes) or they may be asked to remember TV advertisements rather than those appearing elsewhere (aided recall). In the third variant, recognition, the respondent is presented with a picture of an advertisement and asked whether he/she has seen it within the last seven days. This increases the chances of misrecall since a familiar advertisement seen a fortnight ago may be recounted, or the advertisement shown may be confused with a similar one. The errors involved in each technique may, of course, be minimized by using a combination of all three.

A great deal of learning and memory theory is useful in assessing the extent to which repetition contributes to attitude change. In most cases, repetition certainly appears to be positively related to consumers' expressed intentions to buy, and these are often a good guide to purchase behavior. There is always the possibility, however, that constant repetition may lead to boredom and psychological fatigue and that it may then reduce the consumer's intention to buy. The consumer's rate of learning (change in behavior) is, as we have seen, related to the reinforcement through experience of the advertiser's claims. It is likely that repetition to people who do not buy the product or who have had unfavorable experiences with it may only serve to inculcate existing negative attitudes.

But none of these provisos should be allowed to detract from the basic argument that repetition is positively associated with consumer awareness. The consideration raised by learning theory may help managers arrive at an appropriate rate of advertising repetition (see Driver and Foxall 1984, chapters 4 and 5).

SUMMARY

The concept of consumer attitudes refers to the feelings of liking or disliking that consumers hold with regard to products, brands, stores, advertisements or other marketing stimuli. Consumer attitudes are important to marketers because they predispose consumers' intentions and behaviors toward the marketing mix variables of product, price, promotion and place. Consequently, they provide partial explanations for consumer behavior, and they can be influenced by marketing strategies such as advertising or sales promotions. Attitudes are also used frequently to evaluate the effectiveness of such attempts to influence consumer choice in the marketplace.

Attitudes are functionally useful in directing consumers toward products or brands they find useful in satisfying needs and wants. This adaptive function is linked to consumer motivation in that several products/brands may meet the same consumer need, so favorable attitudes toward the ones that do this best can help consumers use their resources of time, energy, money and memory in the most economical ways to accomplish desired goals. Attitudes represent the effects of past personal experience, the communicated experience of others (information), and deductive reasoning on future behaviors. Not only do attitudes influence behavior, but behavior influences the formation of attitudes as consumers learn through personal experience which brands best meet their needs and expectations.

Attitudes are operationalized or measured by means of self-reports. These include rating scales, Likert Summed Scales, bipolar adjective scales such as the Semantic Differential or Stapel Scales. The data gathered by means of these scaling methods is useful to marketers for what they reveal about consumers' beliefs, attitudes and intentions. These elements form the parts of one of the most influential attitude theories in marketing (as well as in the behavioral sciences generally): Fishbein and Ajzen's Theory of Reasoned Action. This complex theory proposes that precise measures of beliefs and social motivations can be used to explain and predict consumer attitudes, which in turn help predict behavioral intentions that approximate behavior itself. This approach is particularly useful to marketers for the insights it gives in evaluating consumers' perceptions of current marketing offerings.

Attitudes are important to marketing management and consumer research because of their expected influence on consumer behavior. Attitudes and their accompanying constructs are used to segment markets, to develop new products and to predict their success, to assess market share, to explain product success and failure, and to evaluate the impact of advertising (Day 1973). Consumer attitudes also form an important part of the models of consumer behavior used to understand and explain consumption. Nevertheless, attempts to predict unfamiliar behavior on the basis of attitude measures are fraught with difficulty. Attitude change does not always result in behavior change; quite often, changes in behavior such as brand trial precede corresponding changes in attitude and intention. This complication only underscores the need for marketers to be aware of the ways in which the market evaluates their products. It also highlights the key role of changes in attitude, subjective norm or behavioral intention in the persuasive process.

Persuasion is the attempt to use information, provided by means of mass media or sales personnel, to influence attitude formation. A model of communication containing the elements of source, message, channel and receiver helps marketers understand how persuasion takes place and how to both evaluate and improve persuasive communications. Techniques such as fear appeals or humor are used to enhance the persuasive ability of advertising. The choice between one-sided and two-sided messages has also been framed within this attitude/communications context. In addition, marketers use this model to explore issues of frequency of ad repetition and to choose the most effective channels or media to use in attempting to persuade consumers. Thus, attitudes represent a primary means of measuring the effectiveness of all aspects of marketing communication. The model of attitude formation proposed in the Theory of Reasoned Action also suggests a variety of attitude change strategies, such as changing brand beliefs, all of which presuppose relatively high levels of consumer involvement with the persuasive message.

Finally, the concept of cognitive dissonance is an important feature of attitude theory for the marketer because of the emphasis it places on consumers' need to maintain cognitive consistency. That is, this theory tells markets that consumers seek to reduce mental discomfort or dissonance that could arise from the presence of conflicting or inconsistent attitudes. Consumers do this by changing their behaviors and attitudes, or by distorting the messages they receive in order to maintain a balance or consistency across the whole system of beliefs, attitudes, intentions and behaviors. Marketers have found that consumers frequently use advertising and the information it contains to justify or reinforce prior behaviors, such as product purchase, and that targeted efforts to support consumer decision may prove to influence future buying behavior.

Part III

The personal consumer

Chapter 6

Personality and cognitive style

THE NATURE OF PERSONALITY

Marketing managers need information about their target markets that will help them perform the jobs of market segmentation and product positioning. Most of what managers know about their consumers can be described as the demographic characteristics of target segments. Statistical data on the age, race, sex, income, educational level, marital status and number of children in the household, for example, form the core of the marketer's knowledge about his or her consumers. For practical marketing problems, however, this useful information falls short of revealing to the manager what his or her target consumer is 'really like'. That is, for the needs of those who wish to design products and promote them, additional information describing the feelings, behaviors, motives and attitudes of consumers is needed to fill out the stark descriptions of consumers revealed by demographic data.

In their search for this information, market researchers have recourse to two other ways of understanding consumers, through personality and lifestyle. Although the distinctions between these two concepts will be made clearer later, it is sufficient for now to remember that personality is a concept borrowed from psychology that refers to inter-individual differences in broad patterns of behavior (Mischel 1976). Lifestyle is an advertising term that refers to the distinctive ways in which consumers live, how they spend their time and money, and what they consider important – their activities, interests and opinions (Wells 1974; see also Mitchell 1983). Marketers would like to divide the consumers who compose the overall market into segments on the basis of some common characteristic such as social class, personality or lifestyle. Other uses for the twin concepts of personality and lifestyle are the development of new products and the selection of media. A quite considerable body of empirical knowledge has been accumulated which links personality traits and types with customers' product and brand preferences and to several other aspects of their behavior.

It seems reasonable to expect that a consumer's personality – distinct outlook, mannerisms and patterns of behavioral responses – should influence his or her product choices: that there should be consistency between the buyer's general manner of responding to the environment and reactions to specific opportunities to purchase and consume. The possibility of using measures of consumers' personalities to guide marketing action – e.g., in the psychographic segmentation of markets, tailoring new brands to the susceptibilities of innovative consumers, and repositioning mature brands – has encouraged research that has attempted to identify relationships between various conceptions of personality and spending behavior. This chapter examines these claims, probes the reasons for poor observed relations between personality and consumer behavior, and shows how current research is making strides toward a more effective demonstration of the links between person and choice.

The concept of personality arises from psychologists' desire to account for the apparent consistencies and regularities of behavior over time and across a variety of situations. For Pervin (1984: 4) 'Personality represents those characteristics of the person or of people generally that account for consistent patterns of behavior'. As such, personality is invoked to explain those aspects of behavior that are relatively stable regardless of context: hence the possibility of employing measures of personality to predict behavior. Personality research also reflects ways in which one individual differs from other people through the measurement of specific configurations of traits and characteristics in any given person's make-up. Thus 'personality' is 'the unique way in which traits, attitudes, aptitudes, and the like are organized in an individual' (Marx and Hillix 1979: 483). Personality is a function of innate drives, learned motives, and experience: 'the relatively stable organization of a person's motivational dispositions arising from the interaction between biological drives and the social and physical environment' (Eysenck *et al.* 1975).

The meaning of personality in behavioral science becomes more clear when we consider the ways in which the concept has been described and operationalized in research. Over the years, several distinct bodies of theory have been developed to describe and explain personality (Hall and Lindzey 1970), several of which have influenced marketing thought and the direction of consumer research (Kassarjian and Sheffet 1991).

One of the earliest theories created to account for personality is the psychoanalytic theory of Sigmund Freud. This theory of the formation and structure of personality which emphasizes the influence of unconscious forces on behavior will be examined extensively in the next chapter, though it is also relevant in the current context. Another approach to personality theory and research involves the classification of various types of personality. For instance, the categorization of people as introverts and extroverts is a well-known example which stems from Carl Jung's psychoanalytic theories. Another example, again a derivative of psychoanalysis, is the model that emerged from the work of Karen Horney (1958), in which individuals are categorized as compliant, aggressive or detached. These type theories may be thought of as attempts to sum up a person's personality by referring to a dominant trait or series of traits. David Riesman *et al.* (1960) uses the notion of social character essentially to sum up the individual's personality type. His system has three categories of person: the tradition-directed, the other-directed and the inner-directed, each of which has implications for attitudes and behavior. Our discussion will return to these various typologies of human personality.

Another dominant theme in the development of personality as an area of scientific study has been trait theory, traits being an individual's characteristic ways of responding to the social and physical environment. Examples are aggression, honesty, anxiety, independence and sociability. Behavioral scientists do not consider any of these to be ethically better or worse than others; they are simply terms that describe a person's behavior. By and large, traits are independent of each other and have to be measured separately.

PERSONALITY RESEARCH IN MARKETING

Personality types

Some consumer researchers have used personality-type variables in their search for links between consumers' personalities and their consumption habits. It is probably fair to say that while this has not of itself transformed personality research into an immediately usable management tool, the results have been somewhat encouraging.

For instance, some researchers have used the paradigm advanced by Karen Horney (briefly mentioned above), classifying consumers into compliant, aggressive or detached types. Compliant individuals are anxious to be with others, to receive love, recognition, help and guidance. Such needs may make them overgenerous and oversensitive, so that they shy away from criticism and allow others to dominate them. They are essentially conformists. Aggressive people tend to be achievement-oriented, desire status, and see life as a competitive game. They seek the admiration of others by being outgoing in their behavior and may exhibit what are often called 'leadership qualities'. Finally, detached individuals try to separate themselves from others both emotionally and behaviorally; they do not seek responsibility or obligations and do not try to impress other people. Each of these personality types contains sufficient unique traits to be conceptually distinct from the others, though in practice it is probable that many individuals possess elements of more than one.

Cohen (1968) was able to match these personality types with product/brand preferences and usage rates. For instance, highly compliant people were more likely than less compliant types to use mouthwash, prefer Dial soap, and drink wine at least several times monthly. Respondents scoring high on aggression bought more men's deodorant than low-aggression types (they also chose Old Spice), while compliant and detached persons drank tea at least several times a week, something the aggressives did far less frequently.

Fruitful as these results appear to be, it is important to note that Cohen presents only selected data and reported no statistically significant relationships for a wide range of products including cigarettes, dress-shirts, men's hairdressing, toothpaste, beer, diet products and headache remedies. Nevertheless, this particular study tends to resurrect personality theory as a meaningful approach to consumer behavior research. Preferences for media offerings were also discovered, taking the personality/consumer choice relationship beyond brand selection and usage rates. Aggressive individuals, for example, preferred exciting television programs such as *The Untouchables* and *The Fugitive* and magazines like

Playboy and *Field and Stream*. Compliant persons more readily chose programs like *Dr Kildare* and *Bonanza* and typically read *Reader's Digest*. The detached subjects had more mixed and ambivalent preferences.

Another personality-type theory applied to consumer choice derives from the behavioral categories put forward by Riesman *et al.* (1960) in *The Lonely Crowd*. This work classifies individuals as tradition-directed (who have a strong personal sense of the past), the inner-directed (who have a strong personal sense of what sort of behavior is correct), and other-directed (whose values, attitudes and behavior are largely acquired from others). Kassarjian (1965) found that when presented with pairs of advertisements, one of which had a built-in inner-directed appeal, the other an other-directed appeal, respondents tended to choose the advertisement that corresponded to their personality type as the one most likely to influence them. Both groups expressed the view that the majority of people were likely to be influenced more by other-directed appeals; but neither group showed greater or more significant media exposure or preferences. (As an example of the difference between pairs of advertisements, Kassarjian states: 'An inner-directed ad for a Book of the Month Club would contain pictures of book jackets about great people and adventures while an other-directed ad would contain pictures of books about everyday people, best sellers, and books on personality improvement.')

This experiment, conducted with American college students as subjects, ignored tradition direction on the grounds of its alleged non-relevance to the American consumer. Tradition orientation might, however, be of some importance to the understanding of European consumers' behavior and even that of some Americans with respect to products of an antique or generally historical character.

Personality traits

Two classic studies that attempt to link traits with product use concern the ownership of cars. Both were carried out with samples of United States car owners and involved preferences toward buying either a Ford or a Chevrolet. Evans (1959) cites as the stimulus for this research the fact that, while mechanically and in design terms these brands of car were almost identical, advertisers had tried to create very different brand images for them based on what they assumed to be profiles of car buyers. Likely Ford owners were popularly portrayed as independent, impulsive, masculine and self-confident, while probable Chevrolet buyers were presented as conservative, thrifty, prestige-conscious, less masculine and moderate. A standard personality test (the Edwards Personal Preference Schedule) was used to measure these personality traits and others that might be relevant. The test was administered to seventy-one Ford owners and sixty-nine Chevrolet owners. In a first trial based solely on the personality test scores of subjects, Evans was able to predict successfully whether an individual owned a Ford or Chevrolet in 63 percent of cases, 13 percent more than would have been the case purely by chance.

A second analysis used only socioeconomic variables to predict correctly 70 percent. A third analysis combined personality scores with socioeconomic measures, but failed to improve the accuracy of predictions beyond that of his first try. Clearly none of these results is sufficiently reliable to be of much value to the car manufacturer who wants to segment his market on the basis of personality variables. A replication of part of this work by Westfall (1962), using the Thurstone Temperament Schedule in place of the Edwards Scale, also failed to distinguish satisfactorily between Ford and Chevrolet owners by personality traits though it succeeded in distinguishing convertible owners from non-convertible owners; persons who scored low on measures of activity, vigor, impulsiveness and sociability had a lower than average chance of owning a convertible. Although providing evidence that personality may be linked to product if not brand choice, even this result is of limited managerial relevance.

Although cars have figured in a number of surveys, a wide range of products and brands have now been covered by tests. During the 1960s and 1970s, dozens of studies tried to link purchase behavior and personality. The result was a mass of evidence showing that personality traits are linked with product and brand choice; however, the associations are, in the main, very weak. Correlation coefficients of the order of 0.3 or below are very common in these studies, showing that the proportion of variability in consumer-purchase patterns attributable to the effects of personality traits is quite small (Tables 6.1 and 6.2).

Reasons for failure

It is true, of course, that no social scientist expects a single variable to be wholly determinative, to explain some aspect of behavior without exception and without reference to other influences. As Kassarjian (1971: 416) concludes his review of such research: 'To

Table 6.1 Personality traits and product usage

Product/behavior	Associated trait(s)	Correlation coefficient
Headache remedies	Ascendancy	−0.46
	Emotional stability	−0.32
Acceptance of new fashions	Ascendancy	0.33
	Sociability	0.56
Vitamins	Ascendancy	−0.33
	Responsibility	−0.30
	Emotional stability	−0.09
	Sociability	−0.27
Cigarettes	None of the four	
Mouthwash	Responsibility	−0.22
Alcoholic drinks	Responsibility	−0.36
Deodorant	None of the four	
Automobiles	Responsibility	0.28
Chewing gum	Responsibility	0.30
	Emotional stability	0.33

Source: Derived from Tucker, W. T. and J. J. Painter (1961), 'Personality and product use', Journal of Applied Psychology, 45.

Table 6.2 Personality and product choice: some examples

Product/brand	Traits	Results
(a) Fords/Chevrolets	Achievement, defense, exhibition, autonomy, affiliation, intraception, dominance, abasement, change, heterosexuality, aggression.	Allowed correct prediction of 13% more buyer's choice than random allocation alone would give.
(b) Car types	Activeness, vigor, impulsiveness, dominance, stability, sociability, reflectiveness.	'No personality differences between Ford and Chevrolet owners'. Low activity related to low convertible ownership.
(c) Magazines Cigarettes	Sex, dominance, achievement, assistance, Dominance, aggression, change, autonomy.	Less than 13% of purchase behavior variance explicable in terms of personality for magazines or cigarettes
(d) Toilet tissue	45 traits	Personality of no value in prediction of brand loyalty, number of units purchased or color of tissue.
(e) Private brands	Enthusiasm, sensitivity, submissiveness.	Less than 5% of purchase variance explained by these 3 traits; other traits of no value.

Sources: Derived from (a) F. Evans (1959), 'Psychological and objective factors in the prediction of brand choice', *Journal of Business*, 39; (b) R. Westfall (1962), 'Psychological factors in predicting brand choice', *Journal of Marketing*, 26; (c) A. Koponen (1960), 'Personality characteristics of purchasers', *Journal of Advertising Research*, 1; (d) Advertising Research Foundation (1964), *Are There Consumer Types*? A. R. F.; (e) J. G. Myers (1967), 'Determinants of private brand attitude', *Journal of Marketing Research*, 4.

expect the influence of personality variables to account for a large proportion of the variance is most certainly asking too much.' In these circumstances, finding any positive relationship at all is more surprising than the lack of definitive results (Foxall and Goldsmith 1988). Moreover, while the disappointing results we have briefly reviewed had the effect of dampening enthusiasm among researchers (Arndt 1986; Wells and Beard 1973), it is possible to detect the reasons for failure and in some instances to rectify them. The main reasons for the relatively anemic showing by personality research in consumer behavior include the following.

• *The psychological tests used in consumer studies were devised for use in clinical psychology rather than marketing research*. While they had been validated for the situations in which they had been developed, the assumption that they would transfer directly to other contexts was naive.

- *The tests have inherently low predictive power.* In their clinical application, the tests do not explain large proportions of variance in criterion variables; the consumer researchers had unrealistic expectations of how they would perform in market research.
- *Marketing researchers neglected to consider the conditions under which the tests were administered.* The subjects in consumer studies, students or otherwise, may have reacted to the clinical tests in ways that confounded the results, acquiescing or giving socially desirable responses that the researchers failed to foresee or control.
- *The tests were used indiscriminately.* That is, many researchers chose to use conveniently administered and scored tests without carefully developing a theoretical rationale as to why the traits measured by a particular inventory could be expected to relate to consumption.
- *The reliability (consistency) of the dependent variables was typically low or unknown.* Many studies used single instances of behavior or single-item measures for dependent variables. These are inherently of low or unknown reliability, a factor which places low upper-limits on the size of any relationship with independent variables such as the scores on personality tests.
- *Personality tests are general in that they apply to global views of behavior rather than narrow behavioral choices.* Pencil-and-paper personality tests are designed to cover as wide a scope of behavior as possible, while the consumption behavior of interest to market researchers is at a very specific level (sometimes individual brands were used). For accurate measurement of the association of two variables, both need to be conceptualized and measured at the same level of generality/specificity.

Recent developments

Recent studies of personality in consumer behavior have sought to avoid past mistakes and to benefit from current theory development. These studies use more specific measures of more precisely defined personality traits and types, which are theoretically relevant to economic behavior rather than relying on post hoc explanations to justify findings from shotgun-type, general scales. More stress is placed on verifying the reliability and validity of both independent and dependent variables. Where possible, multiple measures of behavior rather than single indicators or one-off instances of behavior to enhance dependent variable reliability through aggregation are used (Epstein 1986). The personality scales themselves are less confined to clinical applications and more relevant to the analysis of everyday behaviors including economic actions and choices. Consumer researchers have more modest expectations of the effects of personality factors on consumer choice, and they see personality traits and types as offering only partial explanations interacting with social, cultural and economic moderator variables to yield distinctive patterns of buying behavior (Punj and Stewart 1983).

Several successful recent studies demonstrate empirically the relationship between personality and consumer behavior. Using the well-established, theoretically grounded and widely validated measures of second-order personality types developed by Eysenck and Eysenck (1975), Allsopp (1986a, 1986b) found significant positive correlations of scores on measures of extroversion, emotionalism, tough-mindedness and impulsiveness with alcoholic beverage consumption among 18 to 21 year old males. Based on the patterns of personality test responses – high scorers on three or four of the scales had consumption levels several times greater than high scorers on none – he was able to suggest marketing strategies for pubs linked to psychographic segmentation.

Becherer and Richard (1978) and Snyder and DeBono (1985) have shown that individual differences in self-monitoring, the tendency to observe and control expressive behavior and self-presentation to match social surroundings, may moderate the relationship between certain personality traits and consumption behaviors and may influence individual reception of advertisements. Other studies indicate that venturesomeness and novelty seeking may explain individual differences in learning about and trial of new products. Goldsmith (1987) suggests that high self-monitoring may be linked to willingness to try innovations. Other studies indicate that venturesomeness and novelty-seeking may explain individual differences in learning about and trial of new products (McAlister and Pessemier 1982; Raju 1980).

In the following sections, we describe the findings and implications of recent research that illustrates the new approach. The first is Allsopp's use of the personality *types* defined by Eysenck. The second is the investigation of cognitive/personality *traits*, culminating in studies of the role of *cognitive style* in innovative consumer behavior.

PERSONALITY TYPES: EXTROVERSION, EMOTIONALITY AND TOUGH-MINDEDNESS

Allsopp (1986a) used the Eysenck Personality Inventory (Eysenck and Eysenck 1969, 1976) in an investigation of the determination of beer and cider consumption by personality *types*. Two samples were used to simulate social-class differences in consumption patterns: 174 apprentice craftsmen attending college on a block- or day-release basis, and 173 full-time undergraduate students reading for degrees in subjects that included engineering, business and food technology. Respondents, all of whom were men aged between 18 and 21, completed a retrospective diary of their consumption of alcoholic beverages in pubs during the previous week, provided data on their leisure interests and activities, and completed tests of the following dimensions of personality.

Extroversion-Introversion

The main characteristics of extroverts are their sociability, their need for others to talk to, their activeness and impulsiveness. By contrast, introverts are quiet and retiring, reserved and cautious (Eysenck and Eysenck 1975). Extroverts are believed to have lower levels of cortical arousal than introverts and thus to seek stimulation through externally oriented experience. Introverts, who already have high levels of cortical stimulation, are likely to shy away from loud, exciting and sensational events. The expectation was that high scorers on extroversion (what Eysenck calls the E scale) would consume more alcohol than low scorers: extroverts would presumably be more likely to look for and discover stimulation by drinking in pubs than would introverts.

Emotionality

High scorers on Eysenck's N scale (which stands for neuroticism) tend toward emotional instability. They are anxious, moody, easily depressed, overemotional; in a word, worriers. Low scorers are emotionally stable: calm and even-tempered, infrequent worriers, reacting emotionally only slowly and temporarily. Given Eysenck's theory, the theoretical expectations with respect to alcohol consumption are contradictory. The high-scoring individual might drink in order to find relaxation; but his or her anxiety might inhibit drinking in public situations with their social stresses.

Tough-mindedness

High scorers on Eysenck's psychoticism (or P) scale are extremely antisocial, insensitive to others, even psychotic. The high range of the scale on which such individuals score is intended for clinical applications and is not relevant to consumer research. However, the low to medium range of the scale measures degrees of self-centeredness, independence, innovativeness, and risk taking, all of which are directly useful (Allsopp 1986b). The expectation guiding the research was, therefore, that medium scorers would consume more alcohol than individuals scoring low on this scale.

Impulsiveness and venturesomeness

Impulsiveness (measured by the Imp. scale) and venturesomeness (Vent.) are components of personality that involve sensation seeking. They also correlate closely with the E and P dimensions. High scorers were, therefore, expected to consume significantly more alcohol than low scorers.

Relationship to alcohol consumption

Allsopp found several significant relationships between these personality dimensions and the on-license consumption of beer and cider (Table 6.3). While the correlation coefficients fall well within the usual range for personality research in marketing, several are of high statistical significance. The results thus suggest to marketing managers (or, for that matter, agencies involved in reducing alcohol consumption) criteria for segmenting consumers whose potential for consumption differs substantially. The results for emotionality (N) are not significant – perhaps because the two theoretically possible effects cancel each other out. Nor is the correlation of Vent. scores and consumption significant for the craftsmen. However, the relationships which are significant indicate noteworthy differences between the higher and lower scorers in the expected, theoretically consistent, directions.

The scores for three subsamples of each of the craftsmen and student samples on the four scales that produced significant results are shown in Figure 6.1. For each sample, the subsamples represent approximately equal groupings of low, medium and high scorers. In

Table 6.3 Correlations between total beer and cider consumption and E, P, N, Imp and Vent

	Craftsmen	Students
E	0.23**	0.29***
P	0.26***	0.33***
N	−0.09	0.04
Imp	0.28***	0.44***
Vent	0.06	0.17*

***p<0.001 (two-tailed)
**p<0.01 (two-tailed)
*p<0.025 (two-tailed)

Source: Allsopp, J. F. (1986), 'The distribution of on-licence beer and cider consumption and its personality determinants among young men', *European Journal of Marketing*, 20 (3/4), 55. Reproduced by permission of MCB University Press Ltd.

the case of the students, high scorers consume about twice as much as low scorers on the E, P, and Vent. scales, and about three times as much on the Imp. scale. Among the craftsmen, high scores on the E, P and Imp. scales consume about twice as much as the low scorers; in the case of the Vent. scale, where the relationship is non-significant, high scorers consume about a fifth more than low scorers.

Figure 6.2 shows the combined effect of the two higher order dimensions, E and P. For both samples, the greatest consumption is found among those scoring highest on both scales (E+P+) and the smallest among those with the lowest scores on both scales (E–P–). For the craftsmen, compared with the lowest-scoring group (E–P–), the highest-scoring group (E+P+) consumes three times as much beer and cider. The second highest-scoring group of craftsmen (E=P+) consumes twice as much as the lowest-scoring group. These differences are greater for the student sample: the E+P+ group accounts for about three and one half times as much consumption as the E–P– group, while the E=P+ group drinks three times as much as the E–P– group.

The levels of consumption reported by the higher scorers on all of the relevant scales are shown in Figure 6.3. (For this analysis, the samples were each divided into two subsamples of approximately equal size.) The craftsmen who scored high on two or three of the significant scales consumed about twice as much as those scoring high on one or none. Students who scored high on four scales drank about twice as much beer and cider as those scoring high on none.

The research is theoretically grounded and produced results generally consistent with the expectations. The author shows considerable sensitivity to the transfer of scales produced for general personality research to the consumer behavior context. Although the work relies on self-report data on consumption (something that young men might be expected to exaggerate), there is no reason to believe that craftsmen would lie more than students. (The Eysenck scales include lie scales, scores on which produced no reasons to doubt the general veracity of the respondents). Moreover, Allsopp shows in some detail that the reported levels of consumption are similar to nationally available figures for young men in the social classes investigated (Allsopp 1986a).

The results are also interesting from a managerial point of view, especially in view of the current concern with the design of 'pub atmospheres' and the attempt of breweries to increase their consumers' feelings of security and comfort with their surroundings. It is

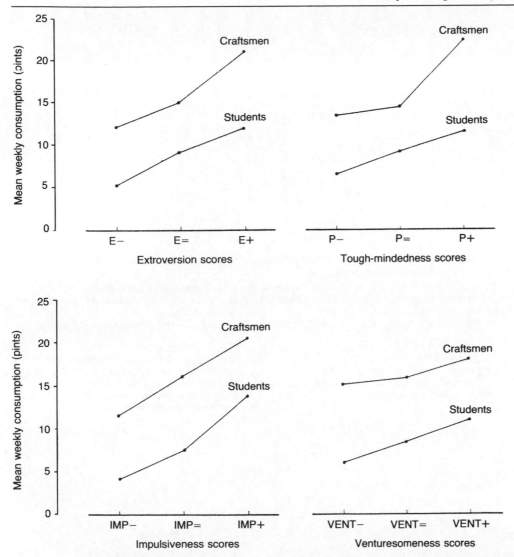

Figure 6.1 Mean weekly consumption for low, medium and high scorers on four personality scales.
Source: Allsopp, J. F. (1986) 'The distribution of on-licence beer and cider consumption and its personality determinants among young men', *European Journal of Marketing*, 20 (3/4), 56. Reproduced by permission of MCB University Press Ltd.
Note: Cut-off points defining low, medium and high scorers on personality scales different for craftsmen and students.

reasonable to expect that different personality-based segments are attracted to different physical and social environments. In particular, the personality types that are clearly related to higher levels of alcohol consumption have also been shown to prefer outdoor leisure pursuits such as sports. This is relevant to the design of pub interiors as well as to the monitoring of clientele to ensure an appropriate ambience of consumers and surroundings (Allsopp 1986a).

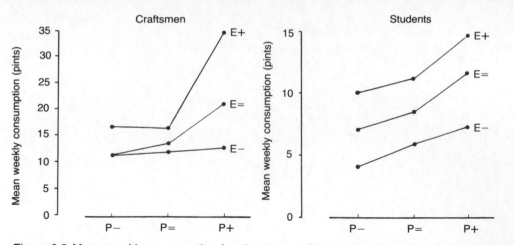

Figure 6.2 Mean weekly consumption for nine personality groups categorized by combinations of extroversion (E) and tough-mindedness (P)

Source: Allsopp, J. F. (1986) 'The distribution of on-licence beer and cider consumption and its personality determinants among young men', *European Journal of Marketing*, 20 (3/4), 57. Reproduced by permission of MCB University Press Ltd.

Note: Cut-off points defining low, medium and high scorers on E and P differed for craftsmen and students.

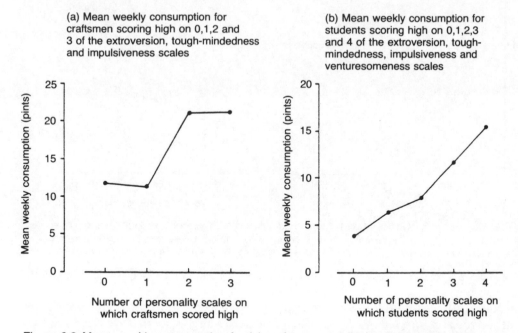

Figure 6.3 Mean weekly consumption for (a) craftsmen and (b) students scoring high on the personality scales.

Source: Allsopp, J. F. (1986) 'The distribution of on-licence beer and cider consumption and its personality determinants among young men', *European Journal of Marketing*, 20 (3/4), 58. Reproduced by permission of MCB University Press Ltd.

COGNITIVE/PERSONALITY TRAITS: THE CASE OF CONSUMER INNOVATORS

An encouraging strand of personality *trait* research involves the investigation of personality traits and types within the framework of consumers' cognitive decision making. Grounded in middle-range cognitive/personality theories and employing test instruments appropriate to the analysis of economic rather than clinical behavior, this approach has yielded a consistent body of knowledge which is particularly relevant to the behaviors of consumer innovators. Though the results of this work frequently rest on weak relationships between dispositional factors and innovative consumer behavior, they show a recurring link between innovativeness and category width, flexibility, tolerance of ambiguity, self-esteem and sensation seeking.

Category width

Category width refers to the extent to which a consumer perceives an innovation as different from the norm established by his or her existing products, brands or consumption patterns. Broad categorizers differentiate less sharply between existing and novel products and perceive less risk in purchasing and consuming divergent items. They are more willing, therefore, than 'narrow' categorizers to embrace discontinuously new products (Donnelly and Etzel 1973; Popielarz 1967; Venkatesan 1973). Donnelly and Etzel (1973) argue that, while broad categorizers prefer genuine new products (those showing radical functional divergence from the existing norm), the more conservative narrow categorizers prefer artificially new products (those that are similar to familiar versions). This strategy appears to reflect narrow categorizers' fear of making mistakes: better for them to avoid some new products that would yield positive benefits than to accept one that had negative consequences.

Broad categorizers are, by contrast, willing to risk making mistakes if this enables them to find some advantageous innovations (Foxall 1988). Broad categorizers are more amenable to change in general and actively seek opportunities to engage in behaviors that offer new experiences (Taylor and Levitt 1967). Narrow categorizers are more cautious in their decision making and will conform with norms established by others in order to avoid social tensions and pressures (Steiner and Johnson 1965). Broad categorizers process and retain more information and more diverse information from the environment (Parsons 1973); they are, therefore, 'attuned to more information impinging on them' (Pinson 1978: 170).

Dogma/rigidity vs. flexibility

Dogmatic consumers are less willing than their more flexible counterparts to accept novelty, whether it is an unfamiliar product class, such as a discontinuous innovation, or the discrepant information embodied in an advertisement. Several empirical studies have shown a tendency for more flexible consumers to prefer new products while the more dogmatic select established or traditional versions (Coney 1972; Jacoby 1971; McClurg and

Andrews 1974; cf. Ostlund 1974). Moreover, more rigid individuals are less likely to accept new or diverse information, showing resistance to change and a fixed, deterministic approach to life (Rokeach 1960).

Tolerance of ambiguity

Consumers highly tolerant of ambiguity show a preference for decision situations in which several potentially contradictory bodies of information must be taken into consideration. Ambiguity and inconsistency play an important motivating role for such people: they easily become bored by problems (or pseudo-problems) that appear routine and offer little challenge by way of novel and discrepant information and choice criteria (Budner 1962; Schaninger and Sciglimpaglia 1981). This does not imply that tolerant consumers necessarily seek more information, but that they are better placed to accommodate and process diverse information with which they are presented (cf. Bettman 1971). Consumers who are intolerant of ambiguity are likely to seek clarity before reaching a decision; they, therefore, may exhibit a high tendency to engage in extended pre-purchase search for and evaluation of information (Cox 1967a).

Less tolerant consumers are likely to view innovations as more discontinuously new and are thus less likely to buy. These consumers are more likely to try to finish incomplete messages (Pinson 1978), to perceive a product as new (Blake *et al.* 1973). Their aversion to ambiguity means they have less experience of new products; this in turn leads them to perceive such items as newer, more discontinuous than do their more tolerant counterparts. Tolerant consumers, however, are attracted to perceived newness and more likely to purchase it (Blake *et al.* 1973). They are likely, therefore, to buy more new products; intolerant consumers, less likely.

Self-esteem vs. anxiety

Self-esteem is related to confidence in one's capacity to evaluate alternatives and reach purchase decisions (Cox 1967b). It is negatively related to anxiety, which is positively related to perceived risk. High-anxiety, low self-esteem individuals experience novel purchase decisions as threatening and are less capable of acquiring and processing information in such contexts (Schaninger and Sciglimpaglia 1981); hence they may be less likely to buy new products.

Sensation seeking

Consumers whose optimum stimulation level is high – i.e., those who prefer a complex and full information environment – are more open to risk taking, trying new products, being innovative, seeking purchase-related information, and acquiring new retailing facilities (Schiffman and Kanuk 1987: 128). These individuals feel comfortable with a highly stimulating environment but are quickly bored in a context that does not supply the required level of arousal. Those whose optimum stimulation level is low in comparison are likely to seek fewer innovations, preferring safe, tried and tested products with predictable consequences in use. The former group explore more (Price and Ridgway 1982), while the latter are content with what they know and can trust.

Cognitive style and innovative consumer behavior

Foxall (1988) and Goldsmith (1983) both offer evidence from independent studies that individual differences in problem solving and decision making of a global nature find expression in variations in the purchases of new brands and products that are relevant to the establishment of segmentation criteria and the pre-launch developing of innovations. In these studies, scores on the Kirton Adaption-Innovation Inventory (Kirton 1976), a self-report measure of individual preferences for styles of intellectual processing (i.e., *cognitive* style) are related to awareness and purchase of new grocery items. Studies such as these are giving substance to the hope that careful use of appropriate tests, the examination of more sophisticated hypotheses, and sophisticated analysis would result in better explanations and applicable findings. The following discussion describes an exemplar of the new approach.

As we noted in Chapter 2, the social and economic characteristics of innovators are known in general terms and usually provide sound indications of the kind of marketing mix that will appeal to this primary market. However, any psychometric assessment that allowed an early, quick, accurate, sensitive and inexpensive identification would be more valuable since it could be employed in the initial stages of new product development prior to major investment in plant and marketing. In view of the history of personality research in marketing, a measure was sought which had been validated over a wide range of behaviors and situations and which, in particular, had relevance to economic problem solving and decision making.

The KAI is a measure of cognitive style which possesses attractive psychometric properties and which has been shown to have a high degree of validity in the sphere of economic behavior, particularly in organizational contexts (Kirton 1987). In addition, KAI scores correlate with numerous measures of personality traits whose validity and reliability are well established. The adaption-innovation theory from which the test derives posits that individuals consistently display one or other of two styles of problem solving and decision making. At one pole of this continuum, the (extreme) Adaptor (low scorer on the KAI) confines his or her problem solving to the frame of reference within which the problem has arisen. Adaptors aim to produce better ways of accomplishing familiar tasks and, in organizational and other social milieus, their solutions can usually be implemented without disrupting established working patterns or networks of interaction. By contrast, the (extreme) Innovator (high scorer on the KAI) is far less likely to seek solutions that can be readily incorporated within existing systems. His or her underlying approach to problem solving is much more likely to result in a complete reevaluation of the entire frame of reference within which the problem has arisen and, in seeking solutions, the Innovator may redefine not only the problem but the context. As a result, Innovators produce different ways of meeting needs and solving problems. (In order to prevent confusion with consumer innovators, i.e., the first buyers of a new brand or product, Adaptors and Innovators are identified in this book with capital initial letters.)

The personality traits associated with these styles of information processing have been confirmed by research conducted by some twenty investigators in eight countries, using two dozen or more psychological tests to produce over sixty correlations. Adaptors have been shown to be more controlled, systematic, consistent, steady, reliable, prudent, sensitive, realistic, efficient and orderly than Innovators. Innovators tend to be more extrovert, less dogmatic, more tolerant of ambiguity, more radical, flexible, assertive, expedient, undisciplined and sensation-seeking than Adaptors (Kirton 1987; Goldsmith 1984). In summary,

> A consistent picture emerges of the intuitive-innovator who pays little attention to routine details, welcomes the new and different, and generates many novel ideas, contrasted with the equally-creative sensing-adaptor, who watches the details, works routinely and steadily, preferring standard solutions to problems.
>
> (Goldsmith 1985a: 103).

As Figure 6.4 shows, cognitive/personality traits that correlate highly with the KAI are the precise cognitive/personality factors related to consumer innovativeness (cf. Foxall 1984b, 1989; Goldsmith 1989; Horton 1979; Midgley 1977; Mudd 1990; Pinson 1978; Pinson *et al.*1988; Rogers 1983). The following discussion first presents evidence linking specific cognitive/personality dimensions with consumer innovativeness and then shows how these traits are related to adaption–innovation.

Category width   Ettlie and O'Keefe (1982) and Goldsmith (1985b) have shown that KAI correlates with readiness to change measured by the Readiness to Change Scale (Hardin 1967), the Change Index (Hage and Dewar (1973), the Innovativeness Scale of Hurt (Hurt, Joseph and Cook 1977) and the Innovation section of the Jackson (1976) Personality Inventory. De Ciantis (1987) reports a negative correlation between KAI and structuring orientation measured by the Revised Bureaucrat-Executive Scale of the management Position Analysis Test (Reddin 1983). Gryskiewicz (1982) shows KAI to correlate negatively with Need for Structure measured by the Wesley Total (Wesley 1953). Kirton (1976) reports a negative correlation of KAI with Wilson and Patterson's (1968) New Measure of Conservatism. There is also a negative correlation between the Locus of Control Scale (Rotter 1966) and KAI (Keller and Holland 1978).

Flexibility   Kirton (1976) has shown that KAI correlates negatively with the Dogmatism Scale of Rokeach (1960) and Goldsmith (1984) reports a negative correlation of KAI with the Dogmatism Scale of Trodahl and Powell (1965). KAI correlates positively with flexibility on the California Psychological Inventory (Gough 1956, 1975); see Gryskiewicz (1982), Gryskiewicz *et al.* (1987), Kirton (1976).

Tolerance of ambiguity   Several studies show KAI to correlate negatively with Intolerance of Ambiguity measured by Budner's (1962) scale (Keller and Holland 1978; Kirton 1976), and by MacDonald's (1970) and Rydell and Rosen's (1966) scales (Kirton 1976). KAI also correlates negatively with Ivancevich and Donnelly's (1974) Need for Clarity Scale (Keller and Holland 1978).

Self-esteem   Gryskiewicz (1982) shows that KAI correlates with both Capacity for Status and Social Presence, measured by Gough's (1956, 1975) California Psychological Inventory. It is also related to Rosenberg's (1965) Self-Esteem Scale (Keller and Holland 1978). KAI is positively related to factors measured by the 16PF Scale (Cattell *et al.* 1970) that imply self-confidence and esteem: humble/assertive, subdued/independent, tenderly emotional/alertly poised, astute/forthright (Gryskiewicz 1982; Kirton and De Ciantis 1986), and negatively to those implying the reverse: self-assured/apprehensive, low/high anxiety (Kirton and De Ciantis 1986).

Sensation seeking KAI correlates positively with Eysenck's (Eysenck and Eysenck 1964) Personality inventory on Extroversion (Kirton 1976) and negatively on Introversion measured by the Strong Campbell Inventory (Campbell 1974); see Gryskiewicz (1982). It correlates also with several relevant 16PF factors: conservative/experimenting, controlled/undisciplined, conscientious/expedient, subdued/independent (Kirton and De Ciantis 1986), shy/adventurous, practical/imaginative, group dependent/self-sufficient, trusting/suspicious (Carne and Kirton 1982). There are also correlations of KAI with the Sensing/Intuition and Judgement/Perception Scales of the Myers–Briggs Type Indicator (Myers 1962); see Carne and Kirton 1982; Gryskiewicz 1982; Goldsmith 1985b); with the Control-Impulse Scale of Tellegan's Research Scale (Gryskiewicz 1982), Risk Taking measured by the Jackson (1976) Personality Inventory (Goldsmith 1984, 1985b); with Sensation Seeking measured by Mehrabian and Russell's (1974) Arousal Tendency Seeking Instrument (Goldsmith 1984, 1985b) and with the General Sensation-Seeking Scale (Zuckerman 1974); see Goldsmith 1986c). Finally, KAI is negatively related to Field Dependence/Independence measured by the Embedded Figures Test of Witkin *et al.* (1971): see Keller and Holland (1978).

Figure 6.4 Cognitive/personality traits associated with adaption–innovation
Source: Foxall, G. R. and S. Bhate (1993) 'Cognitive style and personal involvement of market initiators', *Journal of Economic Psychology*, 11, 1–24. Reproduced by permission.

Relationship to consumer innovativeness

The KAI has been used in consumer research to identify the personality profiles and cognitive styles of innovative buyers of new food products and brands (Foxall and Haskins 1986, 1987). Respondents in the first investigation had purchased at least one of thirteen innovative brands of food products launched within three to four months of research; all but four respondents in the second had purchased at least one of twenty-six food products recently introduced by supermarkets and promoted as conducive to 'healthy eating'. The expectation that guided the research was that these consumer innovators would be innovators in the sense defined by Kirton: as we have seen, the diffusion literature suggests that relative to later adopters, consumer innovators are less dogmatic, more able to cope with abstractions, ambiguity and uncertainty, less fatalistic (and thus presumably more flexible, self-controlled and unsubjugated) and high in achievement motivation and aspiration (Rogers 1983). Furthermore, many marketing studies have indicated (albeit on the basis of numerous small but positive consumers' innovative choices) that consumer innovators are risk-takers, impulsive, active, dominant, inner-directed and self-reliant (Midgley 1977; Foxall 1984b).

In view of this, the results of the investigations are surprising. There was some tendency for the consumer innovators in both samples to be innovative in Kirton's sense also: the KAI means of respondents in both cases show them to be significantly more innovative than members of the general population. However, whilst both samples contained more Innovators than Adaptors, both cognitive styles were substantially represented in each instance; both samples contained Adaptors and Innovators in the ratio of approximately 40:60. The small, positive correlations typical of earlier research are, therefore, explicable in that investigators appear to have been concerned with only one set of personality traits, those of Innovators, and have ignored the role of adaptive consumer innovators.

Also contrary to the expectations that guided the research, Innovators were not responsible for purchasing a larger volume of new brands or products than Adaptors. In both cases, the purchasers of the fewest innovations were Adaptors, and purchasers of intermediate numbers of brands or products were, as expected, Innovators. However, purchasers of the largest volumes of brands or products were not, as anticipated, even more innovative; they were clearly adaptive. Figures 6.5 and 6.6 show the numbers of each brand/product bought by Adaptors and Innovators.

Whilst this is contrary to the weak evidence provided by both diffusion and marketing studies, it is quite readily explicable in terms of adaption–innovation theory. It is well known that many consumer innovators exhibit little or no loyalty, trying novel brands and products frequently but moving on to other innovations and abandoning, at least for the time being, the items that initially attracted them (e.g., Pymont *et al.* 1988). Consumer innovators whose cognitive style is predominantly innovative conform to this stereotype by purchasing a reasonable but intermediate number of innovations, whilst purchasers of just a few, if any, innovations are predictably unadventurous, sound, steady Adaptors. However, the theory proposes that those individuals who decide firmly upon a different lifestyle (such as one that includes a 'healthy' diet) are more likely to be Adaptors, who

Study 1.   Innovative Food Brands

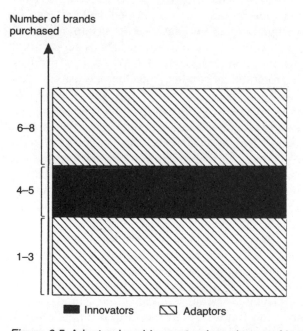

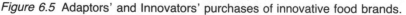

Figure 6.5 Adaptors' and Innovators' purchases of innovative food brands.

Study 2. 'Healthy Food Products'

Number of products
purchased

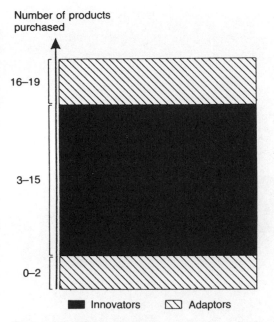

Figure 6.6 Adaptors' and Innovators' purchases of 'healthy' food products.

will thoroughly, patiently and assiduously target and seek out not a few but as many relevant products as possible (Kirton 1987, and personal communication).

These findings are clearly inconsistent with the widespread expectation in marketing circles that the personality profiles of Kirton's Innovators would lead them to be consumer innovators while Adaptors would be later adopters. But they are consistent with adaption–innovation theory which suggests that those Adaptors who were highly committed to the product field would assiduously seek out not a few but the maximally available number of relevant 'healthy' food items (Foxall 1988). Highly involved Adaptors *should*, therefore, show the highest level of innovative purchasing, and this has been borne out in empirical research concerned with the early adoption of healthy food brands (Foxall and Bhate 1993a, 1993b). Figure 6.7 shows the results.

Psychographic segmentation

None of these studies found a significant correlation between KAI and consumer innovativeness, for the simple reason that both Adaptors and Innovators were to be found among the earliest adopters of the new products or brands. However, it is not high correlations that determine the psychographic basis of market segmentation but the existence of

Study 3.   Innovative 'Healthy' Food Brands

Mean number of
brands bought

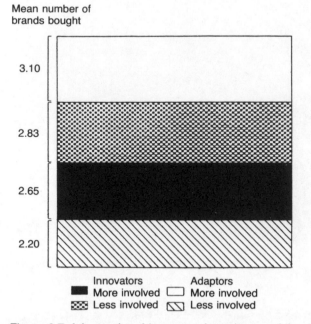

Figure 6.7 Adaptors' and Innovators' purchases of 'healthy' food brands.

separate groups, which differ in that their respective consumer behaviors make it worthwhile to consider various marketing mix approaches (Bass *et al.* 1968). The results do just that: they indicate that consumer innovators may have one of two diametrically opposed personality profiles which imply different styles of cognitive processing. They also help to identify the role of involvement in innovative purchasing for, while involvement makes no difference to the purchase level of Innovators, for Adaptors it marks a crucial distinction. The market for food innovations apparently consists of three distinct segments (Figure 6.8), members of each of which can be expected to show distinctly different patterns of problem solving at each stage of the adoption decision process depending on their adaptive/innovative cognitive style and, in the case of Adaptors, their level of involvement with the product field (Table 6.4).

At the *problem recognition* stage, whereas the less involved Adaptor is unlikely to seek out problems, the Innovator will be constantly on the lookout for them. Adaptors are more likely to recognize as problems those relatively small discontinuities that arise within the current range of their experience and the solutions they apply: they will simply disregard radical discontinuities as irrelevant, impracticable, unworthy of their attention. Innovators, by contrast, recognize discrepancies, invite ambiguities, and show disproportionate interest in problems that require tangential thinking. However, while the less involved Adaptors

MARKET SEGMENTS
(FOODS)

| Less involved adaptors | Innovators | More involved adaptors |

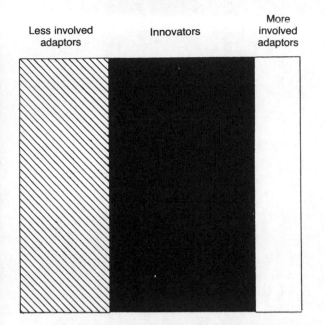

Figure 6.8 Psychographic segments of the market for innovative 'healthy' food brands.

show a lower level of initial motivation than Innovators, the more involved Adaptors, those committed to the product field as a valued means to the end of healthier living, show the highest level of new product awareness of all.

During *search and evaluation*, Adaptors would seek detailed information assiduously, perhaps slowly but certainly carefully, prudently and soundly. Any problem that has arisen will be dealt with within the framework in which it has arisen. Innovators are more likely to seek out diverse solutions, looking not just at alternative brands that promise to solve the problem but at altogether different product classes. They are likely, however, to do so somewhat superficially. Evaluation by Adaptors will be meticulous, rigid, rational and objective, based on existing tried and tested criteria. Innovators, by comparison, will introduce new choice criteria which may conflict with those they have used in the past, make quicker judgments based more on expediency, which may be more short term in their implications. They may change their minds in midstream, pausing to consider new alternatives, and so on. Nevertheless, the more involved Adaptors might be expected to consider more innovations in a product field to which they have become committed and to evaluate them more thoroughly and positively than either of the other groups. Their interest and expertise in the product field might enable them to undertake these procedures as quickly as, or more quickly than, Innovators despite their higher level of efficiency.

Adaptors' *decisions* will be conservative; those of the Innovators, impulsive. Adaptors see more discontinuity in novelty where Innovators treat even discontinuous innovations

Table 6.4 Decision styles of market segments based on adaption–innovation and personal involvement

Adoption Decision Process Stage	Less involved Adaptors	Innovators	More involved Adaptors
Problem recognition	Passive, reactive	Active	Proactive
Search	Minimal, confined to resolution of minor anomalies caused by current consumption patterns	Superficial but extensively based within and across product class boundaries	Extensive within relevant product category: assiduous exploration of all possible solutions within that framework
Evaluation	Meticulous, rational slow and cautious; objective appraisal using tried and tested criteria	Quick, impulsive, based on currently accepted criteria; personal and subjective	Careful, confined to considerations raised by the relevant product category: but executed confidently and (for the Adaptor) briskly within that frame of reference
Decision	Conservative selection within known range of products, continuous innovations preferred	Radical: easily attracted to discontinuously new product class and able to choose quickly within it. Frequent trial, followed by abandonment	Careful selection within a product field that has become familiar through deliberation, vicarious trial, and sound and prudent pre-purchase comparative evaluation
Post-purchase evaluation	Meticulous, tendency to brand loyalty if item performs well	Less loyal; constantly seeking novel experiences through purchase and consumption	Loyal if satisfied but willing to try innovations within the prescribed frame of reference; perhaps tends towards dynamically continuous innovations

Source: Foxall, G. R. and Bhate, S. (1993) 'Cognitive style and personal involvement as explicators of innovative purchasing of "healthy" food brands'. *European Journal of Marketing*. 27 (2). Reproduced by permission of MCB University Press Ltd.

as familiar, connected. But Adaptors for whom the product field has high personal relevance are likely to decide in favor of a larger number of innovations than either less involved Adaptors or Innovators. At the stage of *post-purchase evaluation*, Adaptors will be meticulous, again employing established criteria of appraisal, comparing current outcomes with past experience. They are more likely than Innovators to become and remain brand/store loyal. Innovators will make a more rapid judgment, comparing current performance with the levels of effectiveness they expect in the future, choosing more new products for a short time, and showing little loyalty. But the characteristically adaptive behavior outlined above will be found predominantly among the more involved Adaptors, for whom the product field constitutes an important contributor to personal lifestyles.

Other authors have suggested that different groups of consumer innovators might be distinguished depending upon their decision style (e.g., Hirschman 1984; Venkatraman 1991; Venkatraman and MacInnis 1985; Venkatraman and Price 1990). Some have argued that the pre-purchase and purchase behaviors of innovative consumers differ according to a single trait such as novelty seeking (Hirschman 1980) or sensation seeking (Mittelstaedt *et al.* 1976). However, the investigation reported here has identified three subgroups among market initiators and has done so on the basis of the comprehensive cognitive/ personality profiles detailed by adaption-innovation theory and research, and level of personal involvement with the product field. Each of the three subgroups – the less involved Adaptors, the Innovators, and the more-involved Adaptors – has been shown to have a different consumption level at the market initiation stage of the brand life cycle, and it has been proposed that their pre-purchase and post-purchase decision processes also differ profoundly.

At the empirical level, the findings resolve the problem of low correlations between measures of personality and aspects of consumer behavior which were repeatedly a feature of early research. The low correlations were presumably the outcome of researchers' measuring the traits of personality embodied by Innovators and overlooking those of the Adaptors, who also constituted a substantial part of the market initiator samples investigated. Low correlation of KAI and market initiation would be a problem for this measure only if it operationalized innovativeness alone; however, as a bipolar measure of adaptiveness as well as innovativeness, it has consistently produced results that are intelligible once the coexistence of Adaptors and Innovators among market initiators is recognized.

At the theoretical level, the results have two broad implications. First, they require revision both of the simplistic adoption models that attribute innovative behavior to a single set of intervening 'innovative' personality variables, and of the contingency theories that propose that consumers' innovative behavior can be traced ultimately to a hypothetical construct such as innate or inherent innovativeness. The coexistence of antithetical personality profiles among market initiators imposes new problems of explanation upon both. Second, however, the results offer to reconcile the two strands of thinking inherent in the cognitive and personality strands of dispositional approaches to consumer innovativeness: the view of consumer innovators as impulsive individualists seeking novelty at any cost, and that which portrays them as unable to make a purchase before engaging lengthily in an extended decision process. Clearly, they may be either or both!

Implications for the marketing of innovations

It is useful to consider the probable differences in decision making styles for Adaptors and Innovators as they influence product perceptions and responses to persuasive marketing communications. The following propositional inventory for further research rests on substantial bodies of knowledge concerning the personality basis of adaptive–innovative cognitive style (Goldsmith 1989; Gryskiewicz et al. 1987; Kirton 1989) and the relationship of cognitive style to consumer behavior (Foxall 1988; Foxall and Goldsmith 1988; Pinson 1978; Pinson et al. 1988).

New product perceptions and behavior

An important component of an individual's framework for decision making is his or her category width: the extent to which he or she perceives an innovation to differ from the norm established by existing products or practices. This aspect of the consumer's cognitive framework partly determines the degree of risk he or she perceives in buying and using an innovation. Broad categorizers are more willing than narrow categorizers to embrace innovations that diverge from the norm (Donnelly and Etzel 1973; Venkatesan 1973). Broad categorizers are also likely to adopt genuine innovations (radical or discontinuous), even at the risk of being dissatisfied, while narrow categorizers prefer artificially new items, minimizing the possibility of a mistake. Adaptors are likely to be narrow categorizers, seeking to avoid mistakes even if this means their missing some positive opportunities (Foxall 1988). Their need for structure (Gryskiewicz 1982) and reluctance to change (Goldsmith 1989) leads them to take a more cautious view.

- Adaptors tend, in making decisions, to be conservative, confining their search for information within the frame of reference dictated by their direct personal experience.
- Adaptors' narrow category width means that they are more likely to be attracted to relatively continuous new products (artificial innovations) than genuine (discontinuous) ones.

This may help explain why more involved Adaptors bought the highest numbers of food brands/products, items which at their most radically new tend to be fairly continuous. Adaptors are also more intolerant of change and disruption, unwilling to accept ambiguity, more dogmatic and inflexible than Innovators (Kirton 1976, 1989; Goldsmith 1984, 1989; Gryskiewicz 1982). So, unless they are highly involved in the product field,

- Adaptors will be less amenable to new product trial.
- Adaptors' resulting lack of experience of new products further reinforces their unwillingness to explore.

Innovators, by contrast, are likely to be broad categorizers, risking errors and costs to take advantage of potential positive chances.

- Innovators are likely to try new products, accepting the risk of buying an unsatisfactory item.
- They use more environmental stimuli, taking in more of the data that impinge on them and using them more actively to find a solution.
- Their more abstract thinking leads them to ask more questions, search widely for information, and investigate more relationships.
- Seeing products as more alike than Adaptors, Innovators are less brand loyal.

Persuasive marketing communications

Considerations of category width, boredom with the familiar, and a capacity to work with several paradigms rather than within one framework implies that Innovators would respond more positively than Adaptors to two-sided appeals. It is possible that Innovators actually appreciate messages that embody pro and con arguments and that they become easily bored with repeated messages that are consistent with their current beliefs. Hence:

- Adaptors are more likely than Innovators to respond favorably to one-sided messages, consistent with their current attitudes and habits.
- They are more likely than Innovators to need credible sources of information to handle discrepant advertising messages and to change their attitudes and behavior.
- Innovators, being more flexible, can accommodate more discrepant information.
- Innovators can cope with cognitive dissonance and indeed may be motivated by it.
- They are, therefore, more likely than Adaptors, who have strong needs for clarity, to remember incomplete messages.
- Innovators' tolerance of ambiguity might render them more susceptible to postmodern advertising.

Since Adaptors are more cautious and analytical in their judgments, more reflective and tentative in their decision making, they are open to rational, apparently objective appeals based on reasoned arguments. Hence:

- Adaptors will be more amenable to reasoned argumentative advertising, even if it leads to allegedly incontrovertible conclusions (that would appear dogmatic and authoritarian to Innovators).
- The more impulsive Innovator is likely to be more open to personalized, affective advertising.

SUMMARY

Personality refers either to an extensive range of separate behavioral traits (honesty, perseverance and hostility, for instance) or to overall types of character and response (extrovert and introvert). In spite of some high hopes and prima facie evidence that aspects of consumers' purchase behavior might be closely related to their personality traits, empirical verification of this association is still lacking. A large number of weak relationships have been discovered but it remains to be seen whether this approach will ever enable the majority of markets to be segmented using a pure personality approach. Type theories and the concepts of self-image and ideal self-image throw more light on the psychological dimension of consumers' choices but there is considerable need for further research before marketing practice benefits from these concepts.

In the meanwhile, marketing and advertising managers will continue to make use of psychographic data to guide their decisions in segmenting markets, profiling market segments, and developing advertising and other promotional strategies. There is growing evidence that they can do so, within limits, with confidence. Early studies of personality and consumer behavior were characterized by an atheoretical clinical orientation dominated by subjectivity and eccentricity in interpretation. Later trait-based studies were often naive in their assumption that so broad a measure of an individual as personality would be consistently related to so narrow a behavioral criterion as brand or even product choice. In more recent years, several researchers have attempted to revive the analysis of consumer choice in terms of personality variables by correcting mistakes of the past and by using new theories of personality. Theory-grounded typologies of the higher-order factors which organize series of traits into dominant personality or cognitive styles appear more successful in making sense of consumer decision making than the simple, single-trait studies pursued in the 1960s. Judicious use of personality theory and measures is also capable of showing why earlier research failed to find managerially useful associations, e.g., in the search for the innovative consumer. In contrast to many investigations of putative personality/consumer behavior links, research into the cognitive/personality traits of consumer innovators have produced a consistent body of knowledge.[1]

NOTE

1 Using the KAI to measure differences in adaption–innovation promises to open a new avenue for the study of product adoption by consumer innovators. This perspective, it must be emphasized, views innovativeness as a global personality trait. An alternative approach has been suggested by Goldsmith and Hofacker (1991), who have developed a valid and reliable self-report scale to measure domain-specific innovativeness, a research tool long lacking in consumer and marketing research. Their study shows that the six-item scale is effective in identifying consumer innovators within a specified market, such as for clothing, music recordings, or personal care products. Using this scale in a survey, researchers can now measure domain-specific innovativeness as a characteristic of consumers in much the same way they can measure attitudes or lifestyle.

Chapter 7

Motivation and lifestyle

SHOPPING MOTIVES

As we have seen, much consumer research is devoted to studying *how* consumers behave: the processes of information acquisition and decision making, trial and repeat buying, and the personal factors influencing these processes. We turn now to the question of *why* consumers act as they do: the fundamental motives underlying consumer behavior. Several aspects of consumer information processing are influenced by consumers' needs and goals, in short by their motives (Bettman 1979: 57). Motives are also important to marketing managers. Obviously, the better that marketers understand the needs and wants consumers are seeking to satisfy through purchasing behavior, the better able they will be to meet these needs and wants.

The motives or reasons for shopping are relatively easy to discern. Tauber (1972) proposed that shoppers had a number of personal motivations – the need to play the role of shopper, the need for diversion, the need for self-gratification, the need to acquaint themselves with novel trends, the need for physical activity, and the need for sensory stimulation. They also have social needs: for social experience beyond the home, to communicate with similar individuals, for peer group attraction for status and authority, and for the pleasure provided by bargaining. Recently, the *Wall Street Journal* published an article (Figure 7.1) which confirms the multiplicity of motives which underpin shopping activity.

Fascinating as they are, these accounts of shopping motives at best reveal a limited aspect of the factors responsible for consumers' pre-purchase and purchase behaviors within the retail environment. Discerning the underlying motives that guide and shape consumer behavior in all its aspects is a more complicated affair. Products and services are seldom

BIG SPENDER
AS A FAVORED PASTIME, SHOPPING RANKS HIGH WITH MOST AMERICANS
They Browse, Buy to Dispel Boredom, Find Fantasy; Economists Are Amazed
Staggering Amounts of Debt

By Betsy Morris
Staff Reporter of the *Wall St. Journal*

ATLANTA – Lenox Square mall has been open less than three hours, and members of the David Jackson family have already spent a small fortune and amassed nine shopping bags among them.

Their haul includes fall shoes in suede and snakeskin, an emerald and magenta outfit, a soft black leather purse marked down to $90 from twice that much and some on-sale Easter bunnies for the kids.

None of which the Nashville, Tenn., family really needs, especially after the vacation shopping the Jacksons did on earlier summer trips to Memphis and to Orlando, Fla. 'I get total fulfillment from it,' says Norma Jackson, a Nashville schoolteacher, in trying to explain the family's binge. Adds Mr Jackson, an assistant school principal: 'Shopping is like a drug. It's a temporary high.'

The Jacksons may sound a bit compulsive. But every day, an estimated 15,767 energetic, indefatigable shoppers descend – sometimes by the busload – on Lenox Square, one of Atlanta's hottest shopping spots. And many of them are like the Jacksons: They don't really need what they are shopping for. Often they don't even know what they're after. Some buy things they never wear or rarely use; many buy and then return what they bought, then buy again and return that.

Better than TV

Shoppers' behavior has been a major driving force for the US economy and has made shopping, arguably, the favorite American pastime next to television-watching. Adults (both women and men) average about six hours weekly on shopping for everything. It is impossible to tell what is drudgery and what is pleasure; but according to a study by John Robinson, a sociology professor at the University of Maryland, the time spent shopping is way more than the hour adults spend gardening or reading books, the 10 minutes or less they spend on golf or the 40 minutes spent playing with children.

For some time now, this shopping boom has flown in the face of demographic and economic logic. The archetypal shopper – the female – has gone to work and presumably has more important things to do. Everybody, it seems, is strapped for time. And catalog and home-shopping services offer the convenience that consumers say they so badly want.

Shocking Statistics

Beyond that, who can afford it? While a boon for the economy, this spending spree has helped propel consumer debt to staggering levels and pushed the savings rate to just as shocking lows. In the last month, economists have been saying yet again that they believe consumers are tightening their belts. But earlier this week, the US Commerce Department reported that consumer spending had surged in June, once again defying their predictions.

Economists, many of them amazed at consumers' freewheeling ways, wonder what has kept them going for so long and periodically predict they will exhaust themselves and collapse under the weight of their credit lines. But even if they do slow down, few expect that this year, anyway, they will do anything as dire as save their money or stay home Saturday afternoons.

Shopping has taken on a life of its own. It has attained a pop-culture status that has spawned such bumper stickers as: 'I shop, therefore I am' and 'Born to Shop'. 'It is a lot more than simply providing for necessary things,' say Joseph Smith a psychologist and president of the New York consulting firm Oxtoby-Smith Inc. 'It is obviously fulfilling many needs – a lot of people don't like to confess that.'

Serious Questions

It is also raising some serious questions. 'People are going into debt in incredible levels without making rational decisions about how and why they are spending money,' say Robert Cialdini, a psychologist who teaches at Arizona State University. 'There is a kind of mindless character to it'. While truly compulsive shoppers are a small minority, the number of those who have problems controlling their impulse to buy 'is much, much larger,' says Thomas O'Guinn, advertising professor at the University of Illinois. He adds: 'I would term it a national problem.'

A number of recent studies present the following picture of American shoppers: About 70 percent of all adults visit a regional mall weekly. Most shop at neighborhood shopping centers twice a week. On the average, everybody grocery-shops at least twice a week.

The shopping epidemic can't be explained away just by spendthrift yuppies or the 'me generation'. It has infected everybody. More men are shopping – making up about one-third of the adult mall crowd this year in one survey – up to one quarter in 1981. And judging from the latest generations of shoppers, their numbers are likely to increase. 'Teenage males are becoming extremely fashion-conscious,' says Peter Zollo, executive vice president of Teenage Research Unlimited in Lake Forest, Ill., pointing out that 27 percent don designer jeans and 23 percent use hair-styling mousse.

For teens, both the time spent shopping (two hours a week for boys and four hours a week for girls) and the enjoyment of the pastime are increasing rapidly, Mr Zollo says. Even the elderly – with memories of the Depression fading – are getting looser with their spare change. Shopping has become a favorite of vacationers. And what time-starved working women want even more than extra hours in the day, one study says, is longer shopping hours.

Increasingly, purchases are linked less and less closely to need. 'We're not talking ironing boards that have worn out,' says Isaac Lagnado, the director of research for Associated Merchandising Corp, a merchandising-consulting firm. 'You're talking replacement just for the sake of change. People are buying new sheets not because the old ones wore out but because they're stimulated by a new set of plaid ones.' Long true of apparel, the trend is rapidly spreading to other areas. Six years ago, all but one-quarter to one-third of all houseware purchases were to replace items that had worn out. Today, less than half are replacements.

A tremendous amount of buying is done on impulse. About 53 percent of groceries and 47 percent of hardware-store purchases are spur of the moment, studies say. When Stillerman Jones & Co., a marketing-research firm, asked 34,300 mall shoppers across the country the primary reason for their visit, only 25 percent had come in pursuit of a specific item.

So why, then, do so many people spend so much time shopping? The reasons are many, varied and complex. According to shoppers and those who observe them, shopping can be all things to all people. It can alleviate loneliness and dispel boredom; it can be a sport and can be imbued with the thrill of the hunt; it can provide escape, fulfill fantasies, relieve depression. A closer look at some of these categories follows.

Alleviating Loneliness: For a lot of people, 'shopping appears to be a substitute for a relationship', says Jack Lesser, a marketing professor at Miami University in Ohio, who has found the most avid shoppers are the single, the widowed and the divorced. Kathryn Roth, an art professor swinging through Lenox Square on a recent lunch hour, says she is most prone to shop during evenings 'when I don't have anything to do and don't have anybody to talk to, I go to the mall and look at the people.' And, she says with a sigh, 'I can spend it, and I don't have to tell anybody.'

Dispelling Boredom: Shopping is tailor-made for a video generation that thrives on bright colors and visual distractions. 'I shop when I'm feeling bored or when I feel like I need something new,' says Brad Vroon, a 19-year-old Emory University student. 'If you look in my closet, you'll say I don't need anything. But I get sick of things after a couple of months.' Often he buys things and returns them.

Shopping as a Sport: At Finale on Five, the discount paradise of Rich's downtown department store, the shoppers who cull through tangles of 90 percent-off belts and racks of half-price evening dresses are committed to beating the system. 'To me, shopping is like playing baseball,' says Debra Weston who has snatched up so many prospective purchases that she is sitting cross-legged on the floor, trying to sort them out. Today's homer: 14 pairs of designer socks for $13, marked down from $50. 'I spend a lot of time eyeballing, and I love to find something cheaper at another store,' she says.

At some point, though, one wonders who is beating whom. Last year, Carol Duhart went broke bargain-shopping at Finale on Five. She paid off her debt and is back. 'This place is like a magnet,' says the US government employee. 'It has a weird effect on me.'

Spoils of the Hunt: Mr Smith, the consultant, believes shopping may be the modern manifestation of more primitive roles. He explains: 'Man, the provider, the big daddy, may not be able to bring home a mastodon, but he can sure bring home a VCR or a computer.'

Shopping as an Escape: Holly Tappen, like many working women at times, considers shopping a pleasant, mind-numbing narcotic. 'It's a little vacation from your daily tasks,' says the travel consultant. 'It is absolutely mindless behavior.'

I'm hearing (working) women more and more say, 'I can go into this home-decorating store and it's therapy. I can go into a trance".' says Bill Huckabee, the president of C. W. Rees & Associates Inc., a Columbus, Ohio, retail consulting firm.

Fantasy Fulfillment: The malls are brimming with the fantastic, but perhaps the most dramatic example is Banana Republic, a unit of Gap Inc. It beckons across Lenox Square like Bali Ha'i with a roof made of palm fronds, door handles made out of ivory (presumably) tusks and catalog piles on crates marked 'Chad' and 'the Congo' that are filled with pictures of anywhere but here. It lures even the unlikeliest of passers-by. Gail Thiessen, an art professor, prides herself on being a practical shopper and a real stickler for necessities and bargains. But even she admits a weakness for Banana Republic. 'I think it appeals to the adventuresome soul in everybody,' she says.

Although Brad Clevenger visits Atlanta's Perimeter Mall twice weekly, he only actually buys something about once a month. The rest of the time, he fantasizes. 'I usually come to get something to eat,' says the 18-year-old data processor, 'and then I look for what I can get – what I'd like to have in the future, what I can look forward to. It gives me a goal, something to save my money for.'

Relieving Depression: 'Just the thought of going shopping makes me feel better,' says Mrs Jackson, the Nashville teacher. 'I think about the clothes, the colors. It may not feel better in the long run, but it takes my mind off my problems.'

At Rich's, Linda Smith searches for flaws in a green cocktail dress she is holding up to the light. 'Shopping makes me feel better when I'm depressed and not feeling too good,' says the finance-company manager. 'It's a state of mind, I guess. I don't know why it makes me feel better.'

Shopping is no longer isolated to clearly defined districts. Lenox Square, with its 200–odd stores and shops, could be an entire city all by itself. Instead, it is merely one of 347 shopping centers in the Atlanta area. In one Kroger supermarket, a budget-minded shopper must resist not only gourmet cheeses and pasta but also perfume, television sets and sushi. A local Lechmere store offers not one, not 10, but 32 different personal stereos with headphones, 24 different hair dryers and 16 irons.

'The mass media clearly have done a lot to whip up this shopping orgy,' says Mr O'Guinn, the advertising professor, noting that many TV shows portray a life of opulence. 'Even if you don't believe life is really like that, you sort of operate as if it were.' Mr O'Guinn says, 'I buy a Mercedes not because it is a fine piece of German engineering, but because I value it as a symbol of my success.'

Pavlovian Response

Consumers, though craftier bargain-hunters than they used to be, are nonetheless susceptible to spending if the right buttons are pushed. One recent study indicates, for instance, that they have developed an almost Pavlovian response to credit cards. When asked how much they would pay for an item like a toaster, the participants were consistently bigger spenders when a credit card was pictured nearby (as it is on many cash registers). They would spend $67.33 for the toaster, for instance, three times as much as when credit cards weren't in sight. They were also bigger tippers and more generous charity donors when they saw pictures of credit cards, says Richard A. Feinberg, the Purdue University consumer-sciences and retailing professor who conducted the study.

Mr O'Guinn worries that consumers are caught in a 'hedonic trap' – an ever-spiralling and hopeless search for happiness through the acquisition of things.

Mr Cialdini, the psychologist, believes that consumers are resorting increasingly to what he calls 'click-whir' behavior. Life has become so complex that consumers can't possibly analyze the merits of all of their decisions, he says. So they are more susceptible to certain cues and symbols like 'discount' or 'last day of sale' and take less time to analyze fundamental questions like need or cost. 'When we react to symbols instead of to information, then what we do doesn't make sense anymore,' he says.

Some shoppers doubt their own behavior. 'I really think that the time can be better spent in conversation, writing, painting, reading,' says Ms Tappen, the travel consultant. Says Mr Vroon, the Emory student: 'I don't think all this materialism is so good. It's probably good for the economy, but not real good for people's minds.'

Figure 7.1 'Big Spender' article, *Wall Street Journal*, August 4, 1987
Source: *The Wall Street Journal*, August 4 1987. Reproduced with permission of the *Wall Street Journal* ©1987 Dow Jones & Company, Inc. All rights reserved worldwide.

purchased for their functional values alone; shopping is seldom simply an economic process; and consumption may be undertaken to impress others and raise the consumer's social status, as well as to realize the fruits of his or her labour. While, historically, individuals have frequently enjoyed browsing, purchasing and consuming in these extra-functional ways, the affluent consumers of industrial and post-industrial societies usually seek to acquire the social and psychological values and meanings that derive from the consumption of economic goods. Cars are chosen not just because they make efficient transportation possible but also for the social status or prestige they confer on their owners. A glance at what we wear shows that clothes are not desired simply to hide our nakedness or just for their warmth and protection; style, color and quality reflect the wearer's status, group affiliations, self-image and attitudes, and can be an accurate guide to age, lifestyle and personality (Kaiser 1990). Much the same can be said of the food we eat, the cultural recreations we choose, the gifts we give, the TV programs we watch (Ritson *et al.* 1986).

THE MEANING OF MOTIVATION

Although consumer motives may seem simple and easy to understand, problems often arise in the analysis of motivation because of the interrelationships between conditioning variables. Motives are usually inferred from past behavior, but the job of the applied behavioral scientist calls for the prediction of future behavior from a current set of conditions. Since any single human action is capable of stemming from many motives, it becomes necessary to decide which factors have the most overall significance. Behavior which seems in one context to be motivated by pure altruism may, if all the facts are known,

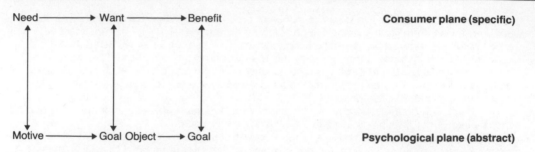

Figure 7.2 Elements in the motivating situation

be caused by avarice. Since the behavioral scientist is seldom aware of 'all the facts', perhaps because questionnaire respondents do not tell the truth, perhaps because they do not know it to tell, accounts of consumer motivation are almost certainly always incomplete. Sometimes this difficulty is expressed in terms that suggest consumer behavior is only weakly motivated compared with other facets of human action. There is, however, no reason to believe that buying is in reality less strongly motivated than any other behavior – only that the means of identifying motives are not yet as sophisticated as one would like.

The study of motivation in consumer research seems to revolve about two fundamental problems. The first is understanding the interrelationships between motives and specific behavior. The second is to develop a typology or list of consumer motives comprehensive enough to capture the wide variety of motivating forces that stimulate and shape behavior.

Motivated behavior is activity that is directed toward the attainment of a goal or an objective (Markin 1977). Two aspects of motivating situations are of particular importance for consumer research. First, there must be a goal or objective that acts as an incentive and which is usually located outside the individual. Second, there is a state or condition within the motivated person that stimulates action, perhaps a social need (like popularity) or a physiological drive (such as thirst). A commonplace example which illustrates the connection between these two elements in motivation is the hungry man who experiences the hunger drive and whose behavior is subsequently channeled toward attaining the goal or incentive of food (see Figure 7.2). The attainment of goals is frequently achieved by acquiring 'goal-objects' which themselves embody, symbolize, or otherwise represent goal attainment. Needs and motives are often treated in the marketing literature as interchangeable terms, but a person is motivated only when his behavior is directed toward the satisfaction or elimination of his needs.

A second useful distinction to be made is the often interchangeable use of the terms 'needs' and 'wants'. In our framework, needs are identified as the felt manifestation of physiological, personal or social motives, and arise from the discrepancy between actual and desired states of being. Needs are the way in which we describe basic activated states in consumers. Wants refer to specific manifestations of needs and may be thought of as the embodiment and expression of abstract motives. Just as specific 'goal-objects' link interior motives to exterior goals, an admittedly tautological dyad, wants connect consumer needs with the specific benefits consumers are seeking via consumption (Hanna 1980). Finally, benefits are whatever customers derive from products; they represent the reasons they want them. Consumers do not want products for themselves; they want the benefits products provide. The hungry consumer is motivated to seek food when certain physiological mechanisms are activated. Thus he needs food, but he may want a hamburger, a pizza, or Chicken à-la-King (specific goal-objects) in different contexts or at different times to satisfy his need. The differing taste and olfactory sensations of these foods are the unique benefits they supply.

For the marketer it is important to realize that needs are few in number and very general in nature, but wants are limitless, contingent and specific. Moreover, while consumer needs may be legitimate from an observer's point of view (after all, people need food), their wants may not meet with our approval (the observer may not agree that their choices to meet these needs are appropriate). This relatively straightforward scheme is also complicated by the fact that multiple needs are often met by the same behavior and that multiple behaviors may be needed to satisfy a single need.

From the marketer's point of view, two features of the motivating situation summarized in Figure 7.2 must be stressed.

- First, marketers need to understand accurately the link between needs and wants for specific product markets. What consumers *say* they want may be at variance with their true underlying needs, or many needs may be expressed by a single want.
- Second, it is important that the marketer be sure to offer a brand of goods or services (goal-objects) that truly provides the benefits that consumers seek and that consumers accurately view the brand in this light.

It should be pointed out that for the consumer researcher, knowledge of consumer motivation comes from two admittedly imperfect sources. Either consumers must reveal accurately and honestly to the researcher the nature of their motivated state (that is, they must tell us why they behave as they do) or their motives must be inferred from observing their behavior (or self-reports of their behavior). In the first instance, consumers may not be willing or able to reveal their true motives. In the second, observation and self-reports contain their own forms of inaccuracy. This measurement activity is complicated further by the fact that there is no universally agreed upon classification or list of human motives. In fact, the variety of perspectives on the nature and number of human motives often leaves the researcher (not to mention the manager) frustrated. The next section presents several theories of motivation.

MASLOW'S HIERARCHY OF NEEDS

The problem facing both the consumer researcher and the marketing manager is that there exists no universally agreed description of human motivation. Several attempts have been made to describe comprehensively the forces that give strength and direction to human behavior, and there is a great deal of overlap across these typologies, reflecting general agreement as to the status of some human motives. The following sections, therefore, will simply describe some of these schemes to give an idea of how some motivation theorists picture the terrain of human motivation.

One of the most widely cited motivational theories is that put forward by Abraham Maslow (1943), who presents the idea that there is a hierarchy of needs in man (Table 7.1)

Table 7.1 Maslow's hierarchy of needs and consumer motivation

Maslow's needs	
Self Actualization	Personal growth – The need to consume products so as to be or become one's own unique self (self-improvement classes)
	Influence over others – The need to feel one's impact on others' consumption decisions (may underlie the behavior of opinion leaders or innovators)
Self-esteem	Recognition from others – The need to consume products so as to be acknowledged by others as having gained a high status in one's community (designer clothes)
Belongingness	Acceptance by others – The need to consume products so as to be associated with a significant other or a special material comfort – The need to consume a large and/or luxurious supply of material possessions (luxury goods, new products)
Safety needs	Material security – The need to consume an adequate supply of material possessions (risk-reducing buyer behavior)
Physiological needs	Physical safety – The need to consume products so as to avoid harm or danger in their use, and to preserve clean air and water in the environment (seat belts, ecologically sound products)

Source: Hanna, G. (1980) 'A typology of consumer needs', in J. N. Sheth (ed.) *Research in Marketing*, 3, Greenwich, CT: JAI Press. Reproduced by permission of JAI Press Inc.

ranging from the lower-order physiological drives (thirst, etc.), through safety needs (e.g., shelter) and affective needs (for love), to the higher-order needs for self-esteem and self-actualization (in essence, being the best of what you are).

The satisfaction of a lower-order need triggers the next level of needs into operation, demanding new patterns of behavior on the part of the individual. Naturally the basic needs must be met first of all – to put it crudely, no one can be expected to be concerned about his esteem while he is hungry. But once the biogenic needs have been satisfied, the individual turns his attention to the fulfillment of more advanced sociogenic requirements. The final stage in the motivational hierarchy is the need for what Maslow calls 'self-actualization'. While he does not define this term with any real degree of precision, it appears to represent the attainment of what other psychologists call self-realization: the process in which the individual has the opportunity to invest all his talents and abilities in activities that he finds meaningful, activities that help him develop his personality, e.g., through leisure activities and creative pastimes, or work.

There are many criticisms of Maslow's theory. At one level, critics point to the behavior of a hungry mother who deprives herself of food in order to feed her needy children – effectively letting her affective needs operate prior to the satisfaction of her own physiological needs. More importantly for marketing, it is worth noting that while firms provide the means of satisfying the biogenic and esteem/affective needs, the quest for self-actualization, if it is a reality at all, would doubtless take the individual into realms where the marketing system is not necessarily able to assist.

Another criticism of Maslow's paradigm is that it is too abstract for use by marketers or consumer researchers, who need a description of human motives more closely oriented to consumer behavior. One attempt to fill in this gap is provided by Hanna's typology of consumer needs, which closely parallels Maslow's yet is more focused on the needs consumers seek to satisfy through purchasing behavior (see Table 7.1).

Despite the criticisms, Maslow's theory is useful in that it makes a distinction between what may be termed physical/inherited needs and learned needs. The latter are not innate but acquired by the individual through social interaction. While marketing effort is highly relevant to the distribution of products like food which satisfy basic needs, the existence of social motives presents an additional dimension to the marketing manager for all products and services. Firms may find it easier to attract consumers' discretionary income by making the most of non-functional product attributes if advertising and other promotional tools can be geared to the stimulation of sociopsychological wants as well as purely physiological needs. This is not new, of course – the contemporary pattern of marketing would not exist had this not been long understood (Levitt 1986). But if this classification of needs tells us little that is novel, it is a reminder of what the marketing manager must try to achieve; also it provides some confirmation of the basic tenets of modern marketing thought.

THE FREUDIAN INTERPRETATION OF MOTIVATION

Conscious and unconscious dimensions of mind

That Freud distinguished conscious and unconscious sources of motivation – 'two states in the same country' – is well known. In fact, his system was always more complicated than this, differentiating several kinds of non-conscious influences on overt behavior, and their relationships with the conscious mind. (For some recent evaluations of Freud's life and thought, cf. Gay 1988; Gellner 1985; Storr 1989; Schellenberg 1978; Stevenson 1974.) The *conscious* mind is the arena in which current thinking and awareness occur. The *preconscious* contains information, ideas, reminiscences that are not currently part of a person's consciousness but of which he or she is capable of becoming aware. A friend's telephone number, your date of birth, and the brand of contraceptives one may use are all amenable to recall even if they are not currently in one's conscious mind. Some of this information may be suppressed, i.e., while it is not currently in awareness, it is available. The *unconscious*, by comparison, contains repressed information, a source of motives not open to recall without many hundreds of hours of psychoanalysis, or 'free association', in which the individual talks spontaneously about his or her earlier life and experiences, eventually (in a successful analysis) uncovering this repressed material. Repressed ideas may be forgotten but they remain active and can be the origin of dreams, neuroses and unhappiness.

Freud believed that the personality consisted of the interaction between three forces: the *id*, demanding gratification of all wishes and desires; the *ego*, the controlling and directing force seeking to moderate the operation of the id; and the *superego*, the moral and judicial part of personality which seeks to align behavior with societal rules. His detailed treatment of unconsciousness distinguishes these levels of personality as three wellsprings of motivation.

The id

The id is the oldest part of the mind, from which the other elements are derived. Emotional and illogical, the id functions on the Pleasure Principle by which it seeks to avoid or minimize pain and to maximize immediate gratification. As the repository of an individual's underlying lusts and antisocial desires, the id comprises the instincts including sex and aggression, that, unchecked, would inspire wanton and utterly self-serving behavior.

The ego

Although newborn humans are motivated primarily by impulses originating in the id, their increasing contact with the objective world, which responds to them on its terms rather than according to their demands, imposes a more rigorous discipline on behavior. Systematic relationships with this world of reality are inculcated as the individual recognizes that the best way to receive food or attention is through performing acceptable actions, even if this means that gratification is sometimes delayed. The resulting Reality Principle is the guiding light of the ego, encouraging realistic and reasonable thoughts and actions. The ego exercises, in the normal personality, as overall controlling and balancing function, determining according to conditions and circumstances whether the basic instinctual motives should be expressed or contained. Hence the urges of the id are constrained and channeled into socially acceptable patterns of behavior.

The superego

The third component of the Freudian personality, the superego, is a sort of socially defined conscience. As such, it is constantly in conflict with the id, acting through the ego which it threatens with punishments like guilt if the id is allowed to get out of hand. Equally, the superego can reward the ego that acts in accordance with its moral precepts, e.g., by resisting temptation, heightening self-esteem for instance in the obedient rational mind. The superego strives for perfection. If its influence is too strong, it engenders timidity, withdrawal. The underdeveloped superego, conversely, leads to a personality and style of behavior dominated by a search for self-gratification. The ego is called upon to provide balance between id and superego, and thereby to promote a normal, healthy personality. Figure 7.3 summarizes the relationship of id, ego and superego to conscious and unconscious minds. It is from this tripartite structure of hypothetical influences on actual behavior that some marketing authors have deduced basic human motives believed to impinge upon purchase and consumption (e.g., Holbrook 1988). Before looking more deeply at the insights Freudian psychology may provide into consumer behavior, it is useful to delve further into the system's explanation of personality development and the emergence of adult motivations.

Stages of psychosexual development

Freud presented a deterministic account of human behavior in which physiologically based instincts were held accountable for internal drives such as hunger, thirst and sex which compel action (Hillner 1984). Behavior is an attempt to reduce these drives among which the sex drive or libido is accorded a special emphasis. The primary influence of the id, and the emergence of ego and superego, are described by Freud by means of a succession of five fixed stages of personal development, each of which is defined by the object that provides libidinal satisfaction. The attainment of a stable adult personality requires a

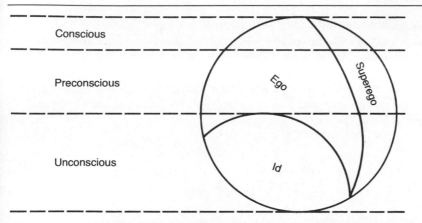

Figure 7.3 Relationship of id, ego and superego to conscious and unconscious phases of mind
Source: Nye, D. (1981) *Three Psychologies: Perspectives from Freud, Skinner, and Rogers*, Monterey, CA:
Brooks/Cole, 18. Copyright © 1993, 1986, 1981, 1975 by Wadsworth, Inc.
Reproduced by permission of Brooks/Cole Publishing Company, Pacific Grove, California 93950.

successful progression through these stages: the oral, the anal, the phallic, latency, and the genital. Fixation at or regression toward one of these stages leads to neurosis denoted by a particular type of personality.

The oral stage

During the oral stage, which covers the first two years of life, the id reigns unopposed; libidinal satisfaction is demanded and obtained through the mouth – by eating, drinking, sucking and so on. These gratifications, provided usually by the baby's mother, the current object of libidinal satisfaction, are sought also by the adult who has fixated at this stage of development. The adult oral personality is disproportionately concerned with activities such as eating and drinking, kissing and smoking. The individual for whom oral gratification has been obtained all too easily tends to assume that life is easy and becomes spoilt and gullible; he or she for whom it has been difficult to obtain oral gratification may become pessimistic about life, assuming it to be hard and unyielding.

The anal stage

Through the anal stage, which extends over the third and fourth years of life, libidinous satisfaction derives from the toileting activities, retention as well as elimination. The adult anal character is obsessed with orderliness, cleanliness and parsimony.

The phallic stage

Beginning at the third or fourth year and extending to the fifth, the phallic stage is marked in boys by Oedipal conflict (i.e., competition for the mother's attention to the point of entertaining murderous intentions toward the father) and in girls by a corresponding

Electra complex (in which the father's exclusive attention is sought). Successful resolution of these complexes encourages identification with the same-sex parent but the stage is characterized by the emergence of the superego in response to the individual's recognition of the seriousness and severity of his or her willingness to kill for gain. Adults who are disproportionately influenced by events at this stage display – according to Freud – behaviors characteristic of the extreme sexual prototype for their gender: the man is excessively masculine, the woman excessively feminine.

Latency

Latency is a culturally rather than biologically defined stage, and persists from the age of 5 to the onset of puberty. The boy or girl identifies with peers of the same sex and adopts a gender-role identity marked by the social characteristics of the ideal sexual prototype. Preferring the company of their own sex, individuals may express negative attitudes toward the opposite sex and develop intellectually and socially in isolation from or in deliberate contrast to its attitudes and behavior.

The genital stage

Adults who fail to progress beyond this stage are unlikely to develop a libidinous interest in the opposite sex. However, for those who do, the genital phase, extending from puberty onwards, is characterized by the acceptance of a member of the opposite sex as the object of the libido. But frustrated sexual desire is likely to lead to 'perversions' or to sublimation, in which sexual energy is displaced into creative, scientific, artistic or literary endeavors.

SOME MARKETING INSIGHTS

Not all psychologists are sympathetic toward Freud; one refers to this account of the human mind as the theory that 'man is essentially a battlefield; he is a dark cellar in which a maiden aunt and a sex-crazed monkey are locked in mortal combat, the affair being refereed by a rather nervous bank-clerk'! (Bannister 1966: 363). The original, clinical psychoanalysis provided a slender basis for marketing thought. Yet, the first major personality theory to influence marketing practice was Freud's. The key feature of his theories that influenced marketing was the role of unconscious wishes and desires in shaping behavior. Much of human behavior is seen as the result of unconscious efforts to control inner drives for sex, hunger and aggression. In the 1950s this set of doctrines was introduced to marketing and advertising under the name of Motivation Research, which is described in more detail below. Led by the psychoanalyst, Ernest Dichter, this school stressed the psychological and symbolic aspects of consumption. Products and brands were interpreted in appropriate symbolic terms and related to unconscious desires of consumers.

Nevertheless, it is difficult to evaluate objectively the contribution of Sigmund Freud's theories and techniques to our understanding of consumer behavior because of the bias shown by so many writers in this area. Some appear to have seen in it the key to all consumer behavior while others take pains to avoid it. But psychoanalysis has moved on in the last fifty or so years to emphasize quite distinct aspects of psychodynamic functioning and behavior. It is also making a strong reemergence in consumer research (e.g., Holbrook 1988; Albanese 1990). However, let us consider briefly the impact of the more traditional psychoanalysis on our understanding of the consumer.

Sexual symbolism

Freudian ideas may influence advertising in particular, suggesting id-directed themes of fantasy, wish fulfillment, and escape from reality. For example, the successful 'I dreamt . . .' campaign of Maidenform Bra, or ads that entice the reader to escape from his/her world and enter a world of fantasy and daydreams, represent Freudian appeals. Appeals to traditions, societal norms and obligations may be especially persuasive to the superego (Glazer 1970).

Indeed, it seems probable that much of the sexual symbolism employed in advertising is derived, consciously or unconsciously, from Freud's emphasis on the human sex drive as a clue to understanding social and individual behavior. However, no acceptable means of measuring the effects of such advertisements on buying has been published. It has been demonstrated, though, that when sex is not relevant to the product in question, its effect on sales cannot be predicted: consumers are quite capable of remembering the sexual allusions rather than the brand (Alexander and Judd 1978). As a result, its use in advertisements – notably, for jeans, perfume, cars – has been justified on the basis of its assumed ability to capture the audience's attention: 'many more consumers enjoy the advertisements than buy the product'. However, it appears from research that when sex is used simply as a means of attracting attention to the ad, brand recall is lower than when it is used to exhibit the functional applications of a product, or to convey fantasy images, or when used symbolically (Yovovich 1983; see also Schiffman and Kanuk 1987: 356). This finding is consistent with Freudian expectations.

Attitudes toward money

There is evidence that attitudes and behaviors toward money stem from the anal stage of development. At this point, the child can for the first time defy its parents by refusing to become toilet-trained. The habit of retention may come to symbolize control over the environment and, especially, over people. In later life, this is manifested in an unwillingness to share (toys, money, time) and, later still, in a preoccupation with saving, parsimony, obstinacy and punctuality (Furnham and Lewis 1986: 62). Nevertheless, convincing evidence of a connection between an 'anal personality', saving and concern with money is lacking (Lea *et al.* 1987: 228).

Excessive gambling may also be interpreted in terms that derive from the theory, as a continuation of the guilt felt on recognizing one's murderous intentions toward the same-sex parent, which is thereafter channeled into a lifelong determination to punish oneself. Rejecting the Reality Principle – since no one can win in the long run – the compulsive gambler neurotically seeks to remove his Oedipus guilt by expressing a desire to lose (Lea *et al.* 1987: 282).

Mass communication

Psychoanalysis probably would have met little interest from marketing writers had it not been for Harold Lasswell's Theory of the Triple Appeal (Lasswell 1948). This states the idea that to be successful any piece of propaganda must appeal to all three elements of the mind; if it appeals to just the id, for instance, its effects will be immediately negated by the superego. This is advanced as a reason why advertising should appeal not only to pleasurable drives but also to behavior that is socially acceptable. A Mars a day helps you work as well as rest and play.

Lasswell's theory has also been used to explain why advertisements which depict the romantic/sexual consequences of the use of products like shampoo or bath soap tend to end with the participants getting married. This may well have appeared so in the 1950s, but changing social mores have surely rendered obsolete this attempt to drag Freud's three elements of human personality into marketing at all costs. Many current advertisements contain sexual imagery and suggestions that are little more than unveiled appeals to the id.

The application of Freudian ideas, however, has been limited, and much of their influence has waned. The concepts were too difficult to apply across the broad field of consumption. Disagreement could arise as to the precise symbolic meaning of a brand because there is no way to evaluate the reliability and validity of the interpretations. Only one consumer could be studied at a time, preventing application to mass-market research and strategy. Nevertheless, Freudian theory did bequeath to marketing research some useful techniques, depth interviews, focus group interviews and projective tests, which are still widely used and make up an important part of the marketing research armamentarium. Despite the applications noted above, however, the most lasting contribution of Freudian thought to marketing and consumer research lies in the area of motivation research, which deserves further discussion.

MOTIVATION RESEARCH

It is apparent from the foregoing that the identification of consumers' motives is a complex business. The difficulties involved in discovering directly the precise motivating factors that shape buying behavior led some marketing psychologists to devise oblique techniques for exposing hidden motives. These methods, known collectively as motivation research techniques, are concerned with a wide range of personality traits and attitudes as well as needs and drives (Gunter and Furnham 1992). The 1950s witnessed a revolutionary transformation in the way managers, especially in marketing and advertising, viewed their relationship with their customers, actual and potential. An increasing imbalance between the excess supply of goods and services over primary demand, coupled with rising levels of education, affluence and exposure to the mass media, transformed the competitive environment, making it far more intensive than before. How to cope with the constantly changing markets and intensive competitive pressures became a matter of crucial concern. The behavioral sciences seemed to many to present a path out of the confusion of this new business environment. As a result, the theories, techniques and attitudes of the scientist began to infiltrate the boardroom and advertising agency.

This interest in behavioral science and 'human engineering' is typified in a series of articles appearing in 1954 in *Business Week* (August 14, 21 and 28), which sought to introduce readers to some of the new concepts and the people who were struggling to bring the insights of social science to bear on a variety of business problems. Whilst not promising sure-fire, fail-safe solutions, the pioneers of this era were able to show that marginal efficiencies in sales and profits could be achieved by spending a portion of the budget along lines suggested by systematic marketing or advertising research directed to answer the fundamental questions about the why and how of consumer purchasing.

One idea in particular which seemed to capture the attention of marketers and advertisers was the concept that personality might play a role in product purchase. This was most likely because, of all the ideas available in the array of psychological theories, personality – the basic notion that individuals differ from one another in systematic and stable patterns of behavior and attitude – is both intuitively appealing and very familiar to most observers. Scientific concepts and measures of personality had been developed in order to account for consistencies in behavior across situations. Moreover, behavioral scientists employing such ideas confirmed what was anyway a widespread belief that patterns of behavior were due to internal motives, needs, beliefs and traits. The possibility that markets could be segmented psychographically, on the basis of groupings of consumers who shared determinative personality traits that could be related to purchase and consumption, loomed large.

In essence, motivation research is an attempt, stimulated by psychoanalytic theory such as Freud's, to uncover the consumer's suppressed and repressed motives (sometimes referred to as conscious and unconscious motives respectively). In suppression, the consumer remains aware of his motives but does not care to admit their existence to others for fear of ridicule, punishment or being ostracized. Information about the motivating factor remains in the conscious mind, however. Repression implies a more serious rejection of knowledge about a motive because the individual will not admit the motive's existence even to himself/herself. The types of technique employed in isolating suppressed and repressed motives are well known and include depth interviews, word association tests, and projective techniques. It is not intended to describe these methods in any detail here, as this is done in most textbooks of marketing research; however, several points are worthy of note. As long as depth interviews do not degenerate into games of verbal wit between interviewer and subjects, or into 'free association' sessions, they can yield useful information which the familiar questionnaire session is unlikely to uncover. Group depth interviews (called focus groups) all have the inherent problem of ensuring sample representativeness. Word association and sentence completion exercises can also provide usable, though obviously partial and impressionistic data.

Projective tests range from Rorschach ink-blot exercises to imaginary buying situations. They include picture story tests (thematic apperception), in which the subject is required to add a story to a series of pictures usually depicting a buying situation, and cartoon tests, in which a consumer is asked to suggest what cartoon characters are saying, or answer a question about the situation depicted. The interviewer may provide, for example, a picture of two women, one fat, the other thin; the respondent is asked to comment on their relative consumption of milk. Other forms of projective test require consumers to ascribe personalities to brands and to describe them as though they were living beings (What is Mr Daz like? What does he wear? What sort of car does he own?), or to write brand obituaries (How did the brand die? Old age or accident?).

An interesting example of a marketer's use of projective tests and the sort of thinking that lies behind them is provided by the McCann-Erickson ad agency (Alsop 1988: 21). Research showed that low-income Southern women strongly believed that a new brand of roach killer sold in little plastic trays was more effective than old-fashioned sprays. But they never bought it, preferring instead the traditional sprays. To try to understand this contradiction, perhaps impervious to direct questioning, researchers asked representative groups of these women to draw pictures of roaches and write stories about them. The results were very informative – all the roaches in the pictures were male, 'symbolizing men who the women said had abandoned them and left them feeling poor and powerless'. The women were said to be expressing their built-up hostility by spraying the roaches and watching them squirm and die!

Evaluating motivation research

During the 1940s, the clinical psychologist Ernest Dichter argued that marketers and advertisers were neglecting the psychological aspects of consumption which play a decisive role in product and brand preferences (Dichter 1949, 1964). The 1950s saw a headlong rush into the use of psychological concepts in the design of marketing and advertising strategies. Levy's classic 1959 *Harvard Business Review* article, 'Symbols for sale', provided a broad summary of the rapidly spreading ideas that consumers bought products for many reasons other than to obtain the functional benefits they represented. So popular was the notion that marketers could identify and manipulate the psychological precursors of consumer behavior that the belief that marketing made unscrupulous use of 'hidden persuaders' to deprive consumers of their freedom of choice in the marketplace gained widespread currency (Packard 1957). No wonder early accounts tended to present it as a 'set of miracle tools available to plumb the depths of the consumer's psyche in some mysterious way' (Engel *et al.* 1968: 69).

From today's perspective, both positions seem naive and unwarranted. Competitive action soon erodes any benefit conferred by the application of behavioral science and consumers have proved remarkably resistant to the efforts of marketers and advertisers to influence them. Far less real power accrued to the users of the psychoanalytically derived tools on which so-called motivation research was founded than many feared at the time; whilst they still play a part (e.g., Heylen, n.d.), their influence has long since peaked. By 1970, motivation research had passed its Messianic phase to become 'absorbed into the repertoire of more mature research practice' (Collins and Montgomery 1970: 11). Motivation research methods based vaguely on psychoanalytical theory and practice cannot achieve in a matter of minutes what trained psychiatrists often cannot do in years, that is, determine the hidden factors that motivate an individual. Testing its validity (i.e., whether it in fact identifies the constructs such as repressed motives that it claims to) is an exceedingly difficult task because of the inherent problems of experimental design and the use of control groups in research.

Motivation research has proved useful in uncovering some of the information that is suppressed by consumers in the normal business of life. Whatever one thinks about the apparatus of the mind proposed by Freud, most would accept that he identified important sources of behavioral motivation that have given rise not only to a comprehensive system of empirical research (Kline 1981; cf. Eysenck 1985) but a useful system of behavioral interpretation. Much of the criticism of the psychodynamically based study of consumer choice stems from the fact that these techniques were frequently misapplied in the marketing context. Different researchers could, moreover, disagree on the interpretation of a single consumer in-depth interview, projective test or whatever, and this led to a lack of reliable findings that could be consistently applied. However, the importance attached to consumers' underlying motives, values and lifestyle perspectives has been vindicated. The use of both direct observation and oblique methods of data gathering continues and has resulted in the classification of consumer segments based on consumers' overall lifestyle patterns.

CONSUMER LIFESTYLES

Although no definition of 'lifestyle' is commonly accepted by all marketers, the term refers in general to unique patterns of activities, interests and opinions that characterize differences among consumers. A consumer's lifestyle reflects the patterns of time, spending and feelings that make up the reality of much of how people live: what they think is important, how they spend their time and money. Identifying labels can be attached to these lifestyle patterns, enabling us to talk conveniently about groups or types of consumers. Hence, marketers can refer to a market segment consisting largely of 'quiet family men', 'contented housewives', 'elegant socialites', or 'frustrated factory workers'. Figure 7.4 reveals five male and five female lifestyle patterns derived from a widely cited commercial study.

THE FEMALE SEGMENTS

Thelma, the old-fashioned traditionalist (25 percent)
This lady has lived a 'good' life – she has been a devoted wife, a doting mother, and a conscientious housewife. She has lived her life by these traditional values and she cherishes them to this day. She does not condone contemporary sexual activities or political liberalism, nor can she sympathize with the women's libbers. Even today, when most of her children have left home, her life is centered around the kitchen. Her one abiding interest outside the household is the church which she attends every week. She lacks higher education and hence has little appreciation for the arts or cultural activities. Her spare time is spent watching TV, which is her prime source of entertainment and information.

Mildred, the militant mother (20 percent)
Mildred married young and had children before she was quite ready to raise a family. Now she is unhappy. She is having trouble making ends meet on her blue-collar husband's income. She is frustrated and she vents her frustrations by rebelling against the system. She finds escape from her unhappy world in soap operas and movies. Television provides an ideal medium for her to live out her fantasies. She watches TV all through the day and into late night. She likes heavy rock and probably soul music, and she doesn't read much except escapist magazines such as *True Story*.

Candice, the chic suburbanite (20 percent)
Candice is an urbane woman. She is well educated and genteel. She is a prime mover in her community, active in club affairs and working on community projects. Socializing is an important part of her life. She is a doer, interested in sports and the outdoors, politics and current affairs. Her life is hectic and lived at a fast clip. She is a voracious reader, and there

are few magazines she doesn't read. However, TV does relatively poorly in competing for her attention – it is too inane for her.

Cathy, the contented housewife (18 percent)
Cathy epitomizes simplicity. Her life is untangled. She is married to a worker in the middle of the socioeconomic scale, and they, along with their several pre-teen children, live in a small town. She is devoted to her family and faithfully serves them as mother, housewife, and cook. There is a certain tranquillity in her life. She enjoys a relaxed pace and avoids anything that might disturb her equilibrium. She doesn't like news or news-type programs on TV but enjoys the wholesome family entertainment provided by Walt Disney, *The Waltons*, and *Happy Days*.

Eleanor, the elegant socialite (17 percent)
Eleanor is a woman with style. She lives in the city because that is where she wants to be. She likes the economic and social aspects of big city living and takes advantage of the city in terms of her career and leisure-time activities. She is a self-confident on-the-go woman, not a homebody. She is fashion-conscious and dresses well. She is a woman with panache. She is financially secure; as a result she is not a careful shopper. She shops for quality and style, not price. She is a cosmopolitan woman who has travelled abroad or wants to.

THE MALE SEGMENTS

Herman, the retiring homebody (26 percent)
Herman is past his prime and is not getting any younger. His attitudes and opinions on life, which are often in conflict with modern trends, have gelled. And he is resistant to change. He is old-fashioned and conservative. He was brought up on 'motherhood and apple pie' and cherishes these values. Consequently he finds the attitudes of young people today disturbing. He realizes he cannot effect any change, and has withdrawn into a sheltered existence of his own within the confines of his home and its surroundings. Here he lives a measured life. He goes to church regularly, watches his diet, and lives frugally. He longs for the good old days and regrets that the world around him is changing.

Scott, the successful professional (21 percent)
Scott is a man who has everything going for him. He is well educated, cosmopolitan, the father of a young family, and is already established in his chosen profession. He lives a fast-paced active life and likes it. He is a man getting ahead in the world. He lives in or near an urban center and seems to like what a big city has to offer – culture, learning opportunities, and people. He also enjoys sports, the out-of-doors, and likes to keep physically fit. He is understandably happy with his life and comfortable in his lifestyle.

Fred, the frustrated factory worker (19 percent)
Fred is young. He married young and had a family. It is unlikely that he had any plans to get a college degree, if he did, he had to shelve them to find work to support his family. He is now a blue-collar worker having trouble making ends meet. He is discontented, and tends to feel that 'they' – big business, government, society – are somehow responsible for his state. He finds escape in movies and in fantasies of foreign lands and cabins by quiet lakes. He likes to appear attractive to women, has an active libido, and likes to think he is a bit of a swinger.

Dale, the devoted family man (17 percent)
Dale is a wholesome guy with a penchant for country living. He is a blue-collar worker, with a high school education. The father of a relatively large family, he prefers a traditional marriage, with his wife at home taking care of the kids. His home and neighborhood are central in his life. He is an easygoing guy who leads an uncomplicated life. Neither worry nor skepticism

are a part of him. He is relaxed and has a casual approach to many things. He is a happy, trusting soul who takes things as they are.

Ben, the self-made businessman (17 percent)
Ben is the epitome of a self-made man. He was probably not born wealthy, nor had he the benefit of higher education, but through hard work and shrewd risk taking, he has built himself a decent life. He has seen the system work. He believes if you work hard and play by the rules you will get your share (and perhaps some more). Therefore he cannot condone hippies and other fringe groups whom he sees as freeloaders. He embraces conservative ideology and is likely to be a champion of business interests. He is a traditionalist at home, and believes it is a woman's job to look after the home and to raise a family. He is gregarious and enjoys giving and attending parties. And he likes to drink.

Figure 7.4 Psychographics and buyer behavior
Source: Mehotra, S. and W. D. Wells (1979) 'Psychographics and buyer behavior: theory and recent empirical findings', in A. G. Woodside, J. N. Sheth and P. D. Bennett (eds) *Consumer and Industrial Buying Behavior*, New York: North Holland, 54–5. Reproduced by permission of the authors.

Similar lifestyle descriptions have been published as the technique has gained considerable application in marketing and advertising over the past two decades (for other examples, see Gunter and Furnham 1992). And no wonder, since lifestyle descriptions offer the marketing manager, advertising director, or copywriter a concrete, flesh-and-blood description of consumers that adds reality to the bare bones of demographic data and involves fewer theoretical and empirical difficulties than the personality approach. Moreover, lifestyles are reflections of self-concept and offer insight into consumer motives, feelings and beliefs unavailable from the purely descriptive demographic data. Also, lifestyle has the advantage of focusing on consumption-relevant activities, interests and opinions. It is thus closer than personality measures to the behaviors (product, brand or store choice) marketers want to understand and predict.

Use of lifestyle profiles is not, however, without difficulties. Lifestyle descriptions sometimes reveal somewhat patronizing attitudes toward consumer groups on the part of marketers and advertisers. They may not represent useful categories by which to classify customers whose wants and aspirations may be changing faster than an ossified lifestyle image gives them credit. The possibility of false segmentation – based on a plausible group of like-minded and similarly behaving customers who, nevertheless, constitute too small a market to make specialized production and marketing profitable – is an ever-present possibility (even the yuppies, whose lifestyles were held to characterize the self-orientation of the 1980s, never accounted for more than a very small proportion of national markets). The components of lifestyle and their interactions are inevitably complex as Figure 7.5, which summarizes some of the relationships among the many variables we have discussed, indicates.

Consumer lifestyles are measured through a technique called 'Psychographics' or sometimes 'AIO Research', standing for (A)ctivities, (I)nterests, and (O)pinions. Using consumer interviews, verbatim statements recorded in focus groups, existing literature, and imagination, researchers write large numbers of statements such as those shown in Figure 7.6 to reflect the AIOs of consumers. Large, representative samples of consumers are asked via a questionnaire to indicate the extent to which they agree or disagree with each statement using 5–7 point Likert-type scales. The resulting data is next analyzed using any

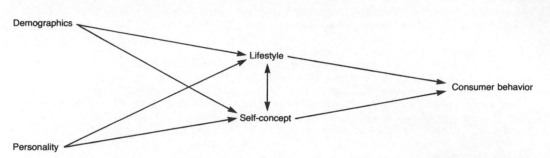

Figure 7.5 The relationships of demographic and personality variables with lifestyle, self-concept, and consumer behavior

of a variety of statistical techniques depending on the researcher's purpose, in much the same way as demographic data is analyzed. One of the important features of psychographic data is that it quantifies certain characteristics of consumers in the same way that demographics quantifies other characteristics.

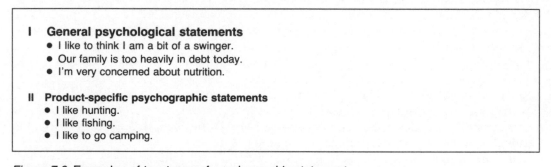

I   General psychological statements
- I like to think I am a bit of a swinger.
- Our family is too heavily in debt today.
- I'm very concerned about nutrition.

II   Product-specific psychographic statements
- I like hunting.
- I like fishing.
- I like to go camping.

Figure 7.6 Examples of two types of psychographic statement
Sources: Drawn from Wells, W. D. (1975) 'Psychographics: a critical review', *Journal of Marketing Research*, 12; and Mehotra, S. and W. D. Wells (1979) 'Psychographics and buyer behavior: theory and recent empirical findings', in A. G. Woodside, J. N. Sheth and P. D. Bennett (eds) *Consumer and Industrial Buying Behavior*, New York: North Holland, 49–65.

In order to segment a market psychographically, for instance, a marketer might use cluster analysis to determine a small set of relatively homogeneous segments or clusters of consumers who tend to agree with certain AIO statements and disagree with others. The output of such an analysis would resemble the segments described in Table 7.1, an example of general segmentation. Another marketer, on the other hand, might use a battery of product-specific AIO statements to profile a known market segment. The heavy users of shotgun ammunition, for example, tend to agree strongly with the statements in the bottom half of Figure 7.6.

Flexible, relatively easy to understand and collect, psychographic data can provide a wealth of information about consumers unavailable through any other means. In addition to its potential as a means of segmenting consumer markets, psychographics can reveal much about consumer motives. For example, a psychographic study showed that an attractive segment of stock-market investors were upwardly mobile, self-made men. Merrill

Lynch had been running ads directed to this segment featuring a galloping herd of bulls and the theme 'Bullish on America' with little effect. To bring the ad closer to the image of the potential client, the simple adjustment was made to feature only a single bull, not a herd, with a new theme: 'A Breed Apart'. The ads produced a dramatic improvement in ad recognition and market share for the company (Atlas 1984).

The most recent systematic application of psychographics comes from the Stanford Research International company which sells a syndicated consumer research program called VALS (Values and Lifestyles) (Mitchell 1983). Combining detailed demographic data with carefully designed AIO statements, this program purports to classify virtually every American into one of nine categories ranging from the need-driven 'Survivors' and 'Sustainers' at the bottom of the socioeconomic scale to a small group (2 percent) of self-actualizers called the 'Integrateds'.

Many companies currently use the VALS data to map social trends, profile market segments, derive product positioning concepts, and inspire advertising themes. The Merrill Lynch example described above was guided by the VALS profile which indicated the target market investor belonged to the 'Achievers' category.

A MULTIDIMENSIONAL APPROACH TO CONSUMER MOTIVATION

Lifestyle segments come and go as social trends arise and decline. As the comparison of US and Canadian consumers indicates, cultural factors impose differences even among societies that are, broadly speaking, closely matched on many materialistic factors. Our final approach to understanding consumer motivation identifies the basic building blocks of any system of consumer motivation and lifestyle. It aims to link the comprehensive theories of human motivation such as those proposed by Maslow and Freud with marketers' needs for a basic understanding of the evaluative factors that underlie *consumer* choice.

This model suggests that the goods and services consumers learn about and purchase satisfy many needs and wants simultaneously. Products are purchased for a variety of reasons as consumers strive to meet a variety of goals. Most theories of motivation applied to consumer behavior suggest that a single product must meet a single need and only that need. A multidimensional perspective, however, acknowledges from the outset that there is no hierarchy of wants, so that a single purchase may satisfy many wants, more or less, at the same time. From this perspective, consumer wants and the ways in which products satisfy these wants are not typed or judged *a priori* to fit into certain rigid categories. Thus, we understand how a product satisfies wants and the nature of these wants only in the act of owning or consuming the product itself. That is, in the eyes of the consumer, a product satisfies whatever wants that consumer feels it satisfies.

For managers, however, a typology of consumers' wants may be useful in order to understand some of the complexities of consumer behavior. Moreover, a limited set of broad consumer needs helps managers think through the consumption process as it develops and to implement appropriate marketing strategies and tactics. Six broad categories of consumer need may be identified:

- physiological needs,
- social needs,
- symbolic needs,

- hedonic needs,
- cognitive needs,
- experimental needs.

Physiological needs

Obviously, much of the want-satisfying quality of goods and services serves strictly utilitarian or functional purposes for consumers. Goods and services solve problems, make life easier, and allow consumers to function in day-to-day life. From Maslow's perspective, they meet the physiological and safety needs. Consumers need food, housing, transportation, etc. The needs that products meet by virtue of their primary or inherent functional characteristics then are met by their functional or utilitarian dimensions.

Social needs

Products also have meaning and satisfy wants through the effect of the product's consumption on the consumer's relationships with other people (Solomon 1983). The products that satisfy functional wants may at the same time act to represent consumers to other people, expressing membership in a social class or other group, or transmitting some other message about the consumer's social relations. We can say that these products fulfill social needs and wants more broadly conceived than Maslow's or Hanna's types.

Symbolic needs

Even more fundamental psychosocial motives such as the need for sex, dominance and so forth, can be expressed via products. It is apparent that we 'regard our possessions as parts of ourselves' (Belk 1988). Thus consumers may buy goods and services to express both to other people and to themselves something about themselves; in this way they seek to convey some of their beliefs or certain aspects of their identity. Products act as symbols of their owners' self-concepts and personality, thereby fulfilling the need to show success, achievement, power, or other dimensions of personality. Products may then meet symbolic needs and wants as they symbolize internal psychological states.

Hedonic needs

A fourth dimension of the want-satisfying nature of products can be described as hedonic. This refers to the fact that many products are consumed because of their sensory benefits – in short, because they taste, feel or smell good to us. These product benefits focus on the sensory quality of products and their consumption (Hirschman and Holbrook 1982). None of the motivational theories of human behavior can account for why consumers like ice cream. Not being bound by theoretical categories, however, consumers find no mystery in this; they will tell you that they like it because it tastes good. This should be reason enough for a category of consumer wants and benefits, and it explains a great deal of consumption behavior not included by Hanna's or Maslow's typologies.

Cognitive needs

The fifth type of need that products can satisfy is the need to know. We can think of this as a rational motive expressing the curiosity consumers have about their world and their desire to understand it. Books, magazines, newspapers, television news programs and documentaries, and informative commercials all appeal to the basic desire many consumers have to learn, find out, explore and know. Marketers who can satisfy consumer curiosity or stimulate the desire to learn and position their brands as a way to satisfy this desire will appeal successfully to this consumer drive.

Experiential needs

The final dimension of consumer wants is called experiential. Many consumer behaviors are primarily undertaken because of the feelings they give consumers. For instance, concerts, sporting events, art exhibitions and parties are all possible objects of consumption because of the way they make consumers feel, because they produce desired emotions or moods. This may be the type of behavior described by Holbrook and Hirschman (1982) when they say that consumption may be seen as 'involving a steady flow of fantasies, feelings, and fun'.

One of the key features of the multidimensional view of consumer motivation is that any single consumption activity may meet many or all of these dimensions of wants simultaneously. An item of clothing, for instance, may be purchased because it will keep us dry and warm (and out of jail), because it has a designer name on it that signifies status, because it makes us feel sexy or competent, because it is comfortable, and because, perhaps as a by-product of these benefits, it is fun to wear. Thus all five wants are satisfied: the physiological, social, symbolic, hedonic and experiential. From the motivational perspective, the job of the researcher and marketer is to discover how much weight each want dimension carries in a specific consumption decision process. This should lead to greater understanding of consumer behaviors in the abstract and to greater marketing efficiency as products are developed to provide the benefits consumers seek.

Examples of multidimensional motivation abound in marketing:

- The fountain pen, increasingly eclipsed since 1939 by Lazlo Biro's invention, made a comeback among American consumers during the late 1980s. Ballpoint pens may be convenient and functional, but cannot compete with the fountain pen in conferring prestige, or in providing opportunities for ritualistic buying and maintenance (Calonius 1989).
- In the realm of mass communications, *Nightmare on Elm Street* films provide chills and thrills (experiential), as well as the ego-satisfaction of having survived the nightmare (symbolic), and may provide a good excuse to grab your date (social) accordingly to Gubernick (1989).
- Sophisticated new homes can be convenient shelters for couples who work at city jobs by day (functions) and at the same time 'suggest that buyers can still have drama, fun and sparkle in their lives' (Simon 1989: 310).
- Recently, large fashion shoe companies in the United States have begun to design and market women's stylish shoes (symbolic and social motives) that are comfortable to wear (hedonic motives) as well! (Geer 1992).

SUMMARY

The identification of factors that motivate consumers to buy is a difficult task because any given piece of human behavior may derive from one of several influences. People may not be aware of their motives or may deliberately misrepresent them to interviewers. Thus, the nature of motivation is usually inferred from observations of the behavior of others, and this leaves much to be desired. Nevertheless, it is known that motivated behavior occurs when an individual perceives a goal (incentive) external to himself and experiences internally a need or drive that stimulates him to reach that goal. Motives can be classed as biogenic (physiological and safety needs) or sociogenic (affective, esteem and actualization needs). Both of these types of motive are useful in marketing planning. Cognitive dissonance may also motivate.

Maslow's theory of human needs is, despite criticisms, a useful starting point for the study of motivation because it involves the basic dichotomy of basic and learned (biogenic and sociogenic) needs. Freudian psychology contains the interesting and potentially useful categories of suppressed and repressed motives. Lasswell's Theory of the Triple Appeal is based on Freud's work but appears to apply to the problems of persuading consumers through advertisements. Motivation research provides a useful starting point for consumer research but its varied techniques do not replace the more traditional methods of marketing research.

A central feature of this chapter is the multidimensional approach to consumer motivation. Basically, this argues that consumer behavior is directed by a host of motivating forces that can best be classified into six categories: physiological, social, symbolic, hedonic, cognitive and experiential. These motives both function simultaneously and may be satisfied simultaneously by goods and services. The article from the *Wall Street Journal* at the beginning of the chapter (Figure 7.1) gives several examples of these phenomena in operation, showing how consumers may derive want satisfactions from marketers' offerings in ways not always obvious to sellers.

For the marketing manager, the basic lesson from the study of motivation in marketing is to be attuned to consumers' needs and wants. While this may sound simple, it is, however, more demanding than it looks because the nature of human motivation is so complex and poorly understood. The multidimensional approach guides the design and implementation of marketing strategies by breaking down that complexity into a basic set of broad consumer motives and showing how they may interact in specific instances of consumer motivation and behavior.

Part IV

Consumers in context

Chapter 8

Retail environments

SITUATIONAL INFLUENCES ON CONSUMER BEHAVIOR

Analysis of consumers' personal and lifestyle characteristics indicates that purchase and consumption decisions are seldom reached in so straightforward a manner as the cognitive models suggest. Consumer researchers have traditionally neglected the influence of environment on purchase and consumption, preferring to concentrate on measuring cognitive states and processes – attitudes, traits and information handling – to account for observed consumer choice. However, both attitude and personality variables, when taken alone, are relatively poor predictors of consumer behavior (Belk 1974, 1975; Foxall 1983; Kassarjian 1971), while other – frequently overlooked – influences on consumer behavior and choice arise from the external environment rather than the psychological makeup of the consumer (Hackett *et al.* 1993). They may act indirectly, as when situational factors interact with brand attitudes and decisions (e.g., Bearden and Woodside 1976; Miller and Ginter 1979; Sandell 1968). Hence unexpected situations may intervene to influence the relationship between behavioral intentions and behavior (e.g., Cote *et al.* 1985; Sheth 1974). Alternatively, the shape and content of consumers' decision processes may differ with such situational factors as the type of product under review (Stoltman *et al.* 1990).

But the social and physical environment may also directly cause, shape, facilitate, activate and direct consumer activities independently of the intrapersonal processes that precede and accompany them (Bonner 1985; Leigh and Martin 1981). In this chapter and the next, therefore, we discuss an additional source of influence on consumer choice: considerations of situation and place, including social and physical environments and locations (Canter 1977; Foxall 1990, 1992; Marans and Spreckelmeyer 1982; Peled 1974). Situational influences may account for 20–45 percent of consumer behavior, while individual differences in such factors as personality and attitude account for 15–30 percent, and interaction between individuals and situations for 30–50 percent (Argyle 1976).

Components of the situation

The situations in which consumer behavior takes place consist of 'all those factors particular to a time and place of observation, which do not follow from a personal (intra-individual) and stimulus (object or choice alternative) attributes' (Belk 1974: 15). Such situations comprise five broadly defined characteristics (Belk 1975).

- *Physical surroundings*, including geographical and institutional location, decor, sounds, lighting, weather, aromas, signs and visible configurations of merchandise, displays or other materials surrounding the stimulus object. Note that merchandise may be stimulus and background as well. Merchandising displays may dispose consumers to buy on impulse (e.g., Wilkinson, Mason and Parksoy 1982). Moreover, consumers have strong preferences for particular retail designs, which can be identified by consumer research and incorporated into marketing programs (Baker *et al.* 1988; Doherty 1991).
- *Social surroundings*, including other persons, their characteristics, roles and interactions, and crowding. Consumers who shop together explore more of the store and are more likely to spend more than planned (Granbois 1968). The creation and maintenance of in-home buying groups, such as Tupperware parties, is a direct response to such tendencies. Crowding in retail contexts influences the amount of time consumers spend shopping, the extent to which they put off purchasing to another occasion, and their willingness to speak to salespersons (Harrell *et al.* 1980).
- *Temporal perspective*, ranging from time of the day to season of the year, time constraints, and elapsed or expected time. Pre-Christmas shopping often differs in style, content and place from that at other times of the year. In-store behavior often takes place within externally imposed time pressures which affect the decision procedure and its outcomes. When consumers are under time pressure, they truncate their external search processes, relying more on memory and experience; they are also likely to reduce the consideration given to evaluating alternative brands, and to make more impulse purchases (Iyer 1989; Mattson 1982).
- *Task definition*, the orientation, intent, role or frame of a person, through which certain aspects of the environment may become relevant. Hence the purchase of particular products or brands can differ according to the situationally determined task orientation of the buyer, such as buying foods for a family meal vs. a formal dinner party, or buying a tie for oneself or as a gift for an acquaintance (Belk 1974; Hornik 1982; Kakkar and Lutz 1975; Rosen and Sheffet 1983).
- *Antecedent states*, which are temporary moods and conditions that 'color' the perception, evaluation and acceptance of the environment present. They may also include factors such as access to credit which facilitate purchase on one occasion over another. Having a bank card or store-issued card may lead to higher levels of in-store purchasing and greater expenditures, while possession of both is likely to lead only to greater levels of purchasing (Hirschman 1979).

This chapter concentrates on the physical context of consumer behavior while the final chapter is concerned with aspects of the social surroundings of consumer choice, viz. the consumer in the social structure. But the other components of Belk's framework should be borne in mind as these accounts unravel: they usefully draw attention to the personal factors that consumers bring with them to the setting and which affect the capacity of the situation to shape their behavior (Russell and Mehrabian 1976). The task definition follows from intra-individual attributes and may be part of the situation. In this sense, it is part of the environment. The same applies to antecedent states. These are intra-individual attributes that may be part of the situation and thus of the environment (Troye 1985). They also help us understand how consumers create as well as react to situations; how they select, avoid and construct situations for themselves and for others (Bowers 1973). The effects of environment on consumer behavior are often determined by the consumer's subjective perception of his or her surroundings rather than by the objective situation (Kakkar and Lutz 1981). Lutz and Kakkar refer to this as the psychological situation and define it as:

> an individual's internal response to, or interpretations of, all factors particular to a time and place of observation which are not stable intra-individual characteristics or stable environmental characteristics, and which have a demonstrable and systematic effect on the individual's psychological processes and/or his overt behavior.
>
> (Lutz and Kakkar 1975a: 495)

THE RETAIL ENVIRONMENT AND CONSUMER BEHAVIOR

The ability of physical surroundings to shape consumer behavior is nowhere greater than in retail environments. The range of social, physical and temporal features of the environment which, singly or in combination, impinge on consumer behavior in such environments is enormous: lighting, aisle width, store size, heating, crowdedness and so on. We first define the components of the consumer environment and then consider the effects of selected aspects of the physical and social retail environments on consumer behavior and choice. At the shopping mall or center level, we discuss the intended effects of micro-retail design and cultural factors on consumer patronage. We also consider the ways in which consumers cognitively map shopping areas and find their way around complex retail settings. Finally, we draw attention to some of the physical (e.g., store design and merchandise layout) and social (crowding) characteristics of retail environments that influence consumers' in-store behavior.

Micro-retail design

It has often been claimed that location is the most important determinant of the success of a retail establishment. If all other factors, such as cost and availability of goods are kept constant, purchases will be made at the nearest shop that stocks the desired product. Moreover, if a choice is available, the largest nearby shop will be selected (Hawkins *et al.* 1983). However, these two variables (nearness and store size) have a smaller effect on the choice of purchase location as the desired product becomes more attractive, and as a consequence, the cost of the desired product rises. Williams (1981), for instance, discovered that as the target of purchases increased, so did the willingness to travel to purchase (cf. Brown 1989).

Selecting a shop for patronage is a two-step process for many consumers. First, the selection of the shopping area (center or mall) is made; second, comes the selection of stores within the area. The precise micro-location of a shop within a shopping area can, therefore, be of vital importance. Shops with windows facing a dense stream of people passing get more customers than shops in side streets outside the flow of people passing. Seeing a shop and seeing products in the windows often leads to visiting the shop and thus to purchasing as though there were a sort of 'impulse entering' of a store without a preformed purchase intent. Entering stores, browsing and buying fulfill consumer needs over and above those that are simply economic and rational. Shoppers' motivations include a search for entertainment, recreation and leisure, all of which complicates the complex modeling of consumers' patronage behavior and the effects of particular systems of retail location which provides a continuing theme in both academic and commercial marketing research (Arnold, Oum and Tigert 1983; Beaumont 1987; Finn and Louviere 1990; Gautschi 1981; Ghosh and Craig 1986; Hortman *et al.* 1990; MacKay 1972; Monroe and Guiltinan 1975; Patricios 1979; Sands and Moore 1980; Timmermans 1993; White and Ellis 1971).

Beliefs about the patronage behavior of consumers are reflected in the design and construction of modern retail environments. The essence of the out-of-town shopping center is its having been deliberately designed, in contrast to the city center shopping district which, by comparison, usually shows signs of having evolved organically. Describing the first as planned, and the second as unplanned, overstates this difference but it is useful to call attention to the overall approach to design generally accorded new, suburban shopping centers as opposed to the necessarily more piecemeal design of urban shopping districts (Davies 1976; Jones 1989; for some specific examples of recent retailing develop-ments, see Doucet *et al.* 1987; Johnson 1987; Whysall 1989). One aspect of such planning involves comprehension of consumers' shopping behavior at the micro-retail level, i.e., within the shopping area. Not only is this underresearched (Brown 1987), but also the assumed patterns of consumer mobility and motivation on which micro-retail design depends rely more on hearsay and causal observation than systematic investigation. We need first to outline the principles on which micro-retail design is accomplished and the presumptions it makes with respect to consumer behavior. We can then consider the findings of studies of consumers' perceptions of, and wayfinding abilities in, two complex retail environments – a new out-of-town shopping center and a high street shopping district in a traditional city – which raise questions for the understanding of how consumers mentally construe and achieve mobility within such contexts.

The fundamental principle of micro-retail design is evident from the structure of the earliest postwar shopping center developments in the United States to the most sophisticated recent examples found on every continent. It is the juxtapositioning of 'anchor' stores, which attract buyers routinely and frequently, with specialist shops whose customers are believed to buy often on impulse, so that people are encouraged to notice and use the latter en route to or from the former (Beddington 1982; Darlow 1972; Johnson 1987; Sim and Way

1989). At its simplest, this takes the form of a single mall, along which smaller tenants are positioned, at each end of which is a variety or department store (Gardner and Sheppard 1989). These larger, magnet or attractor stores need not be placed in the most accessible spots, for large numbers of consumers can be expected to seek them out in order to make indispensable purchases or to compare merchandise with that on offer in similar stores elsewhere (Michell 1986; Scott 1989). The attraction of suitable anchor tenants to shopping centers at their inauguration, and their subsequent retention, have therefore become central concerns of retail center management. The so-called 'low-impulse' trades they represent include not only department stores but, of increasing significance, large, high-quality food supermarkets (Davies 1976; Davies and Rogers 1984; Dawson 1980, 1983; Dawson and Lord 1985).

At the other end of the spectrum, so-called 'high-impulse' trades, which depend heavily on a continuous throughput of potential consumers, and which thus benefit from being located in prominent positions such as along malls and near the entrances to shopping centers, include jewelers, craft shops, clothes stores, photographic equipment specialists and florists. An intermediate group, 'secondary attractors', bring large numbers of potential customers into contact with the specialist stores: they provide services that facilitate customer behavior in one-stop retail developments, and they also employ large numbers of staff who make local purchases during breaks and on their way home. Banks and fast-food outlets obviously come into this category because of the essential consumer services they make available; other stores, such as pharmacies, that offer important non-impulse purchases also belong here, as do office buildings; and, perhaps less evidently, so do large bookshops and travel agencies, which offer a change of pace and increase the overall variety of goods considered on a lengthy shopping trip.

This basic principle of design carries the implication that consumers' behavior is susceptible to the 'cumulative attractiveness' of a variety of stores, and that the tenant mix of shopping centers should be actively managed to promote an optimum level of compatibility among the retailers (Nelson 1958). However, while the widespread advocacy of a planned arrangement of anchor and specialist stores is consistent with commonsense logic, evidence for it relies for the most part on casual observation and anecdote rather than a volume of dependable, systematic knowledge. Although groupings of potentially compatible retailers are frequently encountered, their propinquity may derive from the strictures of local planning regulations rather than their functional interdependence (e.g., Davies 1984).

Consumer mobility

There is some evidence that consumers actually proceed from one type of store to another, though this does not always support the expectation that supermarkets and other attractor stores generate a large amount of traffic for other types of outlet (Brown 1988). Bromley and Thomas (1987: 55) adduce evidence from a study of 'the aggregate behavior of shoppers' that 'a substantial majority confined their shopping to the same type of store as the specified main store visited'. This was found for superstore, DIY, and furniture and furnishings shoppers, and is consistent with the views that consumers gather much of the information on which their purchase decisions are based from in-store situations (Wilkie and Dickson 1991) and that they engage in inter-store information search of a fairly informal kind, especially at the earlier stages of the decision process (Brown 1988; Furse *et al.* 1984; Bloch *et al.* 1986). 'Nevertheless, in each case a significant minority of shoppers generated spin-off shopping linkages to contrasting store types' (Bromley and Thomas 1987: 55). Spinoff linkages are more probable in the case of comparisons of similar products and, therefore, generally concern competitive stores. Spinoffs in which consumers visit contrasting store types are highly limited by the proximity of the shops in question.

An implication is that some consumers (perhaps a significant majority) show less unplanned visiting of stores belonging to different categories than the micro-retail design principles imply. They appear, none the less, to pursue several sources of comparative information on planned major purchases, and this may extend to visiting stores of a different type in several shopping centers (Lord 1987).

Although the patterns of consumer mobility and motivation assumed by the principles of micro-retail design and tenant mix management are supported by commonsense logic and limited observation, systematic evidence for the underlying proposition that consumers perceive complex retail environments in ways compatible with the theory has not been produced. What evidence there is comes mainly from consultants' reports, retailers' informal accounts of their locational experience and aspirations, and consumers' delayed self-reports rather than in the form of the reliable, theoretically derived results of replicated research.

An informative exception is the survey evidence presented by Brown (1987) for retailers' perceptions of micro-retail location and their beliefs about its implications for customer behavior and trade. This confirms a tripartite classification of stores: the anchors that generate trade by providing opportunities for comparison of merchandise and perceptible value-for-money (variety and department stores and, increasingly, large-scale grocery retailers); secondary generators, notably service organizations that act as catalysts to general purchasing (banks, restaurants, fast-food cafés, realtors, travel firms, etc.); and the specialists that provide personal products and services (opticians, clothiers, gift shops, etc.).

The respondents to Brown's survey confirmed the pre-eminent position of the first category, the magnet stores on which the attraction of business in general crucially depends. They drew special attention to the generative effect on trade of the secondary attractors, whose impact was deemed to be strong and growing. In addition, the respondents claimed there was a tendency toward intra-trade consumer behavior – going from one clothier to another, one food store to another, and so on. However, inter-trade linkages were also believed to be important: despite the belief that shopping for convenience goods occurs independently of that for comparison goods, the implication of the survey is that these modes of consumer behavior coexist as routine purchasing gives an opportunity to gather information on a continuous basis about infrequently purchased durable products (cf. Wilkie and Dickson 1991). Finally, the respondents expressed consistent preferences for being located close to food stores, department stores, variety stores, restaurants, banks, and their own direct competitors.

Although these results are derived from a city center shopping location, Belfast, which presents atypical circumstances for consumers, they have been described in some detail on account of their consistency with several assumptions underlying the revealed principles of micro-retail design. Their significance lies in their annunciation of belief in inter-store compatibility, tenant mix optimization, and the resulting cumulative attraction by individuals directly involved in the outcomes of micro-retail design (see, however, Bromley and Thomas 1987; Foxall and Hackett 1992b).

Wayfinding

A factor that influences consumer mobility in retail contexts is the extent to which consumers can visualize and navigate the complexities presented by these physical environments. As public demand has imposed increasing pressure upon limited physical space in built-up areas, so physically extensive, multiple-level developments have become commonplace: diverse, multistorey car parks, shopping developments and international airports are so familiar as to evoke little comment.

One way in which consumers manage such complexity is through the formation of mental or cognitive maps of the retail environment. Cognitive mapping is the process by which people acquire, store, decode and apply information relating to the physical environment (Canter 1977; Downs and Stea 1977; Sommer and Aitkens 1982). Spatial information processing has also been investigated to discern the relationship between environmental cognition and behavior (Golledge 1987; Stea 1974). Cognitive mapping by consumers has been the subject of several studies in which cognitive distance, among other variables, has been identified as determinative of consumers' store selection (Cadwallader 1981; Clark and Rushton 1970; Fingleton 1975; Golledge and Rushton 1976; MacKay et al. 1975). A number of studies have examined consumer cognitive maps of retail locations (Olshavsky et al. 1975; MacKay and Olshavsky 1975). A cognitive map is an internal representation of an external geographical reality, subjective versus objective distances. MacKay and Olshavsky (1975) found that cognitive maps generated by multidimensional scaling from similarity data are better related to shopping preferences and frequencies than actual maps.

Consumer wayfinding, the ability to navigate complex shopping malls and other retail environments, has important implications for consumer choice at both store and product levels. Accuracy in consumer wayfinding depends vitally on the *legibility* of the shopping area and the consequent degree of ease or difficulty consumers encounter in forming useful cognitive maps of retail locations. Legibility depends upon the provision and configuration of:

- *paths*, channels along which a person moves or may potentially move,
- *edges*, linear boundaries that are not considered as paths,
- *districts*, sections of a region which have a two-dimensional extent and into which a person is considered to enter,
- *nodes*, strategic spots in a region such as path junctures,
- *landmarks*, other focal points which are not entered into but which are observed, and
- *locational legibility*, the degree of ease with which a location part may be recognized and can be organized into a coherent pattern or map.

(Lynch 1960)

Stores located in nodal positions (at path junctions) of a shopping center and those which form landmarks are used as reference points in shoppers' cognitive maps and are better remembered than those in other positions in both traditional high street and modern shopping mall locations. Large supermarkets, for instance, are frequently used as landmarks, whilst shops placed at the intersections of pathways and roads form nodes. Both are used by shoppers as reference points in their understanding of the spatial qualities of retail locations. Foxall and Hackett (1992b) compared mapping and wayfinding abilities within a traditional high street (with two dimensions to shop location) and shopping malls (with a third, vertical dimension). They discovered that the location of shop units within the complex retail mall was less accurately and less completely remembered than the relatively simple high street. However, while wayfinding ability (respondents' ability to find their way to specified shops) was substantially better than abstract mapping in both locations, performance on tasks requiring respondents to actually walk to, or imagine walking to, a specified shop location were better within the mall setting.

CHOICE AND LOYALTY

Cultural influences

The physical configuration of shopping areas is only one factor that influences store choice. At a far more general level than we have so far discussed, retailing infrastructures and the patterns of consumer behavior they engender and reflect differ between countries and cultures. This is obviously the case when one compares developed with developing countries, or market economies with centrally planned economies. These differences reflect variations in the economic and cultural environments with their implications for abundance versus scarcity. However, even among Western countries, retailing structures may differ substantially. For instance, a study by Douglas (1976), which investigated the grocery and clothing shopping behavior of working and non-working married women in France and the United States, found that the differences in shopping patterns between the two countries were largely due to variations in the countries' retail structures and environments.

In contrast to their French counterparts, the American homemakers tended to shop for groceries in large supermarkets rather than in neighborhood and corner stores. This finding reflects the prevalence of large shopping malls and supermarkets in the United States, whereas small traditional stores are more common in France. Similar patterns emerged in relation to women's clothing purchases: American homemakers tended to shop more frequently in department and discount stores as opposed to the boutiques typically frequented by French women. Hence differences in shopping behavior are mainly a consequence of the prevailing retailing structure in a country. The high incidence of small independent grocery retailers in France encourages and reinforces fragmented purchasing, while the frequently encountered supermarkets and hypermarkets in the United States make for one-stop shopping. But it could equally be argued that the variations in retail structure and environment result from fundamental differences in consumer attitudes and preferences in these two countries. The built environment can thus be seen as both instigating adaptive behaviors and reflecting social and cultural preferences. Douglas proposes that the explanatory role of the retail environment should take precedence over that accorded underlying attitudes and preferences in the study of factors that influence consumer response patterns. Concentrating on apparent differences in attitudes and behaviors might be misleading, especially when this leads to negative conclusions about the feasibility of influencing or changing these patterns. Furthermore, what is true of the cultural differences that exist between nations can also be true of ethnic and other subcultural variations among consumers within a single country (e.g., Zain and Rejab 1989).

Moreover, the structure of retailing is a product not simply of cultural differences, but additionally of historical development. The department store and the shopping mall originated in the United States and came only later to a Europe still dominated by small shops serving a local clientele. Each of these retailing structures possesses its own life cycle. The classical department store in the United States is now more than one hundred years old and seems to be in the last stage of its life cycle, showing signs of decline. New retailing forms came into existence, such as the discount department store since 1955, the fast-food restaurant since 1960, and the textile supermarket since 1975 (van Raaij and Floor 1983).

Consumers' evaluations of retail structure

Consumers' perceptions of shopping centers and shopping malls and preferences are well researched. Unsurprisingly, such research indicates that consumers prefer roofed-over, pedestrian shopping areas to open-air 'high street' shopping areas with their accompanying car and commercial traffic. Cleanliness, safety, friendly personnel, variety and quality of shops, atmosphere, and good connections with public transportation, and arrangement of shops in the shopping center are found to be the most important attributes of these centers (van Raaij 1983). Van Raaij identified the main components of consumers' satisfaction/ dissatisfaction with six shopping malls in the city of Rotterdam in the Netherlands. The dimensions consumers used to appraise the shopping environment were typical of those reported elsewhere:

- *overall evaluation*, which included quality, variety and arrangement of stores, the helpfulness of personnel, and safety,
- *environment*, which included considerations of traffic noise, proximity and behavior of other customers, shelter, and cleanliness,
- *efficiency*, which included such factors as distances between shops, distance from home, and crowding,
- *accessibility*, which included parking and access to public transportation, and
- *social factors*, including such factors as atmosphere and the friendliness of personnel.

Retail structure variables are inherent in four of the five components (the exception being the social factor). The general evaluation factor largely consists of the arrangement and evaluation of shops: it embodies the 'content' of the shopping area. The environment factor relates to customer well-being and the attractiveness of the area: the 'form' of the shopping area. The third and fourth factors relate to efficiency: the efficiency of reaching the shopping area and of subsequently making use of it. These results provide an empirical structure for consumer evaluations of retail locations. They also indicate that social factors and in-store atmosphere individually and collectively shape consumers' experience within retail settings.

The design of shopping malls and shopping centers increasingly emphasizes the esthetic and recreational considerations implicit in these criteria (Neuman 1986; Small 1993) as in the stylish Galleria in Dallas, Copley Place in Boston, Princes Square in Glasgow, and the atrium at Debenhams in London's Oxford Street (Gardner and Sheppard 1989; Gregorson 1988). Sources of social satisfaction are being enhanced by shopping center managers to the point of excluding some potential occupants (such as teenagers) at certain times; recreational benefits are being incorporated including food courts, art exhibitions, live entertainment and daycare facilities for children; even theme parks are sometimes available, as in the West Edmonton Mall (Bloch, Ridgway and Nelson 1991; Bloch, Ridgway and Sherrell 1989). Consumer research is playing a strong role in the development of such centers (Doherty 1991).

Store loyalty

Consumers' patterns of store selection are similar in several respects to the multibrand buying described in Chapter 2. For a given product, few consumers show undivided loyalty. Even over a period of nearly six months, most consumers who buy the product do so only once or twice at a single supermarket chain (Kau and Ehrenberg 1984). Table 8.1 illustrates this for purchasers of instant coffee at Tesco supermarkets in the United Kingdom, but similar patterns are evident for breakfast cereals, detergents, and canned products such as soups and dog food. Similar patterns are also apparent for the United States (Uncles and Ehrenberg 1988).

On average, instant coffee buyers at a chain buy roughly three times during the 24-week period. Differences in market share between brands correlate closely with their penetration levels, i.e., the proportion of buyers of the product they attract (Table 8.2). As Kau and Ehrenberg point out, this is a comparatively low level of repeat buying and it differs little from chain to chain. A double-jeopardy effect is noticeable, however, in that smaller chains, such as Fine Fare, have fewer buyers who also tend to buy rather less frequently. The data in the final column of Table 8.2 emphasize this tendency. Buyers of instant coffee at Cooperative supermarkets, which have one of the highest market shares, did so on average 3.4 times during the 24 weeks surveyed. But they bought instant coffee in all some 7.4 times on average during that period. The consistency between chains in the extent to

Table 8.1 Frequency distribution of purchases of instant coffee at Tesco in 24 weeks

| | Number of purchases at store | | | | | | | | | |
	1	2	3	4	5	6	7	8	9	10+
Tesco										
O%	38	19	14	9	7	3	4	0	1	5
T%	42	20	11	8	5	4	3	2	1	4
Average chain										
O%	44	19	12	6	3	3	3	3	2	5
T%	43	20	11	8	4	3	2	2	2	5

Source: Kau, A. K. and A. S. C. Ehrenberg (1984) 'Models of store choice'. *Journal of Marketing Research*, 21. Reproduced by permission of the American Marketing Association.
Notes: O = observed percentage of buyers making 1, 2, 3, etc., purchases; T = theoretical NBD.

Table 8.2 Market share, penetration and purchase frequency of instant coffee

	Market share (%)	Penetration (%)		Av. purchase freq. per buyer	
		O	T	O	T
Miscellaneous	21	33	28	2.8	3.3
Cooperative	21	28	29	3.4	3.3
Kwiksave	19	22	26	3.9	3.3
Tesco	14	21	20	3.1	3.2
Asda	11	14	16	3.6	3.1
Symbol	6	10	10	2.9	3.0
Independents	6	11	9	2.4	2.9
Fine Fare	2	5	4	2.1	2.8
Average	12	18	18	3.0	3.1

Source: Kau, A. K. and A. S. C. Ehrenberg (1984) 'Models of store choice'. *Journal of Marketing Research*, 21. Reproduced by permission of the American Marketing Association.
Notes: O = observed; T = theoretical Dirichlet.

Table 8.3 Incidence of 100% loyal buyers of instant coffee in 24 weeks

	% buyers who are sole buyers		Av. no. of purchases per sole buyer	
	O	T	O	T
Miscellaneous	20	24	3.1	3.3
Cooperative	29	24	3.6	3.3
Kwiksave	31	24	3.9	3.3
Tesco	20	22	3.0	3.1
Asda	27	19	3.8	3.1
Symbol	12	19	4.3	2.9
Independents	19	18	2.8	2.9
Fine Fare	16	18	2.7	2.8
Average	22	21	3.4	3.1

Source: Kau, A. K. and A. S. C. Ehrenberg (1984) 'Models of store choice', *Journal of Marketing Research*, 21. Reproduced by permission of the American Marketing Association.
Notes: O = observed; T = theoretical Dirichlet.

which they attract heavy buyers and their consumers' allocation of purchases among chains is particularly noteworthy (Kau and Ehrenberg 1984; see also Wrigley and Dunn 1988).

Comparatively few buyers of the product show exclusive loyalty to a chain during the 24–week period (Table 8.3). Sole buyers are relatively light buyers of the product class, given that they account for only about three purchases on average compared to the seven-plus (Table 8.2) of most buyers.

IN-STORE CONSUMER BEHAVIOR

The in-store environment has both social and physical dimensions. The physical layout of a store may facilitate some consumer behaviors (such as noticing some brands while ignoring those less prominently displayed) and inhibit others (such as leaving without paying). And social factors, such as the degree of crowding in the store, may encourage or impede consumers' progress and willingness to buy.

Physical features of the in-store setting

The retail environment frequently encourages novel consumer information processing by such means as pricing signs and point-of-sale advertising. The way in which merchandise is placed on the shelves may act as a stimulus to problem awareness, decision making and behaviors such as browsing, comparative evaluation, and purchase. The store interior and the presentation of the assortment may affect consumers' momentary states, such as moods, desires and orientation. In department stores these momentary states may vary for the different departments and assortments. In the do-it-yourself department a customer may get into a practical, problem-solving ('informational') orientation, and judge products through this frame. In the cosmetics department the same customer may think about personal care, luxury and social acceptance. This is described as a more 'transformational' orientation. The orientation engendered by the store or department may affect decisions, especially in the case of incompletely planned or unplanned purchases. Unexpected events, such as stock outs, noise, and changed prices, also influence consumer choice.

But the physical environment may also have a direct effect on several facets of consumers' in-store behavior which makes its active management of interest to retailers. It has been argued, for example, that store traffic should be managed in order to expose customers to as much of the retail selling area as possible, since customers who shop from the whole of a store purchase more than those who are exposed only to selected areas; moreover, the duration of time spent in the store correlates with purchase volume (Buttle 1984). Some of the important physical features that may achieve these ends will now be considered in greater depth.

Store layout

Consumers report that they are likely to stay longer in a shopping environment of larger scale, perhaps because it would take longer to explore. They also report that they would be likely to spend more in such environments, perhaps because of the greater variety of products on display and the consequently greater probability of impulse purchases being made (Donovan and Rossiter 1982). But scale is not everything: the way in which a store is laid out can influence consumers' perceptions of the store's 'personalness'. In turn, these perceptions may be an important component of customers' experience of retail settings (Gifford 1987). The size of a store has not been found to have a constant effect upon all shoppers, and needs to be balanced with other sources of consumer satisfaction. For instance, large stores offer better brand and goods choice (a positive feature) but in turn are less personal (a negatively perceived feature).

Sommer *et al.* (1981) noted that several aspects of the layout of a supermarket (e.g., block shape, aisle orientation, linear checkout arrangements) were key factors in the sacrifice of friendliness for traffic efficiency. Other research has taken the layout of store fixtures and fittings as its subject matter. For instance, May (1969) discovered aisle length to be of importance in shopper behavior. If aisles were short then shoppers looked down them rather than walked along them. As a consequence of this, customers within short aisled areas made fewer impulse purchases. Van der Ster and Van Wissen (1983) summarize studies on customer traffic patterns in stores. Customers spending more time in the self-service store pass and see more articles and have thus a higher probability of purchasing these articles, either by impulse or by remembering the need for the product at that moment. Store managers use the layout of the store and background music to keep customers longer in the store without irritating them.

Store layout is a means of keeping customers in the self-service store. Convenience goods such as bread, milk, meat and vegetables are often placed in the far corners of the store, necessitating customers to visit most parts of the store. They are thus confronted with many articles of the assortment. Strong and weak selling areas in the store are distinguished. Strong selling areas are the outer aisles, service areas (e.g., for vegetables, meat and bread), the start and the end of aisles, and the checkout area. Most customers tend to look to the right side of an aisle. The right side, especially at eye level, is thus a strong selling area. It has also been found that the placing of goods at eye level increases sales of that item (Leed and German 1973) and essential or regularly purchased goods which are placed at the rear of the store attract people to them. Weak selling areas are the beginning of the routing, left sides of aisles, floor shelves, inner aisles, and 'dead' areas in the center of the store. The potential of these sources of influence over consumer behavior should not be underestimated as they are readily usable techniques. They are particularly appealing to store owners and managers as they form one of the most cost-effective tools for generating increases in sales (Buttle 1984).

Merchandising and display

The following are among the physical features of the retail environment which are widely held to influence in-store consumer behavior (Buttle 1984):

Store fronts	Display units
Name signs	Display cards
Dump bins	Window stickers
Open/shut signs	Door tickets
Leaflets	Price tickets
Store layout	Shelf positioning
Music	Demonstrations
Shelf-space allocation	Lighting

Essentially they have been considered 'behavior-triggering devices' rather than inescapable determinants of choice. Their common aim is to increase visibility and appeal, and so increase the probability of a sale being made. The obvious assumption is that the more visible the item, the more likely it is to be seen and consequently purchased; the more appealing a manufacturer or retailer is able to make an item, the greater the likelihood of purchase. But the arrangement of the physical environment in this way cannot force sentient beings to conform to the wishes of producers and retailers to sell specific brands. Goods for purchase are seldom displayed in isolation, and the manufacturer is faced with attracting attention to his products from amongst competing brands. Moreover, once having attracted the uncommitted customer's fleeting attention, the brand must appeal in order to become the target of purchase. As the ATR model, discussed in Chapter 2, indicates, repeat buying depends vitally upon the satisfactions provided by the product in use. The retailer's problem is just as great: just as comparatively few consumers are unremittingly brand loyal, so the majority practice multistore purchasing (Kau and Ehrenberg 1984).

Merchandising is the design of the way in which articles are presented in the store to facilitate and stimulate customer purchasing behavior. It has, in particular, been used in the attempt to attract consumers' momentary attention and try to hold it; hence its description as the 'silent salesman', the much-neglected cousin of advertising (Buttle 1984). Like advertising, merchandising may be a cost-effective means of ensuring a vital pre-purchase exposure of products to customers (or potential customers) via persuasive and informative material.

The assumption that attractiveness influences subsequent purchase rests upon the belief that customers may not have decided upon all of the purchases they will make when they enter the store, and that uncommitted consumers may be influenced in their final buying behaviors. Engel et al. (1990), for instance, report that at least half of purchases made in supermarkets are impulse buys in this sense. Iyer (1989) cites studies that have found dramatic proportions of consumers' in-store purchase decisions to result in the unplanned acquisition of products and brands: more than 50 percent in the case of supermarket items (Kollat and Willet 1967), 51 percent in the case of pharmaceuticals, 61 percent of beauty and healthcare products (POPA/Du Pont 1978), and 55 percent for food (Yankelovich et al. 1982). Hence, appealing merchandising displays represent one of the most important forms of communication devices available to retail management. Through the use of window displays, signs and fixtures, attention may be attracted and interested desire created in order to prompt the shopper to inquire about and, the retailer hopes, to purchase the products on display (Cohen 1981).

As promotional devices, displays may be of two broad types: window displays and interior displays. The importance of both of these forms of marketing devices has been described in the merchandising literature about the various types of display stands, their relative and specific usefulness, their intra-store positioning, their seasonal use, and the overall effectiveness of displays. Floor displays can significantly increase the number of units of the displayed product sold (Gagnon and Osterhaus 1985). Merchandising displays of promotional goods placed at the ends of shop aisles may increase the purchase of these goods. However, the same goods are not browsed for within the store, and this may negatively affect the sales of other in-store items. Moreover, there is evidence that although expanded shelf space has a positive – though often modest (Curhan 1973) – effect on sales, special displays are far more effective (Wilkinson, Mason and Paksoy 1982). Other considerations also apply here over and above the effects of display size: for instance, stores that are perceived to be clean are more attractive to customers (Patricios 1979).

Before concluding, however, that most consumer purchases are irrational and that consumers can be easily gulled into buying items for which they have no need, it is important to recognize two facts. First, from a methodological point of view, some of the studies that have linked store display manipulations to dramatic increases in sales are flawed (Doyle and Gidengil 1977: some manipulations of displays have been accompanied by price cuts (e.g., Chevalier 1975) and by increased advertising, making it impossible to isolate the effect of the display changes alone. Second, it is vital to remember that unplanned purchases are not uncaused. Many unplanned purchases are the result of consumers' undertaking active processing of new information, gathered in-store, rather than of their being senselessly exploited by promotional techniques (Park, Iyer and Smith 1989). And consumers have reasons for buying on an unplanned basis: they may have remembered that they have low stocks of the purchased item at home; have recognized their need for a product only when they saw it in the store; they may have been attracted by an excellent price or quality deal; or may have obtained the item for a forthcoming special occasion (Iyer 1989). Though most consumers report having bought unplanned items at least once, the reasons may be quite rational and the behavior an entirely reasonable response to time pressures or other immediate constraints. The notion of irrational 'impulse' buying is, therefore, undoubtedly simplistic.

CROWDING

Crowding, resulting from the density of shoppers within a retail location, is a component of the physical setting of shopping behavior; it is, equally, a component of the social composition of stores. We consider it here in some depth for two reasons. First, it provides an example of the necessity to consider the subjective environment, that perceived by consumers, rather than the so-called 'objective' environment, or that which appears to planners, researchers and retailers. Second, it offers opportunities to marketers to increase consumers' satisfaction with the retail environment, and avoid the problems of consumer alienation (Allison 1978).

Objective shopper density influences perceptions and cognitions of the retail store (Harrell, Hutt and Anderson 1980). In crowded stores it has been found that shoppers often leave earlier than they originally had planned to, and that they often develop negative attitudes toward the store in question. Saergert (1973) found that shoppers within a crowded shoe department located within a department store remembered less detail about both the store's merchandise and layout than did incumbents within similar but less crowded settings. She concluded that a high level of crowdedness was therefore able to affect negatively both consumers' satisfaction with a shopping trip and the resulting image that they carried away with them of the crowded store visited.

Harrell *et al.* (1980) discovered that crowding may have a predictable effect upon behavior in the same negative manner as that already noted by Saergert (1973). However, they found that the effects of crowding upon the feelings or cognitions that an individual had about a store were mediated by the adaptation strategies employed by the individual (e.g., how the individual learned to cope with being in crowded situations). As a consequence of this, both in-store satisfaction and store image may be improved by either reducing crowding or by store management and design which aids the consumer in adapting

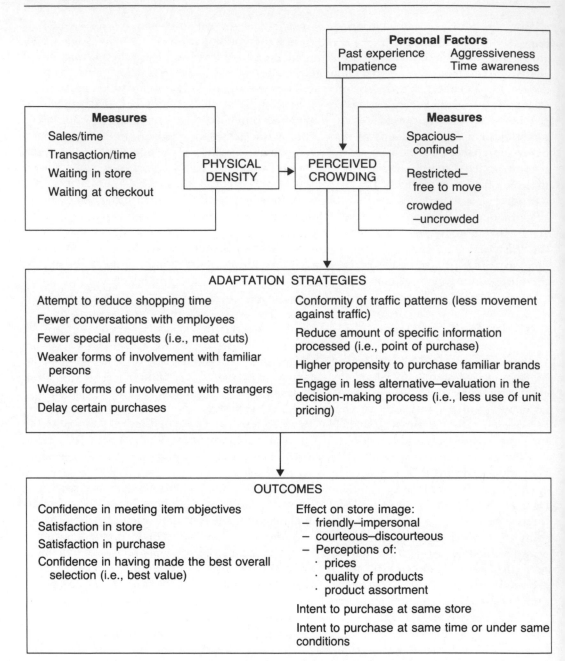

Figure 8.1 Consumer behavior under conditions of crowding
Source: Harrell, G. D. and M. D. Hutt (1976) 'Buyer behavior under conditions of crowding',
Advances in Consumer Research, 3, 38. Reproduced by permission of the Association for Consumer
Research.

to or coming to terms with crowded situations. An alternative interpretation to these findings was also offered by these authors: namely that managers could anticipate changes in consumer shopping patterns and processes under varying levels of crowding and adjust promotion and merchandising policy accordingly.

Crowding is a function not only of the density of the population within a particular retail setting but also of the extent to which it impedes the individual's goal-directed striving. A given level of crowding may or may not interfere with a consumer's achievement of his or her goals. Similarly, population density varies from consumer to consumer in the interference it imposes on his or her in-store interpersonal relationships, susceptibility to anxiety and aggressiveness (Harrell and Hutt 1976). Consumers may adapt to or cope with a crowded environment by allocating less time to each environmental stimulus that reaches their senses (e.g., visiting fewer stores prior to making a purchase decision); by postponing or cancelling the purchase of low-priority products and services; by delegating shopping to others; by avoidance (e.g., of crowded shopping malls); and by limiting social interaction with both acquaintances and strangers in the purchase situation (Harrell and Hutt 1976; Milgram 1970). Harrell and Hutt (1976) present a model of consumer behavior under conditions of crowding which details the kinds of adaptive behavior consumers are likely to engage in: restriction of shopping time, conversation, delaying of some purchases, reducing information processing, and increasing store and brand loyalty (Figure 8.1).

However, while crowding has some deleterious consequences for consumers, such as being jostled and having to put up with noise and movement over which they have no control, there are retail situations in which the presence of some or many others is a positive stimulus to satisfying purchase and consumption. A restaurant which is empty except for oneself or one's party offers little reassurance that the food and service are of high quality, and a football match lacks 'atmosphere' if only a few hundred supporters turn up. Moreover, the subjective experience of crowding may vary according to the efficiency and effectiveness of the retail operation; in other words, the customers' satisfaction with a crowded retail setting depends upon the level of service provided by staff which is, in turn, a function of staffing levels. Ecological psychologists have studied under- and over-manning in a variety of retail environments including stores, restaurants and national parks. Both staff and customers might experience stress as a result of under- or over-staffing in a retail setting, and managers might reduce this by altering the throughput of people in the environment, the capacity of the setting to accommodate and serve them, or the operational efficiency of the organization (Barker 1968; Wicker and Kirmeyer 1977).

ATMOSPHERICS

'Atmospherics' refers to factors that may be designed into or manipulated within retail spaces in order to produce emotional and, in turn, behavioral effects in consumers (Kotler 1973). As Kotler points out, consumers purchase a total product, consisting of not simply the physical item but also the packaging, after-sales deal, advertising, image and – most importantly – the atmosphere of the place in which the transaction takes place. Atmospherics do not, therefore, refer to the objective physical and social factors that constitute store image (see the seminal work of Berry 1968, 1969; Berry and Kunkel 1968) but to the subjective feelings these factors engender in consumers (Donovan and Rossiter 1982), retailers can arrange the visual (including color, brightness and shape), aural (volume and pitch), olfactory (smell, freshness) and tactile (softness, temperature) dimensions of the store atmosphere in order to impact the sensory reactions of consumers and predispose them toward browsing and purchasing (Kotler 1973).

Donovan and Rossiter (1982) have attempted to identify the affective responses elicited by store atmospherics in terms of the three emotional mediates claimed by Mehrabian and Russell (1974) to influence behavior within specific environments. Mehrabian and Russell propose that the emotional response produced within an individual by the environment can be characterized in terms of pleasure, arousal, dominance, or a combination of these three fundamental affective reactions. In turn, these emotional responses determine behavioral responses, notably approach (remaining and behaving in the setting) and avoidance (escaping from or evading the setting). The relevance of this model to the analysis of in-store atmospherics rests on Mehrabian and Russell's inclusion of primary emotional responses as an intervening construct between person and environment on the one hand and behavior on the other hand (Russell and Mehrabian 1978). Not only are pleasure, arousal and dominance cast as the fundamental emotional responses to environments; in addition to their separate and unique effects on behavior, they are posited to have a synergistic effect on behavior. Higher levels of arousal are expected to produce more avoidance behavior in unpleasant settings but greater approach in pleasant surroundings.

The results confirm part of the Mehrabian–Russell model.

- Pleasure, generated within the store, was found to play a strong role in intended approach behaviors, including time spent in the store, purchase level, willingness to exceed planned expenditure levels, interaction with sales assistants, enjoyment of shopping, and disposition to return to the store.
- Arousal, the alertness and excitement generated within the store, is positively related to the intention to spend more time in the store and to interact with salespersons, but its positive effect is confined to stores that are perceived as pleasant.
- These emotional reactions may be 'primary determinants of the extent to which the individual spends beyond his or her original expectations' (Donovan and Rossiter 1982: 54).

These findings are of interest to marketing managers in suggesting how managerial marketing can influence perceptions of, and behavior within, the store. They help contextualize the earlier discussion of the effects of store layout and merchandising on consumer behavior by pointing up the need for high-quality design and in-store conditions. Furthermore, much of the research has involved consumers' intentions to show approach or avoidance reactions rather than their actual behaviors: research in which consumer behavior is the dependent variable is clearly required. Not all research using the Mehrabian–Russell framework in a consumer context has produced such positive results (Kakkar and Lutz 1975; Lutz and Kakkar 1975a, 1975b). Two other points should be noted.

The role of consumer motivation

First, marketing strategies for atmospherics involve the attempt to influence consumers' emotions (rather than their thinking) and thereby to shape their purchase behaviors. However, as we noted in discussing consumers' motivations and lifestyles, consumers may consume environments for their own sake without purchasing. Also, factors other than emotional reactions to atmospherics determine whether sales occur. Consumers' levels of motivation play an important part here, both directly and interactively with emotional responses (Dawson *et al.* 1990). Consumers who are primarily motivated by the product, whose goals on entering a store are principally those of finding and buying the product, have higher levels of pleasure and arousal than those lacking such motivation. Similarly, consumers scoring high on experiential motivation – those who enter stores and shopping centers primarily to experience physical stimuli such as sights and sounds, or for the social environment – have higher levels of pleasure and arousal than consumers who score low on experiential motivation. Product-motivated consumers' shopping trips were more likely to have resulted in making a purchase than those of experience-oriented shoppers. However, although emotions mediated a number of pre-purchase responses, they were least influential in initiating purchase, which were far more amenable to motives than feelings (Dawson *et al.* 1990; cf. Eroglu and Machleit 1990). Moreover, quality of design is a prerequisite of good atmospherics; and consumers' dispositions, especially stimulation needs, may affect their responses (Grossbart *et al.* 1990).

The role of social context

Second, atmospherics depend on the social environment of the store as well as the physical environment. Both store density (the outlet's level of crowding as perceived by its occupants) and design and condition factors (such as lighting, fixtures and sounds) influence emotional reactions and behavior within the store (Grossbart *et al.* 1990). These authors present evidence that design and condition factors in stores (quality of the physical environment as shown by its elicitation of positive emotional reactions) influence consumers' store choice and the time they intend to allocate to shopping. Crowding has the effect of encouraging consumers to do less browsing and comparison shopping, to buy less, to leave the store earlier, postpone shopping, or try another store. However, some customers are more responsive to atmospherics than others and perceive these design/condition and crowding factors more sensitively than others. Those showing higher atmospheric respon- siveness in this way are more likely to restrict their shopping activities to a narrower range of retail outlets. They are 'less open to environmental experiences' and show 'a less urban . . . orientation (which presumes multiple shopping alternatives)' (Grossbart *et al.* 1990: 236). Atmospheric responsiveness appears inversely related to stimulation needs since higher scorers on this dimension are more sensitive to natural environments, averse to physical distractions, extraneous activity and social involvement. They also show some reluctance to change or control environments in order to achieve their goals.

Managerial implications

More generally, marketing managers can influence the situations in which consumer behavior occurs in two principal ways (Branthwaite 1984).

- By controlling the environment: using principles of layout and design to impact consumer behavior directly – e.g., increasing the time consumers spend in supermarkets by reducing (perceived) crowding or adjusting the scale of the store's operations. More subtly, advertising can be used to suggest novel consumption situations, associating luxury products with prestigious surroundings (as in Walls' Vienetta ice cream ads or those for expensive jewelery).
- By generating rules that influence behavior in purchase and consumption settings. For example, patterns of gift giving are often established by advertising that suggests which products make appropriate presents for particular people. Consumption settings not only restrict the range of merchandise available to buy, but they also create social rules that make purchase and use of certain products a vital part of the situation: strawberries and cream at Wimbledon, mints and liqueurs to finalize a dinner party. Branthwaite suggests that the main function of advertising may be to propose such rules rather than to persuade through brand-specific information processing.

SUMMARY

The consumer environment subsumes numerous features of the retail context, all of which potentially influence consumer behavior and choice. Their understanding requires knowledge both of aspects of the physical and social environments and of those internal to the consumer which determine consumers' perceptions. No environment is entirely determinative of consumer behavior but specific environments may activate people (increase their arousal) to think, to feel and to behave. Given the goals of shoppers, some aspects of the consumer environments are more directive of behavior: for instance, signposts, handposts and traffic signs.

Several important questions remain. Environments permit certain behaviors and prohibit other behaviors. But precisely how – and when – does the environment exert influence on cognitions, affect and behavior? Environments may certainly restrict freedom of movement but does the environment cause, permit, facilitate, activate or direct cognitive phenomena and the actions of people, who can think, plan, observe and modify their behavior? Does a merchandise display cause consumers to buy? What ethical issues are raised by managerial attempts to arrange retail settings with the intention of increasing sales and profits?

Chapter 9

Consumers in the social structure

SOCIAL INFLUENCE

All the facets of individual consumer behavior we have discussed – perception, information processing, motivation, personality, and so on – as well as situational influences on choice – are influenced by the social structure in which the consumer is embedded. The social structure consists of the institutions and relationships that bind the individual to the wider society, through which he or she expresses him or herself and in which he or she works out a preferred and valued lifestyle. This chapter is concerned with three broad aspects of the social context of purchase and consumption, beginning with the *social groups*, whose membership influences consumer choice; continuing with a particular group, the *family*, which links the individual consumer to the wider society; and completing the picture with a discussion of aggregate social behavior such as that found in *cultures* and *subcultures*, including those based on *ethnic groupings* and *social classes*.

REFERENCE GROUP INFLUENCES

Groups are of particular interest to consumer scientists and other applied researchers, and to marketing managers because behavior in groups is usually more readily predictable than that of individuals. In everyday conversation, the word 'group' denotes any collection of human beings, from one the size of a football team to one as large as a football crowd or even a nation. In the behavioral sciences, the term has a more specific meaning which limits its scope considerably. In a classic definitional statement, Sprott (1958: 9) wrote that a group is 'a plurality of persons who interact with one another in a given context more than they interact with anyone else. The basic notion is relatively exclusive interaction in a certain context'. A human group involves several people who share common goals or purposes and who interact in the pursuance of these objectives; each member of the group is perceived by others as a member and all members are bound together by patterns and networks of interacting over time.

The interdependence of group members is made enduring by the evolution of a group identity which cements the beliefs, values and norms of the group. The term *reference group* has been used to explain a wide range of human behavior that is pursued in a social context where comparison and aspiration are possible. It requires careful definition. A reference 'group' is any individual or collection of people whom the individual uses as a source of attitudes, beliefs, values or behavior. It may, therefore, be a group to which the individual belongs or one he or she aspires to join. Its essence lies in its use by the individual as a point of comparison for personal attitudes, behavior and performance: a person or people whose social perspectives are assumed by the individual as a frame of reference for his or her own actions.

The implications of reference groups for consumer behavior are extensive. Many purchases are subject to group pressure as consumers try to buy products that others want them to have, that they think will make others accept, approve or envy them, or because they have learned something important about the product from others. Many marketing and advertising strategies use group influences to persuade consumers that the promoted brand is the one endorsed by the group. So advertisements abound with pictures of people purporting to represent groups that are important to consumers. The message is always some variant on the theme: 'Buy this brand because this group recommends it.'

Membership in a group involves the individual in accepting a degree of conformity as the group evolves norms of behavior that define the group's identity by specifying the ideal patterns of behavior that members should perform (frequently called *social roles*). Reference groups influence the behavior of consumers through three primary interpersonal mechanisms. These are usually referred to by the effects observed among consumers: compliance, identification and internalization. Although the mechanisms at work are not the same in each case, on the surface they all tend to produce the identical result, conformity. Indeed, the study of group influences is the study of conformity in human beings. Several classic experiments in social psychology have shown the willingness of individuals to conform in laboratory situations (e.g., Asch 1955; Milgram 1974). These dramatic demonstrations of the willingness of people to agree with the perceptions of others or to obey orders even at variance with their own values and judgments indicate only one extreme of human capacity under closely controlled conditions. But it is undeniable that much consumer choice in affluent economies is imitative, deriving from and serving to reinforce group affiliations and social identities.

One means of inducing conformity among people derives from the power held by groups to reward or punish group members or those who would like to be members. Groups act to create norms of behavior that specify the ideal actions to which members should conform. These norms of behavior are rules and standards of conduct delineating acceptable and unacceptable patterns of group conduct. Reference groups influence individual behavior by establishing and enforcing their norms through the exercise of the ultimate reward, membership, and the threat of the ultimate punishment, denial of acceptance. Normative group influence is reflected in the compliance of people who adjust their behavior to fit group norms in order to attain and maintain group membership and to avoid ostracism. Advertisements sometimes show consumers who buy the right brands being rewarded by group acceptance or being punished by social rejection for failure to buy the brand.

A second avenue by which conformity occurs is through the classic 'referent' power of groups, whereby the individual's liking for the group gives the group the power to influence his or her actions. In this social phenomenon, the group acts as a standard of social comparison; the individual compares his or her behavior to that of the group as a whole and adjusts to match what is observed. The group, in short, acts as a point of reference for the individual. This comparative influence of the group leads to conformity through the process of identification within the individual. Conformity is thus attained by enhancing the self-image of the individual, giving him or her the image desire, or otherwise making the individual more attractive to himself or others. Identification is a common phenomenon among humans as they observe attractive groups and strive to be identified with them. Marketers and advertisers frequently use groups thought to be attractive to their target consumers in brand promotions, thereby showing that purchase and use of the brand will lead to identification with the group.

These first two types of reference group influence suggest that consumers frequently buy brands because they want to be seen as members of attractive groups. However, a final form of group influence leading to conformity depends on the expert power of groups that seem to possess accurate and valuable knowledge in some area of consumer behavior that many consumers either share with the group or currently lack. The expert power accruing to groups by virtue of their special knowledge gives them influence over less knowledgeable consumers, who adjust their behavior to match that of the group because they want to make the right choices and depend on the group's apparent expertise for guidance. This informational influence is an especially powerful force in consumer behavior because consumers regard other people as valuable sources of information.

The process by which consumers adopt the beliefs and behaviors of others because they look to them for guidance in these matters is called internalization because the individual takes the beliefs or behaviors of the group and makes them his or her own, thereby internalizing them. Hence, consumers may act in this way not only because they genuinely agree with the judgment of the group in question but also because this is an efficient and effective way to gain accurate and valuable knowledge. For example, testimonial advertisements feature endorsements of brand excellence based on personal experience. This type of advertisement 'works' partially through the internalization process, as consumers view other consumers who have had experience with a product as possessing expert knowledge about the brand. The testimonial acts to share this knowledge with the viewer, who can then make the information his own (Alsop 1985).

Advertisers who make use of reference group influence must select which of these three types of reference group effects to use in their appeals. The correct choice depends on a firm understanding of the target market and its beliefs, values, knowledge, and attitudes toward the groups considered as reference groups.

- For normative reference group appeals to compliance among consumers, the chief characteristic of the potential reference group ought to be the power of the group to enforce its norms through rewards and punishment. Examples of the use of such appeals in marketing are the ads for personal care products, in which consumers are punished by co-workers or friends for not using anti-dandruff shampoo, deodorant or mouthwash.

- A reference group appeal based upon the comparative influence of the group, and the extent to which the consumer seeks to identify with it, should stress the attractiveness of the group and the desire to be seen as a member thereof. Marketers of many credit cards use the comparative influence of reference groups to sell 'Affinity' cards to consumers. These credit cards feature the logo, colors, name or picture of some group such as a college alumni association, labor union, or professional organization of which the holder would like to be publicly identified as a member (Yang 1986).

- Reference group appeals based upon the informational influence of groups and the consumer's desire to internalize group norms as his or her own should look carefully to the perceived expertise and credibility of the group. An informational appeal using a group having low credibility with consumers is surely going to fail, as is a comparative appeal based on a group consumers find unattractive. Examples of the use of expert power and internalization in advertising are the ads that feature doctors, or actors impersonating doctors, as spokespersons for over-the-counter medicines. Another example would be the use of motor racing stars to endorse car care and other automobile-related products such as tires or gasoline additives.

While conformity is an inevitable feature of social groups, however, absolute compliance is rare. Most people strongly value their independence: even in buying situations in which people choose the same brands as their friends, they often select an alternative color or size. When attempts are made to force compliance with the decisions of others, many individuals will go to lengths to ensure a degree of autonomy: they may show *reactance* by doing precisely the opposite of what they are being pressured into (Venkatesan 1966). Ads sometimes appeal to the desire *not* to be a part of a group by showing how the brand is well suited to individuals who are independent and autonomous: both 'Marlboro Man' and the lone Volkswagen owner exemplify this trend.

Bourne (1956) presents a framework for studying the reference effects of non-membership groups. Identifying conspicuousness as the most pervasive product attribute involved in reference group influence, he pointed out that this has two aspects. Not only must the product be capable of being seen by others; it must also stand out and command attention. The strength of reference group influence differs from product to product; it is likely to be strongest for products and brands about which people have evolved strong norms specifying ideal behavior or usage patterns, and for which they had correspondingly strong brand preferences. The reference group influence might attach mainly to the brand or mainly to the product. For such items as cars, cigarettes and beer, it would be strong for both product and brand; for air conditioners and instant coffee, it would be stronger for the product than the brand; for clothing, furniture, magazines and toilet soap, it would be stronger for the brand than the product; and for canned fruit, laundry soap and radios, it would be relatively weak for both product and brand (cf. Bearden and Etzel 1982). The differences in reference group influence across brands and products might depend on whether they are viewed as luxuries or necessities and whether they are consumed in public or in private. Reference group influence is strongest for publicly consumed luxuries, weakest for privately consumed necessities.

Socially distant reference groups include footballers, filmstars and other celebrities who endorse brands in advertisements on the assumption that they constitute positive reference groups for a large section of the audience. Despite this, however, comparatively little is known about the power to influence a consumer which is possessed by groups he or she evaluates positively and to which he or she would like to belong but with which interaction is greatly limited or impossible. Negative reference groups are also relevant here. These are groups or individuals whose behavior, beliefs, values and so on are repugnant to an individual so that he or she may take active steps not to adopt them. It is probable that consumers select reference groups that are compatible with their self-concepts and ideal self-concepts, and that the use of inconsistent distant 'others' in advertisements may elicit a positive response only in consumers who have already adopted the appropriate groups as personal reference points. Any distant reference group is bound to affect some segment of the market in this way; it is therefore important to take this into consideration in marketing plans.

THE FAMILY AS A CONSUMPTION UNIT

Families exercise some of the most important social or group influences on individual consumption decisions. These influences basically appear in two ways. In the first place, the stage of the family life cycle at which a family is located will determine to some degree the kinds of purchases its members make or contemplate making (Wells and Gubar 1966). The fundamental demographic forces of age, marital status, and presence of children in the family can together play a major role in shaping individual and joint purchase behavior. Marketers and advertisers can use information on the family life cycle to help them develop strategies that conform to the unique needs and circumstances of their target market segments. In addition, as the demographic structures of society change, the family life cycle itself may need to be modified as new types of family form appear (Murphy and Staples 1979). Indeed, as families change, opportunities arise for marketers to develop new products and reposition old ones (Engel *et al.* 1990).

Second, the family (or, at least, the household) often acts as one of the most important reference groups for individual consumers, exercising normative, comparative and informational influences. Much product word-of-mouth communication takes place within families, so this social situation is often pictured in advertisements that show family members discussing products, selecting brands, and consuming in general. Many consumer decisions are taken within the environment of the family and are thus affected by the desires and attitudes of other family members. Many products are purchased on behalf of other members of the buyer's household, perhaps as gifts, and these purchases inevitably reflect some degree of joint decision making. Even the most personal of purchases can be influenced in some details by the behavior of the buyer's family.

The family is also vital because of its mediating function. The culture that consumers are born into, their specific subcultures, social classes and other social groups all shape development both directly and through the agency of the family. Thus the family links the individual with a wider society and it is through this that the individual learns the values, roles, norms, skills, knowledge and practices that are appropriate to adult life. As a result, 'it is through the family that society is able to elicit from the individual his necessary contribution' (Goode 1964: 3). That contribution is inevitably closely bound up with purchasing and consuming.

Family decision making

Kotler (1984: 142–3) distinguishes five buying roles which must be taken into consideration in analyses of family consumption behavior:

- the *initiator* – the person from whom the idea of buying a given product first comes,
- the *influencer* – who consciously or unconsciously affects the shape of the purchase in some way, perhaps by suggesting the brand that ought to be selected or the time of purchase (this person may be an opinion leader),
- the *decider* – who makes any of the main or subsidiary choices that determine the precise nature of the purchase (what, how many, when, where, etc.),
- the *purchaser* – who actually carries out the final act of purchase, and
- the *user* – who makes actual use of the item bought.

These roles can be closely associated with the stages of the consumer decision process. Almost all family decisions are affected by more than one of these consumer roles. The selection of a venue for a family trip, for example, although paid for and purchased by the parents, may be initiated and decisively influenced by the children. Again, the majority of men's toiletry and perfume products are purchased by women: much advertising for these products is, therefore, aimed at the deciders, influencers and buyers rather than the users.

A considerable amount of empirical consumer research has been concerned with the roles of family members, notably husbands and wives, in decision making. The expectation that either husbands or wives would dominate decisions relating to specific products was raised by a study of married couples (in each of which the husband was a graduate student) who were asked how they would spend a windfall (Kenkel 1961). The research was carried out at a time when marital roles were more differentiated than is now usually the case. The money could not be saved or spent on a purchase the couple had already agreed on. The products mentioned by the respondents were classified into five categories: *wife personal* (clothes, jewellery, etc.), *wife household* (washing machine, cooking utensils), *husband* (books, clothes, watch), *joint family* (furniture, TV, car) and *children* (toys, clothes). In 40 percent of the cases, husbands and wives contributed equally to the discussions in terms of the amount of talking each did; in 42 percent, husbands talked more than their wives. When husbands predominated, more items which were husband- or children-specific were agreed upon than when both spouses did about the same amount of talking. In the remaining cases, where wives predominated, more wife-personal goods were decided upon but the husbands still received more items than in the first two cases.

Regardless of the amount of talking done by each spouse, husbands contributed more ideas in 60 percent of cases and, when this occurred, fewer items for children were agreed upon. But when the wives contributed more ideas, more products for the family as a whole were chosen. Women contributed far more to the harmony and smooth running of the conversations by raising their husbands' esteem, being affectionate, laughing or joking. The restricted range of consumer types considered, the hypothetical nature of the situation, and changes in family roles and expectations that have taken place since makes generalization impossible. But even this early study emphasizes that interactions and the scope of decisions taken between family members in consumption planning reflects the self-perceptions and roles of husbands and wives. Davis (1970) raised several interesting issues with respect to the purchase of cars and furniture. The blanket question of whether it was husbands or wives who made the decision was shown to be naive. For cars, husbands decided when to buy in over two-thirds of cases; however, three-quarters of the time, wives decided on other aspects of the decision, such as the color of the car. These figures were identical irrespective of whether the information came from the husband or the wife. In other product fields, however, there were considerable differences in the husbands' and wives' respective perceptions of their roles.

In a more comprehensive study, Davis and Rigaux (1974) analyzed the influence exerted by husbands and wives at different stages of the decision process in order to determine whether there were differences in partners' roles as the procedure unfolded and how each partner perceived their role. Each member of the Belgian couples who participated in the study specified the person who had been dominant in making the overall decision for some twenty-five product areas. Decisions were classified in four ways for the sample as a whole. Two of the categories, those which were *husband-dominant* (for life insurance and other insurance) and *wife-dominant* (for cleaning products, kitchenware, children's clothing, wife's clothing, food and furnishings) are self-explanatory. The joint decisions were split. Product decisions in which husbands and wives contributed jointly in more than half the families surveyed were designated *autonomic* and included cosmetics, non-prescription drugs, appliances, housing upkeep, husband's clothing, alcoholic drinks, garden tools, savings objectives, forms of saving and cars. When less than half the families in the sample contributed jointly to a decision, it was classified as *syncratic*; these decisions were for children's toys, living-room furniture, outside entertainment, vacation, school, housing and TV.

The roles of husband and wives were found to differ slightly at three stages of the decision process: *problem recognition*, the development of a want or need; *information search*, pre-purchase planning and decision making; and *the final decision* or act of purchase. But over the twenty-five decision areas investigated, the prevailing pattern was for husband and wife to assume joint responsibility at all three stages. However, husbands tended to retain dominance over the decision process in the case of insurance products; wives for kitchenware, cleaning products, their own clothes and those of the children, and food.

The final part of the investigation was concerned with role consensus, the extent to which partners agreed on their relative contributions to decision making. Sixty-eight percent of respondents agreed. Both husbands and wives exaggerated their individual roles, however, at the second stage (information search). Overall, the study is valuable for its classification system which has been used in subsequent investigations; for clarifying that it may often be sufficient for market researchers to interview one spouse in order to ascertain the role of both partners in the decision process (cf. Foxall 1980); and for extending this research beyond the United States, where most investigation of this kind has taken place.

Ferber and Lee (1974) tested the proposition that families usually have one member who is responsible for finances as a whole, the 'Family Financial Officer' (FFO). It proved comparatively easy to identify such a spouse among the newly married couples investigated: the role of the FFO was to look after the payment of bills, keep track of expenditure in relation to budgets, and use money left over at the end of the pay period. Over the first two years of marriage, following a period in which joint decision making was emphasized, the role of FFO increasingly accrued to the wife. There was also a tendency for the wife to assume this role when she was 'more quality-minded, more economy-minded, or more bargain-minded', and in families where there was a likelihood of financial disagreements, especially where this involved savings priorities. Couples were more likely to act jointly where both partners shared a savings goal and where their ideas of savings priorities coincided. When the husband assumed the FFO role, savings as a proportion of total income tended to be higher; while car purchases tended to be less frequent in this case, durable purchases as a whole were not affected.

Financial control

Recent sociological research in the United Kingdom reveals a more complicated pattern of responsibility for spending among husbands and wives (Burgoyne 1990; Pahl 1980, 1983, 1988, 1989; Wilson 1987). Particularly relevant are the consequences of the recognition that spending is a function of both the sources of household members' income(s) and the control of money within the home (Pahl 1989). In brief, where the wife controls the family finances (i.e., the money, cash or bank account), she tends also to be responsible for household financial management (the allocation of resources, payment of bills). Where the husband controls the finances, however, he may share some management functions, principally housekeeping (for which the wife may receive a specific allowance), but retains responsibility for paying major bills. Where the wife controls the finances, she also has responsibility for paying major bills as well as day-to-day housekeeping. It is rare for the wife to control the finances while the husband manages them. Further, while the amount spent on house-keeping (mainly food) is related, as would be expected, to the level of household income, it is also linked with the source of that income and the pattern of income control in households (Pahl 1989, 1990).

The patterns and sources of control and their implications for family expenditure are worth considering in detail. Pahl (1990) identifies four patterns of financial control. In the first two, *wife-controlled pooling* and *husband-controlled pooling*, the couples possessed joint bank accounts: the allocation of families to one or other depended on whether the wife reported that she controlled the household's money (wife-controlled pooling) or whether she considered either that her husband controlled the finances or that they were jointly controlled (husband-dominated pooling). In the case of wife-controlled pooling, it was generally the wife who paid the major bills including those for rates (local taxes), fuel, telephone, insurance and rent/mortgage. The tendency was for neither partner to have a separate account and for all financial transactions to be dealt with from the joint account. In the case of husband-controlled pooling, the husband usually paid the major bills.

Lack of a bank account was the result of the couple's being paid in cash and their being too poor to justify a formal banking arrangement, or the result of an objection by one or both partners to a joint account. Where the wife considered her husband to exert total control over the family's financial concerns, the arrangement was designated husband-controlled: the husband usually had his own bank account from which he paid all the main bills. Where the wife considered that she controlled the family finances (situations designated wife-controlled) there was usually no bank account at all and the wife paid all bills in cash. This arrangement was commonest among low-income, working-class families where neither partner had formal qualifications. While the wife paid the main bills, the husband had an allowance set aside for his personal spending. Wife control was, therefore, equivalent to wife management. It contrasts with husband control, which was normally associated with relatively high levels of income. These couples would often set aside a fixed amount for housekeeping which was paid to the wife as an allowance. However, while she paid the routine expenses required for day-to-day living, her husband would typically pay the main bills. These couples, in the majority of which only the husband was earning, generally kept their money separate; if the wife did earn in her own right, her money was typically allocated to housekeeping expenses while her husband paid the main bills.

Wife-controlled pooling was associated with medium levels of income and the employment of both partners, while husband-controlled pooling was more probable among higher-income households, especially if only the husband worked. A general finding that was especially marked among the households with pooling arrangements was that the more the wife contributed to the household income, the more probable it was that she controlled the household finances. If neither partner worked, the wife tended to take this control: the general pattern in such families was of a struggle to survive economically. In pooling arrangements where husbands and wives were of different social classes, the middle-class partner controlled the finances. Similarly for qualifications: the educationally qualified partner tended to take control, though if both partners were qualified, such control was usually exerted by the husband. The general pattern of spending responsibilities by gender is shown in Table 9.1.

Whereas wives tended to pay for food, their own clothing and that of their children, presents and school expenses, husbands tended to pay for their own clothing, the car, repairs and decorating, meals away from home and alcohol. Joint expenditures, a category which was expanded since the early 1970s partly because of an increase in joint accounts (Wilson 1987), were on consumer durables, charity donations and Christmas spending (Table 9.2).

Table 9.1 Control of finances by wife's earnings as a proportion of husband's earnings

	Wife's earnings		
	Over 30% of husband's earnings	*Under 30% of husband's earnings*	*Wife had no earnings*
Wife control	6	–	8
Wife-controlled pooling	12	8	7
Husband-controlled pooling	5	14	20
Husband control	5	5	12
Total number	28	27	47

Source: Pahl, J. (1990) 'Household spending, personal spending and the control of money in marriage'. *Sociology*, 24, 124. Reproduced by permission of the British Sociological Association and Dr J. Pahl.

Table 9.2 Household spending patterns

	Person responsible for spending on each item			
	Wife	Either/both	Husband	N/A other answers
Food	74	18	9	–
Mortgage/rent	31	23	35	11
Rates	33	19	36	12
Fuel	30	27	41	2
Telephone	28	10	41	21
Insurance	28	24	40	9
Clothes (wife)	78	15	7	–
Clothes (husband)	24	27	50	–
Clothes (children)	69	24	7	1
Car or motor bike	4	14	51	31
School expenses	63	13	10	15
Repairs and decorating	14	28	58	1
Consumer goods	12	42	41	5
Children's pocket money	27	27	16	31
Presents	61	36	2	1
Meals out/trips out	4	23	60	13
Holiday expenses	10	35	38	17
Charities	43	48	4	5
Christmas expenses	44	50	5	1
Drinks in house	13	15	36	37
Drinks in pub	2	9	55	34

Source: Pahl, J. (1990) 'Household spending, personal spending and the control of money in marriage', *Sociology*, 24, 126. Reproduced by permission of the British Sociological Association and Dr J. Pahl.
Note: All percentages of total 102.

However, patterns of responsibility for spending differed somewhat with the control of finances:

- Depending on whether or not there was a joint account, the person who controlled the finances paid the major bills such as fuel, rates, mortgage/rent, telephone and insurance.
- Where there was a joint account, and regardless of who controlled it, both partners took responsibility for buying such consumer durables as washing machines and refrigerators.
- Where there was no joint account, husbands were more likely to pay for consumer durables.

The amount spent on housekeeping (principally food) increased with the income of either partner and with overall household income. However, increases in wives' earnings were followed by higher proportional increases in food expenditure. Although husbands contributed more absolutely to housekeeping (they earned on average four times as much), wives contributed a higher proportion of their incomes to housekeeping. Moreover, a greater proportion of household income was spent on housekeeping under wife control or wife-controlled pooling arrangements (though these represented the less affluent households where a higher proportion of income would normally be accounted for in this way).

Men reported that they spent more on personal items and leisure than did women (86 percent compared with 67 percent). However, expenditure on such items is notoriously difficult to ascertain with accuracy: for instance, men overestimated the amount their wives spent in these ways while wives overestimated their husbands' corresponding expenditures. Husbands were more likely to take their leisure spending money from their earnings while wives were more likely to take it from housekeeping money. Somewhat surprisingly, husbands spent more than wives on leisure under wife control or wife-controlled pooling systems, while wives spent more than their husbands under husband control or husband-controlled pooling.[1]

Consumer socialization

The influence of children on family expenditures has long been recognized by advertisers whose appeals to children have had the intention of persuading the parents. The market for children's products has itself grown rapidly in the last several decades and the teenage market in particular is an attractive segment. Despite this, comparatively little is known about the ways in which young people learn to play consumption roles that characterize their adult lives, i.e., consumer *socialization*.

Socialization refers to the process in which individuals learn the attitudes and behavior patterns appropriate to their social roles. Although all of life may be a process of socialization as new roles are acquired and learned, the term is applied especially to 'the process by which the young human being acquires the values and knowledge of his group and learns the social roles appropriate to his position in it' (Goode 1964: 112). *Consumer socialization* is 'the process by which young people acquire skills, knowledge, and the attitudes relevant to their functioning as consumers in the marketplace' (Ward 1974). Children are important to marketers for three fundamental reasons (McNeal 1988).

- They represent a large market in themselves because they have their own money to spend.
- They influence their parents' selection of products and brands.
- They will grow up to be consumers of everything; hence marketers need to start building up their brand consciousness and loyalty as early as possible.

Ward suggests several additional reasons why consumer socialization is relevant to consumer research and marketing management (and, equally, to educational authorities and those responsible for the ethical regulation of marketing).

- Understanding childhood experience may provide a key to the prediction of adult consumer behavior. The way in which the individual originally learns to process information gained from advertisements, for instance, might well affect his or her adult attitudes toward and responses to advertising.
- Knowing how young people acquire the skills, knowledge and attitudes relevant to consumption, and isolating the factors that influence children, should help ensure that marketing campaigns aimed at children become more effective (or stay within the bounds of what is socially and ethically acceptable). Much advertising to children has been

founded on trial and error methods rather than precise knowledge of children's decision processes.

- Child socialization is relevant to understanding family decision making with respect to consumption. While much research has concentrated on husband–wife interaction, comparatively little has been concerned with children's roles.
- Knowledge of consumer socialization is pertinent to formulators of government policy on consumer protection and to those responsible for consumer education, including home economists. Attempts to regulate advertising to children have depended on an imperfect knowledge base as surely as has the marketing planning behind the ads.
- There should be theoretical advantage in understanding more fully the socialization of children into their adult economic roles. Models of the consumption process have not accentuated this aspect of consumer behavior: further research can only increase the predictive capacities of such models.

Based on an extensive literature review, Moschis (1985) proposes a number of ways in which family communication impacts the economic socialization of young people. Parents partially determine their children's ability to appraise advertising information and their consumption motives. They also help shape the preferences of their children for brands and stores. Parental influence has an impact on all stages in the child's decision process but is particularly important for shopping goods rather than convenience or specialty goods and is greater in the case of items engendering more perceived risk. Parental influence also depends on social and demographic factors. Though family influences are generally more important than those of peer groups in early childhood, the influence of parents declines as children get older. Children acquire a considerable degree of independence between the ages of 5 and 9. One reason for this appears to be a failure of parents as a rule to establish their authority in this area: very little purposive training of children as consumers takes place in most families and parents seem to expect their offspring to learn from observation to imitate other family members (McNeal 1964). Moschis argues that parental influence continues longer among middle-class American youths than other groups, and that such influence is greater on boys than girls when the product in question involves high social risk.

Advertising appears to exert a considerable influence over children but it is not certain how young people process or evaluate the claims made by advertisers or how they distinguish the persuasive and informational elements of advertising messages. The precise interrelationship of parental influences and formal communications is also unclear. Children also influence their parents' roles and behaviors, a procedure known as 'reverse socialization'. The range of products where children have actual power to make and implement direct purchase decisions is restricted but young people can have a general influence on household decision making for such items as cars, holidays and even furniture. Mothers who are relatively child-centered (defined as showing greater than average concern for their children's welfare) are less likely to give in to their youngsters' demands for particular types of cereal (Berey and Pollay 1968).

Parents are more likely to yield to children's demands as the children grow older (Ward and Wackman 1972), perhaps because parents believe that their children become more competent judges as they develop, more capable consumers whose views should be taken into active consideration. Children's most frequent influence attempts concern food products and these are also the products on which parents are most likely to yield.

Adult consumer socialization is also worthy of attention. As grown-ups take on new roles, their expected behaviors, including economic activities, are modified. The concept of the family life cycle is useful in organizing the transitions from one type of buying to another as new consumer-related responsibilities are assumed.

CULTURES AND SUBCULTURES

Culture, the most general and pervasive influence of the social structure, consists of the knowledge, behaviors, customs and technologies socially acquired by human beings. Culture is transmitted by social learning, example, instruction and imitation rather than by hereditary means. Although both anthropologists and marketing scientists who have investigated cultures have stressed the differences in beliefs, actions and techniques that mark off one cultural system from another, all cultures actually have much in common. Certain cultural norms appear to be universal including age grading, athletics, bodily adornment, cleanliness, courtship, cosmology, dream interpretation, education, ethics, etiquette, faith healing, funeral rites, incest taboos, marriage, property rights, religious ritual, status differentiation, surgery, tool making and weather control (Murdock 1940). Although these general characteristics are to be found in all societies, they obviously differ in form and detail from one context to another.

The influence of culture

Culture refers to everything that members of a society inherit through social contact with others rather than by biological inheritance. It consists of ideas, techniques, behavior patterns, rules, rituals and customs that are socially transmitted from generation to generation in the process of socialization. Culture is, therefore, *learned*, as a result of social interaction rather than genetic endowment, and it is both deliberately and incidentally *inculcated* in younger members of a social group. Although culture is *ideational*, including the language and other systems of symbols that make consistent social life possible, it is also *adaptive*, capable of changing and evolving as social and other pressures influence it. Culture satisfies both the physical and the derived needs of those who come under its influence, i.e., it is *gratifying*. As a result, it is *integrative* inasmuch as its various elements form a consistent whole which is internalized by the individual who thereby comes to feel that he or she rightly belongs within its confines (Murdock 1940). A cultural system serves to give its members an identity, to tell them who they are or what they are like, and how they should interpret the world around them.

The elements constituting culture are as follows (Johnson 1962):

- *Cognitive and belief elements* Cognitive elements include empirical knowledge of the physical and social worlds, science, technology, practical knowledge, ideas about social structure and organization and the way in which society works. Unlike the cognitive

206 Consumers in context

elements of culture, beliefs are not open to empirical validation or refutation, e.g., religious beliefs and systems of magic. Beliefs are, nevertheless, interwoven with cognitive elements to form knowledge systems that justify and control attitudes and behavior.

- *Values and norms* Values are consensual views about the kind of life individuals should follow: formal and informal rules specifying the goals they should pursue and how they should pursue them. These ideas differ from society to society – competition with others is highly regarded in some cultures, while incurring severe sanctions in others. Norms are defined in two ways: first, they refer to patterns of ideal behavior which a society rewards; second, a norm is a description of the behavior of the majority of a social system's members. Hence, in contrast to the gleaming white teeth featured in toothpaste advertisements in the West, black teeth are admired in some parts of Southeast Asia (Kassarjian and Robertson 1981: 484).

- *Signs*, which include signals and symbols. Signals indicate the existence or presence of a thing, an occurrence or condition, as when a bell signals that dinner is ready or that the next round of a boxing match is about to begin. Street signs, sounds and pictures all function as signals. Symbols are usually verbal and refer to concepts; languages, for instance, are systems of symbols which facilitate communication but which differ considerably from society to society. Kassarjian and Robertson (1981) point out that while a white feather denotes cowardice in England, a yellow feather means the same in America; and, while white represents purity, quality and prestige in the West, it connotes mourning in much of Asia.

- *Non-normative behavior* denotes ways of acting that involve the individual's personal reactions and responses to the culture in which he or she lives. Individual predispositions and personality traits determine non-normative patterns of behavior which are not openly punished by society unless they become so extreme as to threaten major rules, norms, mores or folk ways that have been traditionally established over many generations. Non-normative behavior thus includes those eccentricities that fall within socially defined limits.

The marketing system and the marketer-dominated and buyer-dominated processes of communication involved in consumer socialization are important vehicles of cultural transmission in many societies (Douglas and Isherwood 1980). Television, movies, advertising and the fashion industry among others broadcast common meanings not only of economic goods and services but of many practices and institutions that define modern societies (McCracken 1981). What individuals perceive of their world is not a result of physical factors alone or even of their motives and attitudes. It depends also on their cultural frames of reference, the ways in which values are attached first to products and services and then communicated by those goods as they convey the meanings on which culture depends.

Ethnic subcultures

Just as entire populations that share a common system of beliefs, attitudes, behaviors and social practices are known as 'cultures', so large groups within a society are designated 'subcultures'. Strictly speaking, a subculture is a small-scale society within the total population, containing both sexes, all age groups and institutions found in the total society. In practice, the term is used more loosely than this to refer to any group that has discernible behavioral features which make it worthy of consideration separately from the overall society in which it exists. Subcultures in this broader sense may thus be determined on the basis of religion, area or region of residence: we speak, for instance, of the 'teenage subculture' or of the 'black subculture'. The important feature of this perspective is that these groups exhibit distinctive patterns of values, lifestyles, demographics and consumer behavior that require the marketer to adjust his or her strategy to be specifically congruent with the needs and propensities of the subculture in question. Hence, marketing to teens requires a different appeal from that directed to their parents, even for the same products. Some 'subcultures' are defined largely or entirely by their possession and functional/ conspicuous use of artefacts supplied by the marketing system: camera clubs, punks, motorbike groups, opera buffs, and so on.

Knowledge of subcultures within a company's domestic or overseas markets can provide a basis for differential marketing strategies. Such segmentation requires penetrating marketing analyses that identify the behavioral criteria by which subgroups within the total market can be defined and on which specialized approaches to meeting the consumption preferences of differing segments can be based. In order to appeal successfully to a subculture, the marketing strategy must express or support relevant values, beliefs and lifestyles. Every element of culture that has an impact on consumption makes demands on the sensitivity of differential marketing strategies.

A common mistake is to assume that a so-called subculture is more homogeneous than it really is and to miss the obvious segments that exist within the subsociety. We cannot exemplify this by reference even to all major subcultures within Western societies but we will concentrate on the black subculture in the US. It is usual to imagine that the entire 11 to 12 percent of the American population that is black constitutes a single subculture: in marketing terms, a single segment. In fact, there may be no such thing as a 'black subculture' based solely on race/color as a distinct entity. Certainly, as far as marketing is concerned, there is no single black market. Lifestyle differences may be as pronounced among the members of a subculture as they are within the larger 'mainstream culture' (*Marketing News* 1981).

Afro-Americans are usually cited as the prime example of a subculture within a larger culture that is attractive to marketers because of their substantial spending power. It is easy to think that all black consumers can be grouped together and treated as a distinct market segment. Nevertheless, for marketing purposes it may be more profitable to view the case of black consumers (as is true of all subcultures) from two different perspectives. First, from the segmentation perspective, it only makes sense to treat blacks as a unique segment when they exhibit systematic patterns of product use, attitudes, behavior or values that require a specialized marketing approach. For instance, greater than average television viewership suggests that TV networks should focus greater attention on black viewers (Harris 1990), perhaps even to the point of developing special shows (Freeman 1990). Marketers may, however, incur the wrath of subcultural groups if they single them out as market segments for products that may be potentially harmful, as R. J. Reynolds Tobacco Company discovered to their dismay with the cigarette *Uptown* targeted specifically to blacks. Public pressure based on the argument that such a harmful product should not be pushed on a specific group forced withdrawal of the brand (Quinn 1990).

Generalizations about black consumers should always be tempered by taking into account socioeconomic factors that may be responsible for the unique patterns of behavior that the marketer finds interesting (Engel, Blackwell and Miniard 1990). Heavy consumption of soft drinks among some black consumers may be attributed to younger average age, which is itself linked to this consumption pattern across the population. The same holds true for Hispanic consumers or any other group that marketers are tempted to think of as a homogeneous subculture. The demographic variables of ethnicity, age, national origin, or geography should always be seen in combination with accompanying variables that apply to the society as a whole.

A second perspective marketers may take with regard to the use of subcultures is in developing promotional messages tailored to appeal to their different values, lifestyles and interests without specifically treating them as distinct market segments. Thus advertisements may be changed to make them more convincing to subcultures by using different people in the ad, by including special images and symbols, by translating the ad copy into other languages, and by using targeted media. Hence one can find different versions of the same magazine ad appearing in both mainstream magazines and simultaneously in magazines devoted to particular subcultural groups. Specialty advertising agencies will be commissioned to develop ads that will appeal to a subculture, as when Burrell Advertising Inc. of Chicago, the US's largest black advertising agency, develops TV ads to run side by side with other ads for the same brand. For example, Burrell developed a special Crest toothpaste ad for P&G:

> A black father, en route to his son's concert, muses about the changes parenthood has wrought, including his concerns about the toothpaste his son uses as well as his anxiety about getting to the performance on time . . . Explains Burrell, 'The focus is on the importance of the father figure in the black family. Whites think the spot is nice and touching, but it has a little extra meaning for blacks.'
>
> (Tracy 1985: 47)

Social classes

Social classes are also subcultures; they encompass both genders and all age groups and are distinct components of the system of social stratification. Social stratification represents the hierarchical division of members of a society into relative levels of prestige, status and power. The basic reasoning behind the idea of social stratification is that society can be conceptualized as a series of divisions arranged in a hierarchy, much the same as layers of rock are found in geological stratification. The divisions to which *social* stratification refers, however, are not immutable and the class and power structure is always changing in some degree as a result of upward and downward mobility. This social movement can present the marketer with an opportunity to target groups of consumers moving up and down the social ladder and to develop strategies to appeal to their special needs.

Social class refers to divisions in the population based on objective economic criteria, such as source of income and wealth: occupation usually provides the most useful proxy variable. Definitions of social class thus carry the implication that economic position in society is fundamental to the analysis of social behavior, but members of different social classes can be distinguished also by their differing levels of education and income. Class differences are of interest to marketers because they reflect varied patterns of consumption behavior that are independent of levels of income alone. Because social classes manifest distinctive consumption patterns, they make natural market segments. In addition, their characteristic demographic differences in education, income, occupation and geographic spread provide useful guides for the marketing strategies involved in retail site location, pricing and especially advertising, where knowledge of social class and demographic variations can suggest the tone of voice, appropriate cultural symbols, language, choice of spokespersons, and other aspects of the content and presentation of the message. Thus, knowing the dominant socioeconomic status of a market segment (working class, middle class, etc.) provides the marketer with valuable insights that can help in the design of effective market strategies.

Another dimension of social stratification which is of prime interest to consumer researchers and marketing managers is that of social status. *Social status* refers to the relative honor or prestige that society accords the occupants of a certain social position. Status reflects economic factors but it does not coincide with class. Impoverished aristocrats, to take an extreme example, may well receive status which does not reflect their current wealth but which is based on past wealth, power, manners, accent, behavior and other social criteria held by a particular social system to denote esteem. Similarly, amassing a fortune does not guarantee high status unless the successful person adopts other patterns of behavior that also command prestige. In a society where mobility between the classes exists, there may be a need to show others that one has been upwardly mobile, that he or she has 'arrived', and this is done by means of status symbolism, 'by the use of various symbols (such as material objects, styles of demeanor, taste and speech, types of association and even appropriate opinions)' (Berger 1965: 95). Many products and brands serve as status symbols, the purchase of which may either literally increase the social status or prestige of consumers who buy them or simply symbolize a current status position to others. In both cases, the effect rests upon shared cultural understandings of which products or brands confer status and which detract from it. Such understandings are also inherent in the ways in which marketers try to enhance the status implications of their brands by using perceptual cues such as color (royal blue, gold, silver), country of origin (France, Germany and Japan, for instance, all carry specific connotations that confer prestige), designer name (Calvin Klein, Bill Blass), high price, exclusive distribution, and so on.

Although many social commentators and even some market researchers attempt to play down the influence of class and status, their reality is confirmed by the fact that nearly everyone has some impression of a system of social class and status and of their own position within it. Moreover, most people could readily be able to say where they think various occupational groups should be located within the class system and there is also often wide agreement on this among the groups themselves.

These subjective impressions of the reality of social class and status are substantiated by statistics showing that many social, economic, psychological and physical characteristics of groups of people in the population vary with a more objectively defined class structure.

They include: fertility, birth and mortality rates, educational attainments, patterns of social behavior, religion, divorce rates, the incidence and extent of diseases, occupation and consumption patterns. Class and status differences are apparent not only in product preferences and usage rates but also in such facets of consumer behavior as shopping frequencies, store perceptions and susceptibility to advertising. Moreover, social class offers marketing managers one of the more convenient and dependable means of segmenting markets and, even within the increasingly popular lifestyle segmentation which cuts across class and other criteria, social stratification plays a central role.

Consumer researchers and marketing managers use the descriptive concept of social class to refer to whatever economically defined groupings within society are useful in distinguishing consumption patterns. Like others, they broadly distinguish working, middle and upper classes; these demographically based social worlds reflect differences among consumers (in occupational status, education, income, source of income, house type and dwelling area, and so on) that can be associated with differences in the purchase of products and brands (Coleman 1983). While none of these on its own is wholly indicative of social class, they represent the most direct practical way of making the concept usable in the real world of marketing and consumption. Marketers of many goods and services deliberately attempt to make their offerings appeal to specific social groups. Waterford crystal, for instance, has traditionally appealed to an exclusive, older monied group of consumers, though the company missed the important new market of affluent baby boomers in the 1980s and had to adjust their marketing strategy (particularly new products and advertising) in response

Table 9.3 Social class perceptions of branded goods and services

Product/Service	Upper/ Upper- Middle	Middle	Lower- Middle	Upper- Lower/ Lower	All	Don't Know	Total
a) Beer							
Heineken	88	9	1	–	1	1	100%
Michelob	67		4	1	2	3	100
Coors	22	54	16	2	3	3	100
Bud Light	22	53	14	3	5	3	100
Miller	14	50	22	6	6	2	100
Budweiser	4	46	37	7	4	2	100
Old Style*	3	33	36	22	1	2	100
b) Stores							
Marshall Field	87	10	–	–	–	3	100
Carson Pirie Scott	59	33	3	1	1	3	100
Sears	3	40	44	10	3	–	100
Montgomery Ward	1	35	42	15	1	6	100
K-Mart	–	7	32	57	1	3	100
c) Restaurants							
Wendy's	8	61	15	2	10	4	100
Burger King	3	49	21	10	15	2	100
Denny's	2	49	39	7	2	1	100
							n = (163)

Source: Gronhaug, K. and P. S. Trapp (1989) 'Perceived social class appeals of branded goods and services'. *Journal of Consumer Marketing*, 6, 15. Reproduced by permission of MCB University Press Ltd.

to this group's growing demand for fine crystal (Wilson and Dunkin 1984). Media preferences also differ according to class and presumed status, and this gives rise from time to time to marketing innovations. In the late 1980s, a new magazine was launched to appeal specifically to well-educated, affluent readers: *Fame* was designed for the status-oriented, aggressive spender and overspender (Reilly 1988).

Perhaps more important than whether products and services actually appeal with some degree of exclusivity to specific classes are the perceptions consumers have of the class identities of brands. Gronhaug and Trapp (1989) argue that social class is more predictive of consumers' choices of particular brands of convenience goods because 'attitudes, values, and activities vary across social segments and . . . social class also reflects variations in lifestyle'. They describe a study of consumers' associations of brands with class affiliation in which respondents were asked which social class they thought was most likely to buy or use or go to named brands or places. Table 9.3 summarizes their results.

The results indicate that consumers do link brands of products and services with definite social classes, and that these categories are likely to influence brand choice. Such findings as these are capable of influencing marketing strategies by providing a basis for product positioning, for the design of advertising and other marketing communications (linking the intended consumer behavior to media preferences and symbolism), and to broaden distribution strategies (Gronhaug and Trapp 1989).

SUMMARY

Consumers are influenced by their group memberships and, particularly, by their reference groups. Brand choice, conformity and independence depend to an extent on social affiliations; reference group influences differ from product to product and from brand to brand. Many consumer decisions are made within the context of a single group, the family or household, which links the individual to the wider society. The attitudes and behavior of one family member may affect the purchase and consumption decisions of other family members, while consumer needs and the ability to satisfy them vary with the stage in the family life cycle. Patterns of husband–wife interaction in the consumption decision process are complex. Styles of influence can be identified for most products, however, and responsibility for the outcome of the decision process can be allocated to the wife or the husband or jointly. Financial responsibility and control depend on the working/earning status of the wife compared to that of the husband, and on such factors as education and whether the couple have a joint banking account. The family also provides the forum in which young people are initially socialized by gaining economic knowledge and assuming the roles of consumer, buyer, saver, worker and so on.

Culture adds another dimension to the study of consumer behavior, taking us beyond the individual and his or her immediate social system. Culture includes all those symbols, artefacts and behavior patterns that are passed on socially (rather than inherited biologically) from one generation to the next. It includes beliefs, values and norms, signs and non-normative behavior. Although there are wide differences from one culture to another, there are many cultural universals – items such as mourning and incest taboos – which are found in some form or other in all known cultures. Subcultures are groups within a society that share the social structure of that society but that have a unique lifestyle often based on religion, ethnicity or social class. Ethnic and class-based subcultures are probably the most important for marketing managers to understand and respond to, and this chapter has provided examples of their implications for social perception and behavior, patterns of purchasing, and the use of goods and services.

NOTE

1 Several methodological problems are evident from research on husband–wife interaction in household decision making. A pervasive difficulty is that of deciding whether both spouses should be interviewed and, where they are, ensuring that the interviews are carried out in a similar manner with each. A single partner's perceptions of the decision process might be highly biased: no doubt some of the variations in result stem from inconsistencies in sample composition from survey to survey (Davis 1970; Park 1982). A family's economic behavior is not usually the result of unified or homogeneous planning and action: the role dimensions that have been discussed reflect differing perceptions and differing economic positions and levels of strength. It is obvious that for accurate information on most purchase and saving decisions and behavior, consumer researchers need to interview both spouses, perhaps together as well as separately, and to interpret their findings with a great deal of sensitivity to the economic role structures not only of the family but of the wider industrial society.

   The assumption that the major purchasing decisions are inevitably made by the wife is not always accurate. Where this role does accrue to the wife, conflict may arise as a result of her being not simply an agent for others but responsible in addition for her own needs which have to be satisfied from the same household funds. The assumption is simplistic, despite the continuing tendency to categorize wives as 'family purchasing agents' (Whiteside 1964) or 'consumption administrators' (Galbraith 1976). It is evident from the research reviewed above that despite the closeness of most wives to purchase and consumption decisions and behaviors, these role descriptions do not provide a complete or even reliable guide to the complexities of decision making within the family. Nor do they offer a proper depiction of the roles performed by wives across the spectrum of households' arrangements for financial control and financial management.

   A difficulty with all of the research reviewed here is that despite its indication of the complexities inherent in household decision making, its conclusions are based on small samples which make it impossible to estimate the proportion of each type of decision-unit or form of financial control within the population as a whole.

References

Aaker, D. A. and D. E. Bruzzone (1985) 'Causes of irritation in advertising', *Journal of Marketing*, 49, 47–57.

Ajzen, I. (1985) 'From intentions to actions: a theory of planned behavior', in *Action-control: From Cognition to Behavior*, Heidelberg: Springer, 11–39.

Ajzen, I. (1987) 'Attitudes, traits, and actions: dispositional prediction of behavior in personality and social psychology', *Advances in Experimental Social Psychology* 20, 1–63.

Ajzen, I. and M. Fishbein (1977) 'Attitudinal–behavioral relations: a theoretical analysis and review of empirical research', *Psychological Bulletin*, 84, 888–918.

Ajzen, I. and M. Fishbein (1980) *Understanding Attitudes and Predicting Social Behavior*, Englewood Cliffs, NJ: Prentice-Hall.

Alba, J. W. and J. W. Hutchinson (1987) 'Dimensions of consumer expertise', *Journal of Consumer Research*, 13, March 411–54.

Albanese, P. J. (1990) 'Personality, consumer behavior, and marketing research: a new thoeretical and empirical approach', in E. C. Hirschman (ed.) *Research in Consumer Behavior*, 4, Greenwich, CT: JAI Press, 1–49.

Alexander, M. W. and B. Judd (1978) 'Do nudes in ads enhance brand recall?', *Advertising Age*, 18 February, 47–50.

Alhadeff, D. (1982) *Microeconomics and Human Behavior*, Los Angeles: University of California Press.

Allen, C. T. and T. J. Madden (1985) 'A closer look at classical conditioning', *Journal of Consumer Research*, 12, 301–15.

Allison, N. K. (1978) 'A psychometric development of a test for consumer alienation from the marketplace', *Journal of Marketing Research*, 15, 565–75.

Allison, R. I. and K. P. Uhl (1964) 'Influence of beer brand identification on taste perception', *Journal of Marketing Research*, 1, 36–9.

Allsopp, J. F. (1986a) 'Personality as a determinant of beer and cider consumption among young men', *Personality and Individual Differences*, 7, 341–7.

Allsopp, J. F. (1986b) 'The distribution of on-licence beer and cider consumption and its personality determinants among young men', *European Journal of Marketing*, 20(3/4), 44–62.

Alsop, R. (1985) 'Real people star in many ads, but are they really credible?' *Wall Street Journal*, May 23.

Alsop, R. (1987a) 'More food advertising plays on cancer and cardiac fears', *Wall Street Journal*, 8 October.

Alsop, R. (1987b) 'Don Rickles and Devilish Kid bring dull carpet ads to life', *Wall Street Journal*, 9 July.

Alsop, R. (1988) 'Research probes emotional ties to products', *Wall Street Journal*, May 13.

Alsop, R. (1989) 'Brand loyalty is rarely blind loyalty', *Wall Street Journal*, October 19, B1 and B12.

Antil, J. (1984) 'Conceptualization and operationalization of involvement', *Advances in Consumer Research*, 11, 204–9.

Argyle, M. (1976) 'Personality and social behaviour', in R. Harré (ed.) *Personality*, Oxford: Blackwell.

Arndt, J. (1986) 'Paradigms in consumer research: a review of perspectives and approaches', *European Journal of Marketing*, 20(8), 23–40.

Arnold, S. J., T. H. Oum and D. J. Tigert (1983) 'Determinant attributes in retail patronage: seasonal, temporal, regional, and international comparisons', *Journal of Marketing Research*, 20, 149–57.

Asch, S. E. (1955) 'Effects of group pressure upon the modification and distortion of judgments', in E. E. Macoby, T. M. Newcomb and E. L. Hartley (eds), *Readings in Social Psychology*, Pittsburgh: Carnegie-Mellon Press.

Assael, H. (1987) *Consumer Behavior and Marketing Action*, Boston, MA: Kent.

Atkin, C. K. (1984) 'Consumer and social effects of advertising', in B. Dervin and M. J. Voight (eds) *Progress in Communication Sciences*, Norwood, NJ: Ablex.

Atlas, J. (1984) 'Beyond demographics', *The Atlantic Monthly*, October.

Bagozzi, R. P. (1981) 'Attitudes, intentions and behavior: a test of some key hypotheses', *Journal of Personality and Social Psychology*, 41, 607–27.

Bagozzi, R. P. (1982) 'A field investigation of causal relationships among cognitions, affect, intentions and behavior', *Journal of Marketing Research*, 19, 562–84.

Baker, J., L. L. Berry and A. Parasuraman (1988) 'The marketing impact of branch facility design', *Journal of Retail Banking*, 10, 33–42.

Bandura, A. (1977) *Social Learning Theory*, Englewood Cliffs, NJ: Prentice-Hall.

Bannister, D. (1966) 'A new theory of motivation', in B. M. Foss (ed.) *New Horizons in Psychology*, Harmondsworth: Penguin.

Barker, R. G. (1968) *Ecological Psychology: Concepts and Methods for Studying the Environment of Human Behavior*, Stanford, CA: Stanford University Press.

Barthol, R. P. and M. J. Goldstein (1959) 'Psychology and the invisible sell', *California Management Review*, 1, 30–40.

Bass, F. M., D. J. Tigert and R. T. Lonsdale (1968) 'Market segmentation: group versus individual behavior', *Journal of Marketing Research*, 5, 264–70.

Bauer, R. A. (1960) 'Consumer behavior as risk taking', in R. S. Hancock (ed.) *Dynamic Marketing for a Changing World*, Proc. 43rd Conference, Chicago, IL: American Marketing Association, 389–400.

Baumgarten, S. A. (1975) 'The innovative communicator in the diffusion process', *Journal of Marketing Research*, 12, 12–18.

Bearden, W. O. and M. J. Etzel (1982) 'Reference group influence on product and brand purchase decisions', *Journal of Consumer Research*, 9, 183–94.

Bearden, W. O. and A. G. Woodside (1976) 'Interaction of consumption situation and brand attitudes', *Journal of Applied Psychology*, 61, 764–9.

Beaumont, J. R. (1987) 'Retail location analysis: some management perspectives', *International Journal of Retailing*, 2(3), 22–35.

Becherer, R. C. and L. M. Richard, (1978) 'Self-monitoring as a moderating variable in consumer behavior', *Journal of Consumer Research*, 5, 159–62.

Beddington, N. (1982) *Design for Shopping Centres*, London: Butterworth.

Belch, G. E. (1982) 'The effects of television commercial repetition on cognitive response and message acceptance', *Journal of Consumer Research* 9, 56–65.

Belch, G. E. and E. L. Landon (1977) 'Discriminant validity of a products-anchored self-concepts measure', *Journal of Marketing Research*, 14, 252–6.

Belk, R. W. (1974) 'An exploratory assessment of situational effects in buyer behavior', *Journal of Marketing Research*, 11, 156–63.

Belk, R. W. (1975) 'Situational variables and consumer behavior', *Journal of Consumer Research*, 2, 157–64.

Belk, R. W. (1988) 'Possessions and the extended self', *Journal of Consumer Research*, 14, 139–68.

Belk, R. W., M. Wallendorf and J. F. Sherry (1989) 'The sacred and the profane in consumer behavior: theodicy on the Odyssey', *Journal of Consumer Research*, 16, 1–38.

Bem, D. J. (1972) 'Self-perception theory', in L. Berkowitz (ed.) *Advances in Experimental Social Psychology*, Hillsdale, IL: Erlbaum.

Bentler, P. M. and G. Speckart (1981) 'Attitudes "cause" behaviors: a structural equations analysis', *Journal of Personality and Social Psychology*, 40, 226–38.

Berey, L. A. and R. W. Pollay (1968) 'Influencing role of the child in family decision making', *Journal of Marketing Research*, 5, 70–2.

Berger, P. (1965) *Invitation to Sociology: A Humanistic Perspective*. Harmondsworth: Penguin.

Berry, L. L. (1968) 'Banking, marketing and the image concept', *Arizona Business Bulletin*, 15, 239–44.

Berry, L. L. (1969) 'The components of department store image: a theoretical and empirical analysis', *Journal of Retailing*, 45, 3–20.

Berry, L. L. and J. Kunkel (1968) 'A behavioral conception of retail image', *Journal of Marketing*, 32, 21–7.

Berry, L. L. and J. Kunkel (1970) 'In pursuit of consumer theory', *Decision Sciences*, 1, 25–39.

Bettman, J. R. (1971) 'The structure of consumer choice processes', *Journal of Marketing Research* 8: 465–71.

Bettman, J. R. (1979) *An Information Processing Theory of Consumer Choice*, Reading, MA: Addison-Wesley.

Birdwell, A. E. (1968) 'A study of the influence of image congruence on consumer choice', *Journal of Business*, 41, 1968.

Blackman, D. E. (1980) 'Images of man in contemporary behaviorism', in A. J. Chapman and D. M. Jones (eds) *Models of Man*, Leicester: British Psychological Society.

Blake, B. F., R. Perloff, R. Zenhausern, and R. Heslin (1973) 'The effects of intolerance of ambiguity upon product perceptions', *Journal of Applied Psychology* 58, 239–43.

Bloch, P. H. (1986) 'The product enthusiast: implications for marketing strategy', *Journal of Consumer Marketing*, 3(3), 51–62.

Bloch, P. H., N. M. Ridgway and J. E. Nelson (1991) 'Leisure and the shopping mall', *Advances in Consumer Research*, 18, 445–52.

Bloch, P. H., N. M. Ridgway and D. L. Sherrell (1989) 'Extending the concept of shopping: an investigation of browsing activity', *Journal of the Academy of Marketing Science*, 17, 13–21.

Bloch, P. H., D. L. Sherrell and N. Ridgway (1986) 'Consumer search: an extended framework', *Journal of Consumer Research*, 13, 119–26.

Bogart, L. (1984) *Strategy in Advertising*, 2nd edn, Chicago: Crain Books.

Bonner, F. G. (1985) 'Considerations for situational research', *Advances in Consumer Research*, 12, 368–73.

Booz-Allen & Hamilton Inc. (1981) *New Product Management of the 1980's*, Chicago: Booz-Allen & Hamilton, Inc.

Bourne, F. S. (1956) 'Group influence in marketing and public relations', in R. Likert and S. P. Hayes (eds), *Some Applications of Behavioral Research*, Basle: UNESCO.

Bowers, K. S. (1973) 'Situationism in psychology: an analysis and critique', *Psychological Review*, 80, 307–37.

Branthwaite, A. (1984) 'Situations and social actions: applications for marketing of recent theories in social psychology', *Journal of the Market Research Society*, 25, 19–38.

Bromley, D. F. and C. J. Thomas (1987) 'Clustering advantages for out-of-town stores', *International Journal of Retailing*, 4(3), 41–59.

Brown, J. A. C. (1963) *Techniques of Persuasion*, Harmondsworth: Penguin.

Brown, S. (1987) 'Retailers and micro-retail location: a perceptual perspective', *International Journal of Retailing*, 2(3), 3–21.

Brown, S. (1988) 'Information seeking, external search and "shopping" behaviour', *Journal of Marketing Management*, 4, 33–49.

Brown, S. (1989) 'Retail location theory: the legacy of Harold Hotelling', *Journal of Retailing*, 65, 450–70.

Brown, S. (1992) *Retail Location: A Micro-scale Perspective*, Aldershot: Avebury.

Budner, S. (1962) 'Intolerance of ambiguity as a personality variables', *Journal of Personality*, 30, 29–50.

Burgoyne, C. B. (1990) 'Money in marriage: how patterns of allocation both reflect and conceal power', *Sociological Review*, 38, 634–65.

Burstein, Daniel (1983) 'Using yesterday to sell tomorrow', *Advertising Age*, April 11, M-4.

Busch, P. S. and M. J. Houston (1985) *Marketing Strategic Foundations*, Homewood, IL: Richard D. Irwin.

Buss, D. M. and K. H. Craik (1984) 'Contemporary worldviews: personal and policy implications', *Journal of Applied Social Psychology*, 13, 259–80.

Buttle, F. (1984) 'Merchandising', *European Journal of Marketing*, 18(5), 4–25.

Cacioppo, J. T. and R. E. Petty (1984) 'The elaboration likelihood model of persuasion', *Advances in Consumer Research*' 11, 668–72.

Cadwallader, M. (1981) 'Towards a cognitive gravity model: the case of consumer spatial behaviour', *Regional Studies*, 15, 175–84.

Calonius, E. (1989) 'Mightier than the ballpoint: fountain pens are back', *Newsweek*, July 3, 63.

Campbell, D. P. (1974) *Strong Campbell Interest Inventory*, Stanford, CA: Stanford University.

Canter, D. (1977) *The Psychology of Place*, London: Architectural Press.

Carne, J. C. and M. J. Kirton (1982) 'Styles of creativity: test score correlations between the Kirton Adaption–Innovation Inventory and the Myers-Briggs Type Indicator', *Psychological Reports*, 50, 31–6.

Cattell, R. B., H. W. Eber and M. M. Tatsouka (1970) *Handbook for the Sixteen Personality Factor Questionnaire*, Champaign, IL: IPAT.

Celsi, R. L. and J. C. Olson (1988) 'The role of involvement attention and comprehension processes', *Journal of Consumer Research* 15, 210–33.

Chaffee, S. H. and C. Roser (1986) 'Involvement and the consistency of knowledge, attitudes, and behaviors', *Communication Research*, 13, 373–99.

Chan, K. K. and S. Misra (1990) 'Characteristics of the opinion leader: a new dimension', *Journal of Advertising*, 19(3), 53–60.

Chevalier, M. (1975) 'Increase in sales due to in-store display', *Journal of Marketing Research*, 12, 426–31.

Childers, T. (1986) 'Assessment of the psychometric properties of an opinion leadership scale', *Journal of Marketing Research*, 13, 184–8.

Churchill, G. A. (1991) *Marketing Research*, 5th edn, Chicago: The Dryden Press, 448–64.

Clancy, K. J. and R. S. Shulman (1991) *The Marketing Revolution: A Radical Manifesto for Dominating the Marketplace*, New York: Harper Business.

Clark, W. A. and G. Rushton (1970) 'Models of intra-urban consumer behavior and their implications for central place theory', *Economic Geography*, 46, 486–97.

Cohen, J. B. (1968) 'The role of personality in consumer behavior', in H. H. Kassarjian and T. S. Robertson (eds) *Perspectives in Consumer Behavior*, Hindsdale, IL: Scott Foresman.

Cohen, J. B. (1979) 'The structure of product attributes: defining attribute dimensions for planning and evaluation', in A. D. Shocker (ed.) *Analytic Approaches to Product and Marketing Planning*, Cambridge, MA: Marketing Science Institute, 54–86.

Cohen, P. (1981) *Consumer Behavior*, New York: Random House.

Coleman, R. P. (1983) 'The continuing significance of social class in marketing', *Journal of Consumer Research*, 10, 265–80.

Colley, R. H. (1961) *Defining Advertising Goals for Measured Advertising Results*, New York: Association of National Advertisers.

Collins, L. and C. Montgomery (1970) 'Whatever happened to motivation research?', *Journal of the Market Research Society*, 12, 5–14.

Colloquy (1993) *The Quarterly Frequency Marketing Newsletter*, 4(1).

Coney, K. A. (1972) 'Dogmatism and innovation: a replication', *Journal of Marketing Research* 9, 453–5.

Cooper, R. (1976) 'Introducing successful new industrial products', *European Journal of Marketing*, 10, 299–329.

Copulsky, W. and K. Marton (1977) 'Sensory cues: you've got to put them together', *Product Marketing Magazine*, January.

Cote, J. A., J. McCullough and M. Reilly (1985) 'Effects of unexpected situations on behavior-intention differences: a garbology analysis', *Journal of Consumer Research*, 12, 188–94.

Cox, D. (1963) 'The audience as communicators', in *Toward Scientific Marketing*, Chicago: American Marketing Association.

Cox D. F. (1967a) 'Synthesis – perceived risk and information handling', in D. F. Cox (ed.) *Risk Taking and Information Handling in Consumer Behavior*, Boston, MA: Harvard University Press, 603–39.

Cox, D. F. (1967b) 'The influence of cognitive needs and styles on information handling in making product evaluations', in *Risk Taking and Information Handling in Consumer Behavior*, (ed.) D. F. Cox, Boston, MA: Harvard University Press, 370–92.

Crespi, I. (1961), 'Use of a scaling technique in surveys', *Journal of Marketing*, 25, 69–72.

Csikszentmihalyi, M. and E. Rochberg-Halton (1981) *The Meaning of Things: Domestic Symbols and the Self*, Cambridge: Cambridge University Press.

Curhan, R. (1973) 'Shelf space allocation and profit maximization in mass retailing', *Journal of Marketing*, 37, 54–60.

Dagnoli, J. (1989) 'Kool tries to update image', *Advertising Age*, September 30.

Dale, R. (1985) *The Sinclair Story*, London: Duckworth.

Danko, W. D. and J. M. MacLachan (1983) 'Research to accelerate the diffusion of a new innovation', *Journal of. Advertising Research*, 23, (3), 39–43.

Darden, W. R. and F. D. Reynolds (1971) 'Shopping orientations and product usage rate', *Journal of Marketing Research*, 8, 505–8.

Darlow, C. (1972) (ed.) *Enclosed Shopping Centres*, London: Architectural Press.

Davidson, J. H. (1976) 'Why most new consumer goods fail', *Harvard Business Review*, 54(2), 11–21.

Davies, R. L. (1976) *Marketing Geography: with Special Reference to Retailing*, Corbridge: RPA.

Davies, R. L. (1984) *Retail and Commercial Planning*, London: Croom Helm.

Davies, R. L. and D. S. Rogers (1984) (eds) *Store Location and Store Assessment Research*, Chichester: Wiley.

Davis, H. L. (1970) 'Dimensions of marital roles in consumer decision making', *Journal of Marketing Research*, 7, 246–60.

Davis, H. L. (1976) 'Decision making within the household', *Journal of Consumer Research*, 2, 241–60.

Davis, H. L. and B. P. Rigaux (1974) 'Perceptions of marital roles in decision processes', *Journal of Consumer Research*, 1, 51–62.

Dawson, J. A. (1980) (ed.) *Retail Geography*, London: Croom Helm.

Dawson, J. A. (1983) *Shopping Centre Development*, New York: Longman.

Dawson, J. A. and D. Lord (1985) *Shopping Centre Development: Policies and Prospects*, London: Croom Helm.

Dawson, S., P. H. Bloch and N. M. Ridgway (1990) 'Shopping motives, emotional states, and retail outcomes', *Journal of Retailing*, 66, 408–27.

Day, G. S. (1973) 'Theories of attitude structure and change', in S. Ward and T. S. Robertson (eds), *Consumer Behavior: Theoretical Sources*, Englewood Cliffs, NJ: Prentice-Hall, 303–53

De Ciantis, S. (1987) 'The relationship between leadership style, cognitive style and learning style: an exposition of management style dimensions', unpublished PhD thesis, Hatfield: The Hatfield Polytechnic.

De Sarbo, W. S. and R. A. Harshman (1985) 'Celebrity-brand congruence analysis', in J. H. Leigh and C. R. Martin (eds), *Current Issues in Research in Advertising*, Ann Arbor, MI: University of Michigan.

Dhalla, N. K. and S. Yuseph (1976) 'Forget the product life cycle concept', *Harvard Business Review*, 54(1), 102–12.

Dichter, E. (1949) 'A psychological view of advertising effectiveness', *Journal of Marketing*, 14, 61–6.

Dichter, E. (1964) *Handbook of Consumer Motivations*, New York: McGraw-Hill.

Dickson, P. R. (1982) 'Person-situation: segmentation's missing link', *Journal of Marketing*, 46, 56–64.

Dickerson, M. L. and J. W. Gentry (1983) 'Characteristics of adopters and non-adopters of home computers', *Journal of Consumer Research*, 10, 225–35.

Doherty, P. A. (1991) 'Consumer research and its role in shopping center development', *Advances in Consumer Research*, 18, 453–61.

Dolich, I. L. (1969) 'Congruence relationships between self images and product brands', *Journal of Marketing Research*, 6, 80–4.

Donnelly, J. H. (1970) 'Social character and acceptance of new products', *Journal of Marketing Research*, 7, 111–13.

Donnelly, J. H. and M. J. Etzel (1973) 'Degrees of product newness and early trial', *Journal of Marketing Research*, 10, 295–300.

Donnelly, J. H. and J. M. Ivancevich (1974) 'A methodology for identifying innovator characteristics of new brand purchasers', *Journal of Marketing Research*, 11, 331–4.

Donovan, R. J. and J. R. Rossiter (1982) 'Store atmosphere: an environmental psychology approach', *Journal of Retailing*, 58, 34–57.

Doob, A. N., J. M. Carlsmith, J. L. Freedman, T. K. Landauer and S. Tom (1969) 'Effect of initial selling price on subsequent sales', *Journal of Personality and Social Psychology*, 11, 345–50.

Doucet, M. J., A. H. Jacobs and K. G. Jones (1987) 'Megachains and the Canadian retail environment', *International Journal of Retailing*, 3(4), 5–23.

Douglas, M. and B. Isherwood (1980) *The World of Goods*, Harmondsworth: Penguin.

Douglas, S. (1976) 'Cross-national comparisons and consumer stereotypes: A case study of working and non-working wives in the U.S. and France', *Journal of Consumer Research*, 3, 12–20.

Downs, R. M. and D. Stea (1977) *Maps in Mind*, New York: Harper and Row.

Doyle, P. and B. Z. Gidengil (1977) 'A review of in-store experiments', *Journal of Retailing*, 53, 47–62.

Drayton, J. (1976) 'Consumer behaviour: the state of the art', *Proceedings of the Marketing Education Group Annual Conference*, Glasgow.

Driver, J. C. and G. R. Foxall (1984) *Advertising Policy and Practice*, New York: Holt, Rinehart and Winston.

Drucker, P. F. (1985) *Innovation and Entrepreneurship*, London: Heinemann.

Dumaine, B. (1991) 'Closing the innovation gap', *Fortune*, December 2, 56–62.

East, R. (1990) *Changing Consumer Behaviour*, London: Cassell.

Economist, The (1992) 'Strategic shopping', September 26, 82–7.

Ehrenberg, A. S. C. (1972) *Repeat Buying*, Amsterdam: North Holland.

Ehrenberg, A. S. C. (1974) 'Repetitive advertising and the consumer', *Journal of Advertising Research*, 14, 25–34.

Ehrenberg, A. S. C. and G. J. Goodhardt (1979), *Essays on Understanding Buyer Behavior*, J. Walter Thompson Co. and Market Research Corporation of America.

Ehrenberg, A. S. C., G. J. Goodhardt and T. P. Barwise (1990) 'Double jeopardy revisited', *Journal of Marketing*, 54, 82–91.

Engel, J. F. (1963) 'Are automobile purchasers dissonant consumers?' *Journal of Marketing*, 27, 55–8.

Engel, J. F., D. T. Kollat and R. D. Blackwell (1968) *Consumer Behavior*, New York: Holt, Rinehart and Winston.

Engel, J. F., D. T. Kollat and R. D. Blackwell (1973) *Consumer Behavior*, 2nd edn Hindsdale, IL: Holt, Rinehart, and Winston.

Engel, J. F., R. D. Blackwell and P. Miniard (1990) *Consumer Behavior*, 6th edn, Hindsdale, IL: The Dryden Press.

Epstein, S. (1986) 'Does aggregation produce spuriously high estimates of behaviour stability?' *Journal of Personality and Social Psychology*, 50, 1119–1210.

Eroglu, S. A. and K. A. Machleit (1990) 'An empirical study of retail crowding: antecedents and consequences', *Journal of Retailing*, 66, 33–45.

Etgar, M. and N. K. Malhotra (1978) 'Consumers' reliance on different product quality cues: a basis for market segmentation', in S. C. Jain (ed.) *Research Frontiers in Marketing: Dialogues and Directions, 1978 Educators' Proceedings*, Chicago: American Marketing Association, 143–7.

Ettlie, J. E. and R. D. O'Keefe (1982) 'Innovative attitudes, values and intentions in organizations', *Journal of Management Studies,* 19, 163–82.

Evans, F. (1959) 'Psychological and objective factors in the prediction of brand choice', *Journal of Business*, 32, 340–69.

Eysenck, H. J. (1985) *Decline and Fall of the Freudian Empire*, London: Viking.

Eysenck, H. J. *et al.* (1975) *An Encyclopaedia of Psychology*, London: Fontana.

Eysenck, H. J. and S. B. G. Eysenck (1964) *Manual of the Eysenck Personality Inventory*, London: University of London Press.

Eysenck, H. J. and S. B. G. Eysenck (1969) *Personality Structure and Measurement*, London: Routledge and Kegan Paul.

Eysenck, H. J. and S. B. G. Eysenck (1975) *Manual of the Eysenck Personality Questionnaire*, London: Hodder and Stoughton.

Eysenck, H. J. and S. B. G. Eysenck (1976) *Psychoticism as a Dimension of Personality*, London: Hodder and Stoughton.

Faison, E. W. (1961) 'Effectiveness of one-sided and two-sided mass communications in advertising', *Public Opinion Quarterly*, 16, 248–55.

Featherstone, M. (1991) *Consumer Culture and Postmodernism*, London: Sage.

Fennell, G. (1980) 'The situation', *Motivation and Emotion*, 4, 299–322.

Ferber, R. and L. C. Lee (1974) 'Husband-wife influences in family purchasing behavior', *Journal of Consumer Research*, 1, 43–50.

Ferster, C. and B. F. Skinner (1957) *Schedules of Reinforcement*, New York: Century.

Festinger, L. (1957) *A Theory of Cognitive Dissonance*, Stanford, CA: Stanford University Press.

Fingleton, B. (1975) 'A factorial approach to the nearest centre hypothesis', *Transactions of the Institute of British Geographers*, 65, 131–9.

Finn, A. and J. Louviere (1990) 'Shopping center patronage models: fashioning a consideration set segmentation solution', *Journal of Business Research*, 21, 259–75.

Fishbein, M. (1973) 'The prediction of behavior from attitudinal variables', in C. D. Mortenson and K. K. Sereno (eds), *Advances in Communication Research*, New York: Harper and Row, 3–31.

Fishbein, M. (1975) 'Attitude, attitude change, and behavior: a theoretical overview', in P. Levine (ed.) *Attitude Research Bridges the Atlantic*, Chicago: American Marketing Association, 3–15.

Fishbein, M. and I. Ajzen (1975) *Belief, Attitude, Intention, and Behavior: An Introduction to Theory and Research*, Reading, MA: Addison-Wesley.

Fisher, A. B. (1985) 'Coke's brand-loyalty lesson', *Fortune*, August 5, 44–6.

Foxall, G. R. (1980) *Consumer Behaviour: A Practical Guide*, London: Routledge.

Foxall, G. R. (1983) *Consumer Choice*, London: Macmillan; New York: St Martin's.

Foxall, G. R. (1984a) *Corporate Innovation*, London: Routledge.

Foxall, G. R. (1984b) 'Consumers' intentions and behaviour', *Journal of the Market Research Society*, 26, 231–41.

Foxall, G. R. (1988) 'Consumer innovativeness: creativity, novelty-seeking, and cognitive style', in E. C. Hirschman and J. N. Sheth (eds) *Research in Consumer Behavior*, vol. 3, Greenwich, CT: JAI Press, 79–113.

Foxall, G. R. (1989) 'Adaptive-innovative cognitive styles of market initiators', in M. J. Kirton (ed.) *Adaptors and Innovators: Styles of Creativity and Problem-Solving*, London: Routledge, 125–57.

Foxall, G. R. (1990) *Consumer Psychology in Behavioral Perspective*, New York: Routledge.

Foxall, G. R. (1992) 'The Behavioral Perspective Model of purchase and consumption: from consumer theory to marketing practice', *Journal of the Academy of Marketing Science*, 20, 189–98.

Foxall, G. R. (1993) 'The situated consumer: a behavioral interpretation of purchase and consumption', in R. W. Belk (ed.) *Research in Consumer Behavior*, vol. 6, Greenwich, CT: JAI Press.

Foxall, G. R. and S. Bhate (1991a) 'Cognitive style, personal involvement and situation as determinants of computer use', *Technovation*, 11, 183–200.

Foxall, G. R. and S. Bhate (1993a) 'Cognitive styles and personal involvement of market initiators', *Journal of Economic Psychology*, 11, 1–24.

Foxall, G. R. and S. Bhate (1993b) 'Cognitive styles of use-innovators for home computing software applications: implications for new product strategy', *Technovation*, 13, 153–66.

Foxall, G. R. and S. Bhate (1993c) 'Cognitive style and personal involvement as explicators of innovative purchasing of "healthy" food brands', *European Journal of Marketing*, 27(2).

Foxall, G. R. and J. R. Fawn (1992) 'An evolutionary model of technological innovation as a strategic management process', *Technovation*, 12, 191–202.

Foxall, G. R. and R. E. Goldsmith (1988) 'Personality and consumer research: another look', *Journal of the Market Research Society*, 30, 111–25

Foxall, G. R. and P. M. W. Hackett (1992a) 'The factor structure and construct validity of the Kirton Adaption-Innovation Inventory', *Personality and Individual Differences*, 13, 967–76.

Foxall, G. R. and P. M. W. Hackett (1992b) 'Consumers' perceptions of micro-retail location: wayfinding and cognitive mapping in planned and organic shopping environments', *International Review of Retail, Distribution and Consumer Research*, 2, 309–28.

Foxall, G. R. and C. G. Haskins (1986) 'Cognitive style and consumer innovativeness: an empirical test of Kirton's adaption–innovation theory in the context of food purchasing', *European Journal of Marketing*, 20(3/4), 63–80.

Foxall, G. R. and C. G. Haskins (1987) 'Cognitive style and discontinuous consumption: the case of "healthy eating"', *Food Marketing* 3(2), 19–32.

Frank, R. E., W. F. Massy and D. G. Morrison (1986) 'The determinants of innovative behavior with respect to a branded, frequently purchased food product', in F. G. Smith (ed.) *Proceedings of the American Marketing Association*, Chicago: IL: American Marketing Association, 312–23.

Fredericks, A. J. and D. L. Dossett (1983) 'Attitude-behavior relations: a comparison of the Fishbein–Ajzen and Bentler–Speckart models', *Journal of Personality and Social Psychology*, 45, 501–12.

Freeman, L. (1990) 'P&G eyes TV show for blacks', *Advertising Age*, September 26, 53.

Furnham, A. and A. Lewis (1986) *The Economic Mind*, Brighton: Wheatsheaf.

Furse, D. H., G. N. Punj and D. W. Stewart (1984) 'A typology of individual search strategies among purchasers of new automobiles', *Journal of Consumer Research*, 10, 417–31.

Gabor, A. (1988) *Pricing: Concepts and Methods for Effective Marketing*, Aldershot: Gower.

Gagnon, J. P. and J. T. Osterhaus (1985) 'Effectiveness of floor displays on the sales of retail producers', *Journal of Retailing*, 61, 104–16.

Galbraith, J. K. (1976) *Economics and the Public Purpose*, Harmondsworth: Penguin.

Gardner, C. and J. Sheppard (1989) *Consuming Passion: The Rise of Retail Culture*, London: Unwin Hyman.

Gärling, T., E. Lindberg and T. Mantyla (1983) 'Orientation in buildings: effects of familiarity, visual access, and orientation aids', *Journal of Applied Psychology*, 61, 1–18.

Gatignon, H. and T. S. Robertson (1985) 'A propositional inventory for new diffusion research', *Journal of Consumer Research*, 11, 849–67.

Gatignon, H. and T. S. Robertson (1991) 'Innovative decision processes', in T. S. Robertson and H. H. Kassarjian (eds) *Handbook of Consumer Behavior*, Englewood Cliffs, NJ: Prentice–Hall, 316–46.

Gautschi, D. A. (1981) 'Specification of patronage models for retail center choice', *Journal of Marketing Research*, 18, 162–74.

Gay, P. (1988) *Freud: A Life for Our Time*, London: Dent.

Geer, C. T. (1992) 'Sensible and chic', *Forbes*, December 7, 222.

Gellner, E. (1985) *The Psychoanalytic Movement*, London: Paladin.

Gemunden, H. G. (1985) 'Perceived risk and information search: a systematic meta-analysis of the empirical evidence', *International Journal of Research in Marketing*, 2, 79–100.

Gerth, H. and C. W. Mills (1948) *From Max Weber: Essays in Sociology*, London: Routledge and Kegan Paul.

Ghosh, A. and C. S. Craig (1986) 'An approach to determining optimal locations for new services', *Journal of Marketing Research*, 23, 354–62.

Gifford, R. (1987) *Environmental Psychology: Principles and Practices*, Boston: Allyn and Bacon.

Giges, N. (1987) 'Buying linked to self-esteem', *Advertising Age*, April 13, 68.

Glazer, R. (1970) *The New Advertising*, Washington, DC: Citadel Press.

Goldsmith, R. E. (1983) 'Dimensions of consumer innovativeness: an empirical study of open processing', PhD dissertation, University of Alabama, 1983.

Goldsmith, R. E. (1984) 'Personality characteristics associated with adaption–innovation', *Journal of Psychology*, 117, 159–65.

Goldsmith, R. E. (1985a) 'Personality and adaptive–innovative problem solving', *Journal of Social Behavior and Personality*, 1, 95–106.

Goldsmith, R. E. (1985b) 'A factorial composition of the KAI inventory', *Educational and Psychological Measurement*, 45, 245–50.

Goldsmith, R. E. (1986a) 'Convergent validity of four innovativeness scales', *Educational and Psychological Measurement*, 46, 81–7.

Goldsmith, R. E. (1986b) 'Adaption–innovation and cognitive complexity', *Journal of Personality*, 119, 461–7.

Goldsmith, R. E. (1987) 'Self-monitoring and innovativeness', *Psychological Reports*, 60, 1017–18.

Goldsmith, R. E. (1989) 'Creative style and personality theory', in M. J. Kirton (ed.) *Adaptors and Innovators: Styles of Creativity and Problem Solving*, London: Routledge, 37–55.

Goldsmith, R. E. (1991) 'The validity of a scale to measure global innovativeness', *Journal of Applied Business Research*, 7, 89–97.

Goldsmith, R. E. and R. Desborde (1991) 'A validity study of a measure of opinion leadership', *Journal of Business Research*, 22, 11–19.

Goldsmith, R. E. and J. Emmert (1990) 'Measuring product category involvement', *Proceedings of the Southern Marketing Association*, 46–9.

Goldsmith, R. E. and J. Emmert (1991) 'Measuring product category involvement: a multi-trait, multi-method study', *Journal of Business Research*, 23, 363–71.

Goldsmith, R. E and C. F. Hofacker (1991) 'Measuring consumer innovativeness', *Journal of the Academy of Marketing Science*, 19, 209–21.

Goldsmith, W. and D. Clutterbuck (1985) *The Winning Streak*, Harmondsworth: Penguin.

Goldstein, K. M. and S. Blackman (1978) *Cognitive Style: Five Approaches and Relevant Research*, New York: Wiley.

Golledge, R. G. (1987) 'Environmental cognition', in D. Stokols and I. Altman (eds), *Handbook of Environmental Psychology*, vol. 1, New York: Wiley, 131–74.

Golledge, R. G. and G. Rushton (1976) (eds) *Spatial Choice and Spatial Behavior: Geographic Essays on the Analysis of Preferences and Perceptions*, Columbus, OH: Ohio State University Press.

Goode, W. J. (1964) *The Family*, Englewood Cliffs, NJ: Prentice-Hall.

Gordon, W. C. (1989) *Learning and Memory*, Pacific Grove, CA: Brooks/Cole.

Gorn, G. J. (1982) 'The effects of music in advertising on choice behavior: a classical conditioning approach', *Journal of Marketing*, 46, 94–101.

Gough, H. G. (1956/1975) *California Psychological Inventory*, Palo Alto: Consulting Psychologists' Press.

Graham, J. (1988) 'Stores see loyal customers slip away', *Advertising Age*, July 11.

Granbois, D. H. (1968) 'Improving the study of customer in-store behavior', *Journal of Marketing*, 32, 28–32.

Green, P. E. and D. S. Tull (1978) *Research for Marketing Decisions*, Englewood Cliffs, NJ: Prentice-Hall.

Green, P. E., A. Maheshwari and V. R. Rao (1969) 'Self-concept and brand preference: an empirical application of multidimensional scaling', *Journal of Marketing Research*, 4, 343–60.

Greenwald, A. G. and C. Levitt (1984) 'Audience involvement in advertising: four levels', *Journal of Consumer Research*, 11, 581–92.

Gregorson, J. (1988) 'Tailoring a fashion mall to its urban setting', *Building Design and Construction*, 19, 74.

Gronhaug, K. and P. S. Trapp (1989) 'Perceived social class appeals of branded goods and services', *Journal of Consumer Marketing*, 6, 13–18.

Grossbart, S., R. Hampton, B. Rammohan and R. S. Lapidus (1990) 'Environmental dispositions and customer response to store atmospherics', *Journal of Business Research*, 21, 225–41.

Grubb, E. L. (1965) 'Consumer perception of self concept and its relationship to brand choice of selected product types', *Proc. American Marketing Association*, Chicago: AMA.

Grubb, E. L. and G. Hupp (1968) 'Perception of self, generalized stereotypes and brand selection', *Journal of Marketing Research*, 5, 58–63.

Grubb, E. L. and B. L. Stern (1971) 'Self-concept and significant others', *Journal of Marketing Research*, 8, 382–5.

Gruenwald, G. (1988) *Managing New Products*, Lincolnwood, Ill: NTC Business Books.

Gryskiewicz, S. S. (1982) 'The Kirton Adaption–Innovation Inventory in creative leadership development', *Proc. British Psychological Society*, Brighton: University of Sussex.

Gryskiewicz, S. S., D. W. Hills, K. Holt and K. Hills (1987) *Understanding Managerial Creativity: The Kirton Adaption–Innovation Inventory and Other Assessment Measures*, Greensboro, NC: Center for Creative Leadership.

Gubernick, L. (1989) 'It's great for a date', *Forbes*, February 6, 110–12.

Guilford, J. P. (1980) 'Cognitive styles: what are they?', *Educational and Psychological Measurement*, 40, 715–35.

Gunter, B. and A. Furnham (1992) *Consumer Profiles: An Introduction to Psychographics*, London and New York: Routledge.

Hackett, P., G. R. Foxall and W. F. Van Raaij (1993) 'Consumers in retail environments', in T. Garling and R. G. Golledge (eds) *Behavior and Environment: Psychological and Geographical Approaches*, Amsterdam: North Holland, 378–99.

Hage, J. and R. Dewar (1973) 'Elite values versus organizational structure predicting innovation', *Administrative Science Quarterly*, 18, 279–90.

Hammons, K. (1991) 'Has-beens have been very good to Hasboro', *Business Week*, August 5, 76–77.

Hall, C. S. and C. Lindzey (1970) *Theories of Personality*, New York: Wiley.

Hanna, G. (1980) 'A typology of consumer needs', in J. N. Sheth (ed.) *Research in Marketing*, vol. 3, Greenwich, CT: JAI Press.

Hansen, F. (1976) 'Psychological theories of consumer choice', *Journal of Consumer Research*, 3, 117–42.

Hardin, E. (1967) 'Job satisfaction and desire for change', *Journal of Applied Psychology*, 51, 20–7.

Harrell, G. (1986) *Consumer Behavior*, Harcourt Brace Jovanovich.

Harrell, G. and P. D. Bennett (1974) 'An evaluation of the expectancy-value model', *Journal of Marketing Research*, 11, 269–78.

Harrell, G. and M. Hutt (1976) 'Buyer behavior under conditions of crowding: an initial framework', *Advances in Consumer Research*, 3, 36–9.

Harrell, G., M. Hutt and J. Anderson (1980) 'Path analysis of buyer behavior under conditions of crowding', *Journal of Marketing Research*, 17, 45–51.

Harris, K. (1990) 'Money talks', *Forbes*, May 28, 40.

Hastorf, A. H. and H. Cantril (1954) 'They saw a game: a case study', *Journal of Abnormal and Social Psychology*, 49, 129–34.

Hawkins, D. I., R. J. Best and K. A. Coney (1983) *Consumer Behavior: Implications for Marketing Strategy*, Plano, TX: Business Publications.

Hebdige, D. (1979) *Subculture: The Meaning of Style*, London: Methuen.

Heylen, P. (n.d.) *Libido als Drijfveer van het Konsumentengedrag*, Antwerp: Psycho-analytische Diagnostiek.

Higgins, K. (1984) 'Foil's glitter attracts manufacturers who want upscale buyers', *Marketing News*, February 3.

Hillner, K. P. (1984) *History and Systems of Modern Psychology: A Conceptual Approach*, New York: Gardner Press.

Hintzman, D. L. (1978) *The Psychology of Learning and Memory*, New York: Freeman.

Hirschman, E. C. (1979) 'Differences in consumer purchase behavior by credit card payment system', *Journal of Consumer Research*, 6, 58–66.

Hirschman, E. C. (1980) 'Innovativeness, novelty seeking and consumer creativity', *Journal of Consumer Research*, 7, 283–95.

Hirschman, E. C. (1981) 'Technology and symbolism as sources for the generation of innovations', *Advances in Consumer Research*, 9, 537–41.

Hirschman, E. C. (1984) 'Experience seeking: a subjectivist perspective of consumption', *Journal of Business Research*, 12, 115–36.

Hirschman, E. C. (1985) 'Primitive aspects of consumption in modern American society', *Journal of Consumer Research*, 12, 142–54.

Hirschman, E. C. and M. Holbrook (1982) 'Hedonic consumption: emerging concepts, methods, and propositions', *Journal of Marketing*, 46, 92–101.

Hirschman, E. C. and M. Holbrook (1992) *Postmodern Consumer Research: The Study of Consumption as Text*, Newbury Park, CA: Sage.

Holbrook, M. (1988) 'The psychoanalytic interpretation of consumer behavior: I am an animal', in E. C. Hirschman and J. N. Sheth (eds) *Research in Consumer Behavior*, vol. 3, Greenwich, CT: JAI Press, 149–78.

Holbrook, M. and E. C. Hirschman (1982) 'The experiential aspects of consumption: consumer fantasies, feelings and fun', *Journal of Consumer Research*, 9, 132–40.

Horney, K. (1958) *Neurosis and Human Growth*, New York: Norton.

Hornik, J. (1982) 'Situational effects on the consumption of time', *Journal of Marketing*, 46, 44–55.

Hortman, S. McC., A. W. Allaway, J. B. Mason and J. Rasp (1990) 'Multisegment analysis of supermarket patronage', *Journal of Business Research*, 21, 209–23.

Horton, R. L. (1979) 'Some relationships between personality and consumer decision making', *Journal of Marketing Research*, 16, 233–46.

Houston, M. J. and M. L. Rothschild (1978) 'Conceptual and methodological perspectives on involvement', in S. C. Jain (ed.) *1978 Educators' Proceedings*, Chicago: American Marketing Association, 184–7.

Hovland, C. I., I. L. Janis and H. H. Kelley (1948) *Experiments on Mass Communication*, Princeton, NJ: Princeton University Press.

Howard, J. A. (1977) *Consumer Behavior: Application of Theory*, New York: McGraw-Hill.

Howard, J. A. (1983) 'Marketing theory of the firm', *Journal of Marketing*, 47, 90–100.

Howard, J. A. (1989) *Consumer Behavior in Marketing Strategy*. Englewood Cliffs, NJ: Prentice-Hall.

Howard, J. A. and J. N. Sheth (1969) *The Theory of Buyer Behavior*, New York: Wiley.

Huber, J., M. B. Holbrook and S. Schiffman (1982) 'Situational psychophysics and the vending-machine problem', *Journal of Retailing*, 58, 82–94.

Hughes, G. D. (1971) *Attitude Measurement for Marketing Strategies*, Glenview, IL: Scott, Foresman.

Hughes, G. D. and J. L. Guerrero (1971) 'Automobile self-congruity models reexamined', *Journal of Marketing Research*, 9, 125–7.

Hughes, G. D. and P. A. Naert (1970) 'A computer controlled experiment in consumer behavior', *Journal of Business*, 43, 354–72.

Hurt, H. T., K. Joseph and C. D. Cook (1977) 'Scales for the measurement of innovativeness', *Human Communication Research*, 4, 58–65.

Iuso, W. (1975) 'Concept testing: an appropriate approach', *Journal of Marketing Research*, 12, 228–31.

Ivancevich, J. M. and J. H. Donnelly (1974) 'A study of role clarity and need for clarity for three occupational groups', *Academy of Management Journal*, 17, 28–36.

Iyer, E. S. (1989) 'Unplanned purchasing: knowledge of shopping environment and time pressure'. *Journal of Retailing*, 65, 30–40.

Jackson, D. N. (1976) *Jackson Personality Inventory Manual*, Goshen, NY: Research Psychologists' Press.

Jacoby, J. (1971) 'Personality and innovation proneness', *Journal of Marketing Research*, 8, 244–7.

Jacoby, J. and R. Chestnut (1978) *Brand Loyalty Measurement and Management*, New York: Ronald/John Wiley.

Jacoby, J. and W. D. Hoyer (1982) 'Viewer misconception of televised communication', *Journal of Marketing*, 46, 12–26.

Jacoby, J., D. Speller and C. Kohn (1974) 'Brand choice as a function of information load', *Journal of Marketing Research*, 11, 154–65.

Jacoby, J., R. W. Chestnut and W. Silberman (1977) 'Consumer use and comprehension of nutrition information', *Journal of Consumer Research*, 4, 119–28.

Jacoby, J., W. D. Hoyer and D. A. Sheluga (1980) *The Misconception of Televised Communication*, New York: American Association of Advertising Agencies.

Johnson, D. B (1987) 'The West Edmonton Mall – from super-regional to mega-regional shopping center', *International Journal of Retailing*, 2(2), 53–69.

Johnson, H. M. (1962) *Sociology*, London: Routledge and Kegan Paul.

Johnson, T. (1984) 'The myth of declining brand loyalty', *Journal of Advertising Research*, 24(1), 9–17.

Jones, K. and J. Simmons (1990) *The Retail Environment*, London: Routledge.

Jones, P. (1989) 'The modernisation and expansion of central shopping centres', *Service Industries Journal*, 9, 399–405.

Kahle, L. R. (1984) *Attitudes and Social Adaptation: A Person–Situation Interaction Approach*, Oxford: Pergamon.

Kaiser, B. (1990) *The Social Psychology of Clothing*, Englewood Cliffs, NJ: Prentice-Hall.

Kakkar, P. and R. J. Lutz (1975) 'Toward a taxonomy of consumption situations', *Combined Proceedings*, Chicago: American Marketing Association.

Kakkar, P. and R. J. Lutz (1981) 'Situational influence on consumer behavior: a review', in H. H. Kassarjian and T. S. Robertson (eds) *Perspectives in Consumer Behavior*, Glenview, IL: Scott, Foresman.

Kassarjian, H. H. (1965) 'Social character and differential preference for mass communications', *Journal of Marketing Research*, 2, 146–53.

Kassarjian, H. H. (1971) 'Personality and consumer behavior: a review', *Journal of Marketing Research*, 8, 409–18.

Kassarjian, H. H. and T. S. Robertson (1981) (eds) *Perspectives in Consumer Behavior*, Glenview, IL: Scott, Foresman.

Kassarjian, H. H. and M. J. Sheffet (1991) 'Personality and consumer behavior: an update', in *Perspectives in Consumer Behavior*, Englewood Cliffs, NJ: Prentice-Hall, 281–303.

Katz, D. (1960) 'The functional approach to the study of attitudes', *Public Opinion Quarterly*, 24, 163–204.

Kau, A. K. and A. S. C. Ehrenberg (1984) 'Patterns of store choice', *Journal of Marketing Research*, 21, 399–409.

Keggeris, R. J., J. F. Engel and R. D. Blackwell (1970) 'Innovativeness and diffusiveness: a marketing view of the characteristics of earliest adopters', in D. T. Kollat, R. D. Blackwell and J. F. Engel (eds) *Research in Consumer Behavior*, New York: Holt, Rinehart and Winston, 671–89.

Keller, R. T. and W. E. Holland (1978) 'A cross-validation study of the Kirton Adaption–Innovation Inventory in three research and development organizations', *Applied Psychological Measurement*, 2, 563–70.

Kempner, T. (1976) *A Dictionary of Management*, London: Penguin.

Kenkel, W. F. (1961) 'Husband–wife interaction in decision-making and decision choices', *Journal of Social Psychology*, 54, 117–35.

Key, B. W. (1970) *Media Sexploitation*, Englewood Cliffs, NJ: Prentice-Hall.

Key, B. W. (1973) *Subliminal Seduction*, Englewood Cliffs, NJ: Prentice-Hall.

Key, B. W. (1980) *The Clam-plate Orgy and Other Subliminal Techniques for Manipulating your Behavior*, Englewood Cliffs, NJ: Prentice-Hall.

Khale, L. R. (1984) *Attitudes and Social Adaptation: A Person–Situation Interaction Approach*, Oxford: Pergamon.

King, C. W. and J. O. Summers (1970) 'Overlap of opinion leadership across consumer product categories', *Journal of Marketing Research*, 7, 43–50.

Kirton, M. J. (1976) 'Adaptors and innovators: a description and measure', *Journal of Applied Psychology*, 61, 622–9.

Kirton, M. J. (1987) *KAI Manual*, Hatfield: Occupational Research Centre.

Kirton, M. J. (1989) 'A theory of cognitive style', in M. J. Kirton (ed.) *Adaptors and Innovators: Styles of Creativity and Problem-Solving*, London: Routledge, 1–36.

Kirton, M. J. and S. De Ciantis (1976) 'Cognitive style and personality: the Kirton Adaption–Innovation and Cattell's Sixteen Personality Factor inventories', *Personality and Individual Differences*, 7, 141–6.

Kline, P. (1981) *Fact and Fantasy in Freudian Theory*, London: Methuen.

Kollat, D. T. and R. P. Willet (1967) 'Customer impulse purchase behavior', *Journal of Marketing Research*, 4, 21–31.

Konrad, W. (1990) 'The real thing is getting real aggressive', *Business Week*, November 26, 94–6.

Kotler, P. (1973) 'Atmospherics as a marketing tool', *Journal of Retailing*, 49, 48–64.

Kotler, P. (1984) *Marketing Management: Analysis, Planning and Control*, Englewood Cliffs, NJ: Prentice-Hall.

Krugman, H. E. (1965) 'The impact of television advertising: learning without involvement', *Public Opinion Quarterly*, 29, 249–56.

Kuczmarski, T. D. (1988) *Managing New Products*, Englewood Cliffs, NJ: Prentice-Hall.

Labay, D. G. and T. C. Kinnear (1981) 'Exploring the consumer decision process in the adoption of solar energy systems', *Journal of Consumer Research*, 8, 271–8.

Lambkin, M. and G. Day (1988) 'Evolutionary processes in competitive markets: beyond the product life cycle', *Journal of Marketing*, 53, 4–20.

Landon, E. L. (1974) 'Self concept, ideal self concept, and consumer purchase intentions', *Journal of Consumer Research*, 1, 44–51.

Lasswell, H. (1948) *The Analysis of Political Behaviour*, London: Routledge and Kegan Paul.

Lastovicka, J. L. and E. H. Bonfield (1982) 'Do consumers have brand attitudes?', *Journal of Economic Psychology*, 2, 57–75.

Laurent, G. and J. Kapferer (1988) 'Measuring consumer involvement profiles', *Journal of Marketing Research*, 22, 41–53.

Lavidge, R. J. and G. A. Steiner (1961) 'A model for predictive measurement of advertising effectiveness', *Journal of Marketing*, 25, 59–62.

Lazarsfeld, P. F., B. R. Berelson and H. Gaudet (1944) *The People's Choice*, New York: Columbia University Press.

Lea, S. E. G., R. M. Tarpy and P. Webley (1987) *The Individual in the Economy*, Cambridge: Cambridge University Press.

Leed, T. W. and G. A. German (1973) *Food Merchandising: Principles and Practices*, New York: Chain Store Age Books.

Leigh, J. H. and C. R. Martin (1981) 'A review of situational influence paradigms and research', in B. E. Enis and K. J. Roering (eds), *Review of Marketing 1981*, Chicago: American Marketing Association, 57–74.

Levitt, T. (1983) 'The globalization of markets', *Harvard Business Review*, May/June.

Levitt, T. (1986) *The Marketing Imagination*, New York: The Free Press.

Levy, S. (1959) 'Symbols for sale', *Harvard Business Review*, 37(4), 117–24.

Liesse, J. (1991) 'Brands in trouble', *Advertising Age*, December 2, 16.

Likert, R. (1932) 'A technique for the measurement of attitudes', *Archives of Psychology*, 22, No. 140 (whole issue).

Lord, J. D. (1987) 'Cross shopping flows among Atlanta's regional shopping centres', *International Journal of Retailing*, 1(1), 33–54.

Lutz, R. J. (1991) 'The role of attitude theory in marketing', in H. H. Kassarjian and T. S. Robertson (eds) *Perspectives in Consumer Behavior*, Englewood Cliffs, NJ: Prentice-Hall, 4th edn, 317–39.

Lutz, R. J. and P. Kakkar (1975a) 'The psychological situation as a determinant of consumer behavior', *Advances in Consumer Research*, 2, 439–53.

Lutz, R. J. and P. Kakkar (1975b) 'Situational influence in interpersonal persuasion', *Advances in Consumer Research*, 3, 370–8.

Lynch, K. (1960) *The Image of the City*, Cambridge, MA: MIT Press.

Lynch, J. G. and T. K. Srull (1982) 'Memory and attentional factors in consumer choice: concepts and research methods', *Journal of Consumer Research*, 9, 18–37.

McAlister, L. and E. Pessemier (1982) 'Variety seeking behaviour: an interdisciplinary review', *Journal of Consumer Research*, 9, 311–22.

McClure, P. J. and J. K. Ryans (1968) 'Differences between retailers' and consumers' perceptions', *Journal of Marketing Research*, 5, 35–40.

McClurg, J. M. and I. R. Andrews (1974) 'A consumer profile analysis of the self-service gasoline customer', *Journal of Applied Psychology* 59: 119–21.

McCracken, G. (1981) 'Culture and consumption: a theoretical account of the structure and movement of the cultural meaning of consumer goods', *Journal of Consumer Research*, 13, 71–84.

MacDonald, A. P. (1970) 'Revised scale for ambiguity tolerance', *Psychological Reports*, 26, 791–8.

McGuire, W. J. (1976) 'Some internal psychological factors influencing consumer choice', *Journal of Consumer Research*, 2, 302–19.

MacKay, D. B. (1972) 'A microanalytic approach to store location analysis', *Journal of Marketing Research*, 9, 134–40.

MacKay, D. B. and R. W. Olshavsky (1975) 'Cognitive maps of retail locations: an investigation of some basic issues', *Journal of Consumer Research*, 2, 197–205.

Mackay, D. B., R. W. Olshavsky and G. Sentell (1975) 'Cognitive maps and spatial behavior of consumers', *Geographical Analysis*, 7, 19–34.

Mackenzie, S. N. (1986) 'The role of attention in mediating the effect of advertising on attribute importance', *Journal of Consumer Research*, 13, 174–95.

McKinnon, G. F., J. P. Kelly and E. D. Robison (1981) 'Sales effects of point-of-purchase in-store signing', *Journal of Retailing*, 57, 49–63.

McNeal, J. U. (1964) *An Exploratory Study of the Consumer Behavior of Children*, Austin, TX: University of Texas at Austin.

McNeal, J. U. (1988) 'The children's market', *Incentive*, September, 87–94.

McSweeney, F. K. and C. Bierley (1984) 'Recent developments in classical conditioning', *Journal of Consumer Research*, 11, 619–31.

Maier, N. R. F. (1965) *Psychology in Industry*, New York: Houghton-Mifflin.

Malhotra, N. K. (1988) 'Self-concept and product choice: an integated perspective', *Journal of Economic Psychology*, 9, 1–28.

Mancuso, J. R. (1969) 'Why not create opinion leaders for new product introductions?', *Journal of Marketing*, 33, 35–9.

Marans, R. W. and K. F. Spreckelmeyer (1982) 'Measuring overall architectural quality: a component of building evaluation', *Environment and Behavior*, 14, 652–70.

Marketing News (1981) 'New survey reveals five lifestyle segments of age 18–49 black women', *Marketing News*, August 21, 6.

Markin, J. (1977) 'Motivation in buyer behavior theory: from mechanism to cognition', in A. Woodside, J. N. Sheth and P. D. Bennett (eds) *Consumer and Industrial Buying Behavior*, Amsterdam: North Holland.

Marks, A. P. (1989) 'The Sinclair C5 – an investigation into its development, launch and subsequent failure', *European Journal of Marketing*, 23(1), 61–71.

Marx, M. H. and W. A. Hillix (1979) *Systems and Theories in Psychology*, 3rd edn, New York: McGraw-Hill.

Maslow, A. (1943) *Motivation and Personality*, New York: Harper.

Mattson, B. E. (1982) 'Situational influences on store choice', *Journal of Retailing*, 58, 46–58.

May, F. E. (1969) 'Buying behavior: Some research findings', in J. U. McNeal (ed.), *Dimensions of Buying Behavior*, New York: Appleton-Century-Crofts.

Mehotra, S. and W. D. Wells (1979) 'Psychographics and buyer behavior: theory and recent empirical findings', in A. G. Woodside, J. N. Sheth and P. D. Bennett (eds) *Consumer and Industrial Buying Behavior*, New York: North Holland, 54–5.

Mehrabian, A. and J. A. Russell (1974) *An Approach to Environmental Psychology*, Cambridge, MA: MIT Press.

Messick, S. (1976) *Individuality in Learning: Implications of Cognitive Styles and Creativity for Human Development*, San Francisco: Jossey-Bass.

Messick, S. (1984) 'The nature of cognitive styles: problems and promise in educational practice', *Educational Psychologist*, 19, 59–74.

Michell, G. (1986) *Design in the High Street*, London: Architectural Press.

Midgley, D. F. (1974) *Innovation in the Male Fashion Market*, Amsterdam: ESOMAR.

Midgley, D. F. (1977) *Innovation and New Product Marketing*, London: Routledge.

Midgley, D. F. and G. R. Dowling (1978) 'Innovativeness: the concept and its measurement', *Journal of Consumer Research*, 4, 229–40.

Milgram, S. (1970) 'The experience of living in cities', *Science*, 167, 1461–8.

Milgram, S. (1974) *Obedience and Authority*, London: Tavistock.

Miller, A. (1990) 'You are what you buy', *Newsweek*, June 4, 59–60.

Miller, G. A. (1956) 'The magic number seven, plus or minus two: some limits on our capacity for processing information', *Psychological Review*, 63, 81–97.

Miller, K. E. and J. L. Ginter (1979) 'An investigation of situational variation in brand choice behavior and attitude', *Journal of Marketing Research*, 16, 111–23.

Milliman, R. A. (1982) 'The effect of background music upon the shopping behavior of supermarket patrons', *Journal of Marketing*, 46, 86–91.

Mischel, W. (1968) *Personality and Assessment*, New York: Wiley.

Mischel, W. (1976) *Introduction to Personality*, New York: Holt, Rinehart and Winston.

Mitchell, A. A. (1979) 'Involvement: a potentially important mediator of consumer behavior', *Advances in Consumer Research*, 6, 191–6.

Mitchell, A. (1983) *The Nine American Lifestyles*, New York: Macmillan.

Mitchell, R. (1986) 'How Pontiac pulled away from the pack', *Business Week*, August 25, 56–7.

Mittal, B. (1988) 'The role of affective choice mode in the consumer purchase of expressive products', *Journal of Economic Psychology*, 9, 499–524.

Mittal, B. and M.-S. Lee (1989) 'A causal model of consumer involvement', *Journal of Economic Psychology*, 10, 363–89.

Mittelstaedt, R. A. and R. E. Stassen (1990) 'Shopping behavior and merchandising strategies', *Journal of Business Research*, 21, 243–58.

Mittelstaedt, R. A., S. L. Grossbart, W. W. Curtis and S. P. DeVere (1976) 'Optimal stimulation level and the adoption decision process', *Journal of Consumer Research*, 3, 84–94.

Moeser, S. D. (1988) 'Cognitive mapping in a complex building', *Environment and Behavior*, 20, 29–49.

Monroe, K. B. (1973) 'Buyers' subjective perceptions of price', *Journal of Marketing Research*, 10, 70–80.

Monroe, K. B. and J. P. Guiltinan (1975) 'A path-analytic exploration of retail patronage influences', *Journal of Consumer Research*, 2, 19–28.

Moore, T. E. (1982) 'Subliminal advertising: what you see is what you get', *Journal of Marketing*, 46, 38–47.

Moore, W. L. (1982) 'Concept testing', *Journal of Business Research*, 10, 267–78.

Moran, D. J. (1980) 'Packaging can lend prestige to products', *Advertising Age*, January 7.

Moschis, G. P. (1985) 'The role of family communication in consumer socialization of children and adolescents', *Journal of Consumer Research*, 11, 898–913.

Mudd, S. A. (1990) 'The place of innovativeness in models of the adoption process: an integrative review', *Technovation*, 10, 119–36.

Murdock, G. P. (1940) 'Uniformities in culture', *American Sociological Review*, 5, 346–55.

Murphy, P. E. and W. A. Staples (1979) 'A modernized family life cycle', *Journal of Consumer Research*, 6, 12–22.

Myers, I. B. (1962) *The Myers–Briggs Type Indicator*, Palo Alto, CA: Consulting Psychologists' Press.

Myers, J. H. and W. H. Reynolds (1967) *Consumer Behavior and Marketing Management*, New York: Houghton-Mifflin.

Nelson, R. L. (1958) *The Selection of Retail Locations*, New York: Dodge.

Neuman, N. S. (1986) 'Semiotics of architectural ornament', *Architecture and Behavior*, 3, 37–53.

Nicosia, F. M. (1966) *Consumer Decision Processes*, Englewood Cliffs, NJ: Prentice-Hall.

Nord, W. and J. P. Peter (1980) 'A behavior modification perspective on marketing', *Journal of Marketing*, 44, 36–47.

Ogilvy, J. (1990) 'This postmodern business', *Marketing and Research Today*, February, 4–21.

Ohmae, K. (1982) *The Mind of the Strategist: Business Planning for Competitive Advantage*, Harmondsworth: Penguin.

Olshavsky, R. W. and D. H. Granbois (1979) 'Consumer decision making – fact or fiction?', *Journal of Consumer Research*, 6, 93–100.

Olshavsky, R. W., D. B. MacKay and G. Sentell (1975) 'Perceptual maps of retail locations', *Journal of Applied Psychology*, 60, 80–6.

Osgood, C. E., G. J. Suci and P. H. Tannenbaum (1957) *The Measurement of Meaning*, Urbana, IL: University of Illinois Press.

O'Shaughnessy, J. (1987) *Why People Buy*, New York: Oxford University Press.

Ostlund, L. E. (1974) 'Perceived innovation attributes as predictors of innovativeness', *Journal of Consumer Research*, 1, 23–9.

Packard, V. (1957) *The Hidden Persuaders*, Harmondsworth: Penguin.

Pahl, J. (1980) 'Patterns of money management within marriage', *Journal of Social Policy*, 9, 313–35.

Pahl, J. (1983) 'The allocation of money and the structuring of inequality within marriage', *Sociological Review*, 31, 237–62.

Pahl, J. (1988) 'Earning, sharing, spending: married couples and their money', in R. Walker and G. Parker (eds) *Money Matters*, London: Sage.

Pahl, J. (1989) *Money and Marriage*, London: Macmillan.

Pahl, J. (1990) 'Household spending, personal spending and the control of money in marriage', *Sociology*, 24, 119–38.

Park, C. W. (1982) 'Joint decisions in home purchasing: a muddling-through approach', *Journal of Consumer Research*, 9, 151–62.

Park, C. W., E. Iyer and D. C. Smith (1989) 'The effects of situational factors on in-store grocery shopping behavior: the role of store environment and time available for shopping', *Journal of Consumer Research*, 15, 422–33.

Parsons, R. J. (1973) 'Category width and the learning of multiattribute paired associates', *Journal of General Psychology* 89: 133–40.

Patricios, N. N. (1979) 'Human aspects of planning shopping centres', *Environment and Behavior*, 11, 511–38.

Payton, T. H. (1988) 'The electric car – some problems of driver attitudes and product fit', *Journal of the Market Research Society*, 30, 73–85.

Peled, A. (1974) 'A theory of spatiality of situations empirically tested in the experience of passengers in air terminals', PhD thesis, University of Strathclyde, Glasgow.

Pervin, L. (1984) *Personality*, 4th edn, New York: Wiley.

Peter, J. P. and W. Nord (1982) 'A clarification and extension of operant conditioning principles in marketing', *Journal of Marketing*, 46, 102–7.

Peters, M. P. and M. Venkatesan (1973) 'Expioration of variables inherent in adopting an industrial product', *Journal of Marketing Research*, 10, 312–15.

Peters, T. J. (1988) *Thriving on Chaos*, New York: Alfred A. Knopf.

Peters, T. J. and R. H. Waterman (1982) *In Search of Excellence*, New York: Harper and Row.

Petty, R. E., J. T. Cacioppo and D. Schumann (1983) 'Central and peripheral routes to advertising effectiveness: the moderating role of involvement', *Journal of Consumer Research*, 10, 135–46.

Pinson, C. (1978) 'Consumer cognitive styles: review and implications for marketers', in E. Topritzhofer (ed.) *Marketing: Neue Ergenbnisse aus Forschung und Praxis*, Wiesbaden: Gabler, 163–84.

Pinson, C. and E. L. Roberto (1988) 'Consumer behavior and the marketing activities of firms', in

W. F. van Raaij, G. M. van Veldhoven and K.-E. Wärneryd (eds) *Handbook of Economic Psychology*, Dordrecht: Kluwer, 294–331.

Pinson, C., N. K. Malhotra and A. K. Jain (1988) 'Les styles cognitifs des consommateurs', *Recherche et Applications en Marketing*, III, 53–73.

Pollay, R. W. (1986) 'The distorted mirror: reflections on the unintended consequences of advertising', *Journal of Marketing*, 50, 18–36.

POPA/Du Pont (1978) 'Marketing emphasis', *Product Marketing*, 61–4.

Popielarz, D. T. (1967) 'An exploration of perceived risk and willingness to try new products', *Journal of Marketing Research*, 4, 368–72.

Pratkanis, A. R. (1991) 'Subliminal sorcery then and now: who is seducing whom?', *Proceedings of the Society for Consumer Psychology*, 84–6.

Prato-Previde, G. (1984) 'Adattatori ed innovatori: i risultati della standardizzione italiana del KAI', *Ricerche di Psichologia*, 4, 81–134.

Price, L. L. and L. F. Feick (1984) 'The role of interpersonal sources in external search: an informational perspective', *Advances in Consumer Research*, 9, 250–5.

Price, L. L. and N. M. Ridgway (1982) 'Use innovativeness, vicarious exploration and purchase exploration: three facets of consumer varied behavior', *Proceedings of the 48th Educators' Conference*, Chicago: American Marketing Association, 56–60.

Punj, G. N. and D. W. Stewart (1983) 'An interaction framework of consumer decision making', *Journal of Consumer Research*, 10, 181–96.

Pymont, B. C., R. P. Morgan and J. R. Bond (1988) 'The application of micro-modelling to predicting total market mix potential', *Journal of Marketing Management*, 3, 278–95.

Quinn, M. (1990) 'Don't aim that pack at us', *Time*, January 29, 60.

Rajaniemi, P. (1992) 'Conceptualization of product involvement as a property of cognitive structure', *Acta Wasaensia*, 29.

Raju, P. S. (1980) 'Optimum stimulation level: its relationship to personality, demographics, and exploratory behaviour', *Journal of Consumer Research*, 7, 272–82.

Reddin, W. J. (1983) 'Management effectiveness and style – individual or situation', PhD thesis, University of New Brunswick.

Reilly, P. (1988) 'A new claim to "Fame": high-price talent used to lure upscale readers', *Advertising Age*, July 11, 34.

Ries, A. and J. Trout (1980) *Positioning: The Battle for your Mind*, New York: McGraw-Hill.

Ries, A. and J. Trout (1986) *Marketing Warfare*, New York: McGraw-Hill.

Riesman, D., N. Glazer and R. Denney (1960) *The Lonely Crowd*, New Haven, CT: Yale University Press.

Ritson, C., L. Goffman and J. McKenzie (eds) (1986) *The Food Consumer*, Chichester: Wiley.

Robertson, T. S. (1967a) 'The process of innovation and the diffusion of innovation', *Journal of Marketing*, 31, 14–19.

Robertson, T. S. (1967b) 'Determinants of innovative behavior', *Proceedings of the American Marketing Association*, (ed.) R. Moyer, Chicago: American Marketing Association, 328–32.

Robertson, T. S. (1971) *Innovative Behavior and Communication*, New York: Holt, Rinehart and Winston.

Robertson, T. S. (1976) 'Low commitment consumer behavior', *Journal of Advertising Research*, 16, 19–24.

Robertson, T. S. and H. Gatignon (1985) 'Competitive effects on technology diffusion', *Journal of Marketing*, 50, 1–12.

Robertson, T. S. and J. N. Kennedy (1969) 'Prediction of consumer innovators: application of multiple discriminant analysis', *Journal of Marketing Research*, 5, 64–9.

Robertson, T. S., J. Zielinski and S. Ward (1984) *Consumer Behavior*, Glenview, IL: Scott, Foresman.

Rockwell, J. R. and M. C. Particelli (1982) 'New product strategy: how the pros do it', *Industrial Marketing*, May, 49–53.

Rogers, E. M. (1983) *The Diffusion of Innovations*, New York: Free Press.

Rokeach, M. (1960) *The Open and Closed Mind*, New York: Basic Books.

Rosen, D. L. and M. J. Sheffet (1983) 'The effect of situation on the use of generic grocery products', *Educators' Proceedings*, Chicago: American Marketing Association, 1–4.

Rosenberg, M. (1965) *Society and the Adolescent Self-Image*, Princeton, NJ: Princeton University Press.

Ross, I. (1970) 'Self-concept and brand preferences', *Journal of Business*, 44, 38–50.

Ross, I. (1975) 'Perceived risk and consumer behavior: a critical review', *Advances in Consumer Research*, 2, 1–19.

Rothschild, M. L. and W. C. Gaidis (1981) 'Behavioral learning theory: its relevance to marketing and promotion', *Journal of Marketing*, 45, 70–8.

Rotter, J. B. (1966) 'Generalized expectancies for internal versus external control of reinforcement', *Psychological Monograph*, 80 (whole no. 609).

Rudmin, F. W. (1991) *To Have Possessions: A Handbook on Ownership and Property*, special issue of the *Journal of Social Behavior and Personality*, Corte Maderia, CA: Select Press.

Russell, J. A. and A. Mehrabian (1976) 'Environmental variables in consumer research', *Journal of Consumer Research*, 3, 62–3.

Russell, J. A. and A. Mehrabian (1978) 'Approach-avoidance and affiliation as functions of the emotion-eliciting quality of an environment', *Environment and Behavior*, 10, 355–87.

Ryan, M. A. and E. H. Bonfield (1975) 'The Fishbein extended model of consumer behavior', *Journal of Consumer Research*, 2, 118–36.

Ryan, M. A. and E. H. Bonfield (1980) 'Fishbein's intentions model: a test of external and pragmatic validity', *Journal of Marketing*, 44, 82–95.

Rydell, S. T. and E. Rosen (1966) 'Measurement and some correlates of need cognition', *Psychological Reports*, 90, 139–65.

Saergert, S. (1973) 'Crowding: cognitive overload and behavioral constraint,' in W. Preiser (ed.), *Environmental Design Research*, vol. 2, Stroudsberg, PA: Dowden, Hutchinson and Ross, 254–61.

Salmon, C. T. (1986) 'Perspectives on involvement in consumer and communication research', *Progress in Communication Sciences* 7, 243–68.

Sandell, R. G. (1968) 'Effects of attitudinal and situational factors on reported choice behavior', *Journal of Marketing Research*, 5, 405–8.

Sands, S. (1980) 'Test marketing: can it be defended?', *Quarterly Review of Marketing*, 5, 1–10.

Sands, S. and P. Moore (1980) 'Store site selection by discriminant analysis', *Journal of the Market Research Society*, 23, 41–51.

Scammon, D. (1977) '"Information load" and consumers', *Journal of Consumer Research*, 4, 148–55.

Schaninger, C. M. and D. Sciglimpaglia (1981) 'The influence of cognitive personality traits and demographics on consumer information acquisition', *Journal of Consumer Research*, 8, 208–16.

Schellenberg, J. A. (1978) *Masters of Social Psychology*, New York: Oxford University Press.

Schewe, C. D. and W. R. Dillon (1978) 'Marketing information system utilization: an application of self-concept theory', *Journal of Business Research*, 6, 67–79.

Schiffman, L. G. (1990) 'Uptown's fall bodes ill for niche brands', *Wall Street Journal*, January 22.

Schiffman, L. G. and L. L. Kanuk (1987) *Consumer Behavior*, Englewood Cliffs, NJ: Prentice-Hall.

Schlueter, S. (1992) 'Get to the "essence" of a brand relationship', *Marketing News*, January 20, 4.

Schram, E. W. and D. F. Roberts (1971) *The Process and Effects of Mass Communication*, Champain, IL: University of Illinois Press.

Schwadel, F. (1989) 'Little touches spur Wal-Mart's rise', *Wall Street Journal*, September 22.

Scitovski, T. (1992) *The Joyless Economy: The Psychology of Human Satisfaction*, New York: Oxford University Press.

Scott, N. K. (1989) *Shopping Centre Design*, London: Van Nostrand.

Scott, C., D. M. Klein and J. Bryant (1990) 'Consumer responses to humor in advertising: a series of field studies using behavior observation', *Journal of Consumer Research*, 16, 498–501.

Serafin, R. (1988) 'Oldsmobile goes for youth in major repositioning bid', *Advertising Age*, September 12, 3.

Sheppard, B. H., J. Hartwick and P. R. Warshaw (1988), 'The Theory of Reasoned Action: a meta-analysis of past research with recommendations for modifications and future research', *Journal of Consumer Research*, 15, 325–43.

Sheth, J. N. (1974) (ed.) *Models of Buyer Behavior*, New York: Harper and Row.

Shye, S. (1978) *Theory Construction and Data Analysis in the Behavioral Sciences*, New York: Jossey Bass.

Sim, L. L. and C. R. Way (1989) 'Tenant placement in a Singapore shopping centre', *International Journal of Retailing*, 4(3), 4–16.

Simon, R. (1989) 'Hit the prospect at every emotional level', *Forbes*, January 9, 310–11.

Sirgy, M. J. (1980) 'Self-concept in relation to product preference and purchase intention', in V. V. Bellue (ed.) *Developments in Marketing Science*, vol. 3, Marquette, MI: Academy of Marketing Science, 350–4.

Sirgy, M. J. (1982) 'Self-concept in consumer behavior: a critical review', *Journal of Consumer Research*, 9, 287–300.

Skinner, B. F. (1953) *Science and Human Behavior*, New York: Macmillan.

Small, R. G. (1993) 'Consumption and significance: the shape of things to come', *Scandinavian Journal of Management*, 9 (2), 89–99.

Smith, W. R. (1956) 'Product differentiation and market segmentation as alternative marketing strategies', *Journal of Marketing*, 21, 3–8.

Snyder, M. and K. G. DeBono (1985) 'Appeals to image and claims of quality: understanding the psychology of advertising', *Journal of Personality and Social Psychology*, 49, 586–97.

Soleri, P. (1969) *Arcology: The City in the Image of Men*, Cambridge, MA: The MIT Press.

Solomon, R. (1983) 'The role of products as social stimuli: a symbolic interactionism perspective', *Journal of Consumer Research*, 9, 319–29.

Sommer, R. and S. Aitkens (1982) 'Mental mapping of two supermarkets', *Journal of Consumer Research*, 9, 211–15.

Sommer, R., J. Herrick and T. R. Sommer (1981) 'The behavioral ecology of supermarkets and farmers' markets', *Journal of Environmental Psychology*, 1, 13–19.

Sprott, W. J. H. (1958) *Human Groups*, Harmondsworth: Penguin.

Stea, D. (1974) 'Architecture in the head: cognitive mapping', in J. Lang, C. Burnette, W. Moleski and D. Vachon (eds) *Designing for Human Behavior*, Stroudsberg, PA: Dowden, Hutchinson and Ross.

Steadman, M. (1969) 'How sexy illustrations affect brand recall', *Journal of Advertising Research*, 6, 15–19.

Steiner, I. D. and H. H. Johnson (1965) 'Category width and response to interpersonal disagreements', *Journal of Personality and Social Psychology*, 2, 290–2.

Stern, B. L., R. F. Bush and J. F. Hair (1977) 'The self-image store-image matching process: an empirical test', *Journal of Business*, 50, 63–9.

Sternthal, B. and C. S. Craig (1973) 'Humor in advertising', *Journal of Marketing*, 37, 12–18.

Sternthal, B. and C. S. Craig (1974) 'Fear appeals: revisited and revised', *Journal of Consumer Research*, 1, 22–34.

Sternthal, B. and C. S. Craig (1982) *Consumer Behavior: An Information Processing Perspective*, Englewood Cliffs, NJ: Prentice-Hall.

Stevenson, L. (1974) *Seven Theories of Human Nature*, New York: Oxford University Press.

Stoltman, J. J., J. W. Gentry, K. A. Anglin and A. C. Burns (1990) 'Situational influences on the consumer decision sequence', *Journal of Business Research*, 21, 195–207.

Stone, G. P. (1954) 'City shoppers and urban identification: observations on the social psychology of city life', *American Journal of Sociology*, 60, 48–53.

Storr, A. (1989) *Freud*, Oxford: Oxford University Press.

Strand, P. (1988) 'Hiram Walker plots strategy: Distiller seeks premium positioning', *Advertising Age*, June 6, 24.

Stroud, R. (1988) 'How to exploit popularity, *Advertising Age*, 18 April, 75.

Swasy, A. (1990) 'How innovation at P&G restored luster to washed-Up Pert and made it No. 1', *Wall Street Journal*, December 6.

Tauber, E. (1972) 'Why do people shop?', *Journal of Marketing*, 36, 47.

Tauber, E. (1975) 'Why concept and product tests fail to predict new product results', *Journal of Marketing*, 39, 69–71.

Tauber, E. (1977) 'Forecasting sales prior to test market', *Journal of Marketing*, 41, 80–4.

Tauber, E. (1981) 'Utilization of concept testing for new-product forecasting: traditional versus multiattribute approaches', in Y. Wind, V. Mahajan and R. N. Cardozo (eds) *New-Product Forecasting*, Lexington, MA: Lexington Books, 173–85.

Taylor, J. (1977) 'A striking characteristic of innovators', *Journal of Marketing Research*, 14, 104–7.

Taylor, R. L. and E. E. Levitt (1967) 'Category breadth and the search for variety of experience', *Psychological Record*, 17, 349–52.

Timmermans, H. (1993) 'Retail environments and spatial shopping behavior', in T. Garling and R. G. Golledge (eds) *Behavior and Environment: Psychological and Geographical Approaches* Amsterdam: North Holland, 342–77.

Tracy, E. J. (1985) 'Black-and-white magic in Chicago', *Fortune*, September 2, 47.

Treece, J. B. (1989) 'Teaching an Oldsmobile new tricks', *Business Week*, September 25.

Trodahl, V. and F. Powell, (1965) 'A short form dogmatism scale for use in field studies', *Social Forces*, 44, 211–14.

Troye, S. V. (1985) 'Situationist theory and consumer behavior', in: J. N. Sheth (ed.), *Research in Consumer Behavior*, Vol. 1, Greenwich, CT: JAI Press, 285–321.

Tucker, W. T. and J. Painter (1961) 'Personality and product use', *Journal of Applied Psychology*, 45, 325–9.

Uncles, M. and A. S. C. Ehrenberg (1988) 'Patterns of store choice: new evidence from the USA', in N. Wrigley (ed.) *Store Choice, Store Location and Market Analysis*, London and New York: Routledge, 272–99.

Urban, G. L. and J. R. Hauser (1980) *Design and Marketing of New Products*, Englewood Cliffs, NJ: Prentice-Hall.

Van der Ster, W. and P. Van Wissen (1983) *Marketing & Detailhandel* [Marketing & Retail Trade], Groningen, The Netherlands: Wolters-Noordhoff.

Van Raaij, W. F. (1983) *Shopping Center Evaluation and Patronage in the City of Rotterdam*, Papers on Economic Psychology, no. 27, Rotterdam: Erasmus University, October.

Van Raaij, W. F. and J. M. G. Floor (1983) 'Retailing developments in the Netherlands', *International Journal of Physical Distribution and Materials Management*, 13(5–6), 128–37.

Venkatesan, M. (1966) 'Consumer behavior: conformity and independence', *Journal of Marketing Research*, 3, 384–7.

Venkatesan, M. (1973) 'Cognitive consistency and novelty-seeking', in S. Ward and T. S. Robertson (eds) *Consumer Behavior: Theoretical Sources*, Englewood Cliffs, NJ: Prentice-Hall, 354–84.

Venkatraman, M. P. (1991) 'The impact of innovativeness and innovation type on adoption', *Journal of Retailing*, 67, 51–67.

Venkatraman, M. P. and D. MacInnis (1985) 'The epistemic and sensory exploratory behaviors of hedonic and cognitive consumers', *Advances in Consumer Research*, 11, 102–7.

Venkatraman, M. P. and L. L. Price (1990) 'Differentiating between cognitive and sensory innovativeness: concepts, measurement and implications', *Journal of Business Research*, 20, 293–315.

Verhallen, T. M. M. and R. G. M. Pieters (1984) 'Attitude theory and behavioral costs', *Journal of Economic Psychology*, 5, 223–49.

Vokey, J. R. and J. D. Read (1985) 'Subliminal messages: between the devil and the media', *American Psychologist*, 40, 1231–9.

Wall Street Journal (1990) 'Sear's glitzy ads target affluent fashion market', August 15.

Walker, R. and B. Cude (1983) 'In-store shopping strategies: time and money costs in the supermarket', *Journal of Consumer Affairs*, 17, 356–69.

Ward, S. (1974) 'Consumer socialization', *Journal of Consumer Research*, 1, 1–10.

Ward, S. and D. B. Wackman (1972) 'Children's purchase influence attempts and parental yielding', *Journal of Marketing Research*, 9, 316–19.

Wells, W. D. (1974) *Life Style and Psychographics*, Chicago: American Marketing Association.

Wells, W. D. and A. D. Beard (1973) 'Personality and consumer behavior', in S. Ward and T. S. Robertson (eds) *Consumer Behavior: Theoretical Sources*, Englewood Cliffs, NJ: Prentice-Hall, 141–99.

Wells, W. D. and G. Gubar (1966) 'Life cycle in marketing research', *Journal of Marketing Research*, 3, 335–63.

Wesley, E. L. (1953) 'Preservative behavior in a concept-formation task', *Journal of Abnormal and Social Psychology*, 8, 129–34.

Westfall, R. (1962) 'Psychological factors in predicting brand choice', *Journal of Marketing*, 26, 34–40.

White, L. A. and J. B. Ellis (1971) A system construct for evaluating retail store market locations', *Journal of Marketing Research*, 8, 43–6.

Whiteside, H. O. (1964) 'Integrating the roles of the household purchasing agent', in R. Cox (ed.) *Theory in Marketing*, New York: Irwin.

Whysall, P. (1989) 'Commercial change in a central area: a case study', *International Journal of Retailing*, 4(1), 45–61.

Wicker, A. W. (1969) 'Attitudes vs. actions', *Journal of Social Issues*, 25, 41–78.

Wicker, A. W. and S. Kirmeyer (1977) 'From church to laboratory to national park: a program of research on excess and insufficient populations in behavior settings', in D. Stokols (ed.) *Perspectives on Environment and Behavior: Theory, Research and Application*, New York and London: Plenum Press, 69–96.

Wilkie, W. L. and P. R. Dickson (1991) 'Shopping for appliances: consumers' strategies and patterns of information search', in H. H. Kassarjian and T. S. Robertson (eds), *Perspectives in Consumer Behavior*, New York: Prentice-Hall, 1–26.

Wilkinson, J. B., J. B. Mason and C. H. Paksoy (1992) 'Assessing the impact of short-term supermarket strategy variables', *Journal of Marketing Research*, 11, 72–86.

Williams, R. (1981) 'Outshopping: problem or opportunity?', *Arizona Business*, 27, 9.

Wilson, A. B. and A. Dunkin (1984) 'Waterford learns its lesson: snob appeal isn't enough', *Business Week*, December 24, 63–4.

Wilson, G. (1987) *Money in the Family: Financial Organisation and Women's Responsibility*, Aldershot: Avebury.

Wilson, G. D. and J. R. Patterson (1968) 'A new measure of conservatism', *British Journal of Social and Clinical Psychology*, 7, 274–9.

Wilson, G. D., D. T. Matthews and J. W. Harvey (1975) 'An empirical test of the Fishbein Behavioral Intentions Model', *Journal of Consumer Research*, 1, 39–48.

Wind, Y. (1981) *Product Policy: Concepts, Methods, and Strategy*, Reading, MA: Addison-Wesley.

Wind, Y., V. Mahajan and R. N. Cardozo (eds) (1981) *New-Product Forecasting*, Lexington, MA: D. C. Heath.

Witkin, H. A., P. K. Oltman, E. Raskin and S. A. Karp (1971) *Manual of the Embedded Figures Test*, Palo Alto: Consulting Psychologists' Press.

Worcester, R. and J. Downham (1978) *Consumer Market Research Handbook*, London: Van Nostrand.

Wrigley, N. and R. Dunn (1988) 'Models of store choice and market analysis', in N. Wrigley (ed.) *Store Choice, Store Location and Market Analysis*, London: Routledge, 251–71.

Yang, J. E. (1986) 'Group "affinity" is used to sell credit cards', *Wall Street Journal*, October 9.

Yankelovich, Skelley and White Inc. (1982) *Supermarket Shoppers in a Period of Uncertainty*, Washington, DC: Food Marketing Institute.

Young, P. T. (1961) *Motivation and Emotion*, New York: Wiley.

Yovovich, B. G. (1983) 'Sex in advertising – the power and the perils', *Advertising Age*, May 2, M4–5.

Zaichkowsky, J. L. (1984) 'Conceptualizing and measuring the involvement construct in marketing', PhD thesis, Los Angeles: University of California.

Zaichkowsky, J. L. (1985) 'Measuring the involvement construct', *Journal of Consumer Research*, 12, 341–52.

Zaichkowsky, J. L. (1986) 'Conceptualizing involvement', *Journal of Advertising*, 15, 4–14.

Zaichkowsky, J. L. (1987) 'The Personal Involvement Inventory: reduction, revision and application to advertising', *Discussion Paper no. 87–08–08*, Simon Fraser University, Faculty of Business Administration.

Zain, O. M. and I. Rejab (1989) 'The choice of retail outlets among urban Malaysian shoppers', *International Journal of Retailing*, 4(2), 35–45.

Zajonc, R. B. and H. Markus (1982) 'Affective and cognitive factors in preferences', *Journal of Consumer Research*, 9, 123–31.

Zaltman, G. (1965) *Marketing: Contributions from the Behavioral Sciences*, New York: Harcourt Brace Jovanovich.

Zeithaml, V. A. (1982) 'Consumer response' to in-store price information environments', *Journal of Consumer Research*, 8, 357–69.

Zuckerman, M. (1974) 'The sensation seeking motive', *Progress in Experimental Personality Research*, 7, 74–148.

Index